DOWNSTART

By Brian Inglis

THE FREEDOM OF THE PRESS IN IRELAND
THE STORY OF IRELAND
SIR ROGER CASEMENT
NATURAL AND SUPERNATURAL
THE HIDDEN POWER
THE UNKNOWN GUEST: THE MYSTERIES
OF INTUITION
TRANCE

Downstart

The Autobiography of
Brian Inglis

Chatto & Windus
LONDON

1948–1989

For Margaret, beloved

Published in 1900 by
Chatto & Windus Ltd
30 Bedford Square
London WC1B 3SG

A CIP catalogue record for this book is available from the British Library.

ISBN 0 7011 3390 2

Printed in Great Britain by
Mackays of Chatham plc,
Chatham, Kent
Typeset at The Spartan Press Ltd
Lymington, Hants

Contents

Acknowledgements

I suppose the person I have most to thank is my mother; separated as we were for most of the time, in my childhood and youth, she kept almost everything I wrote, or was connected with me – school reports, and such. This collection, coupled with the fact she persuaded me to keep a diary, has provided many salutary instances of memory's fallibility. For reminders of Malahide, too, I have to thank Mrs Win McLeod – Win Knowles in her Malahide days – for the detailed and delightful nostalgic account she sent me after reading *West Briton*.

Michael Charlesworth read and commented upon the chapter on Shrewsbury; Alan Wood, the chapter on Coastal Command; I am grateful for their suggestions. Tony Gray's unpublished work on the *Irish Times* has been a considerable help. And I must thank Ruth Dudley Edwards for wading through the proofs, along with Bernard Levin, whose caustic marginal comments I would, as usual, have been glad to include.

Prologue

In 1961 somebody suggested to the publisher, Hutchinson, that they should bring out a series on endangered human species, as seen through the eyes of men or women who had grown up in them during their decline – such as the Raj, in India. Iain Hamilton, then senior editor with the firm, asked me to contribute one on the 'Protestant Descendancy': the Anglo–Irish in Ireland following the Treaty of 1921 which set up the Irish Free State. It was not to be an autobiography so much as a camera-lens view; what he had in mind, as I recall, was very much the kind of book David Thomson was later to write, *Woodbrook*, though with a rather wider range of people and places.

For some reason – Sir Robert Lusty, head of Hutchinson at the time, cannot recall why – the project was abandoned before any of the series had been published. Having written a specimen chapter, I was reluctant to waste it; I asked Faber & Faber, who had published my potted history *The Story of Ireland*, if they would take it on. They liked the idea, but the outcome was a book with a different slant. The early part stayed; the rest became a description of Irish, mainly Dublin, life, seen through the eyes of a journalist working on the *Irish Times* between 1946 and 1953.

West Briton had the good fortune to appear at the same time as Brendan Behan's *Borstal Boy*. A number of literary editors paired them for review purposes; *West Briton* shared in the publicity. From time to time, later, I would be asked whether there could be a paperback; and eventually my agent Felicity Bryan, then with Curtis Brown, suggested this to Faber. They turned the idea down, as did

Carmen Callil when it was tried on Chatto & Windus. Carmen, however, suggested I should make a revised version. *West Briton* had dealt only with my life in Ireland; why not fuse it in with the English side, school, university, war service in the RAF, and carry it on after 1953, to cover what has happened since?

This I have tried to do. There are additions to the original Irish side, thanks to the appearance of memoirs, autobiographies, biographies and obituaries which have provided fresh information, along with letters and word of mouth; but I have to admit to the inclusion of many episodes in more or less the same form as they appeared in *West Briton*, occasionally in the same words, when it seemed silly to change them simply for the sake of change. I have tried to make the joins between the English and Irish aspects seamless; but where they show, I hope this will be forgiven.

1

Vera and Claude

In 1907 Claude Cavendish Inglis, at the age of twenty-four, had just taken up his post in the Public Works Department in India when he received a letter from Dublin

> Dear Inglis
> This is to let you know that both Mrs Blood and I disapprove of and object to the correspondence which appears to be carried on between you and Vera
> Yours truly
> J. R. Blood

Many Dublin parents would have been delighted, at that time, to find that their twenty-year-old daughter was carrying on with Claude Inglis. His father Malcolm had made a substantial reputation, largely thanks to taking on the unremunerated but influential post of Hon. Secretary to the Irish Liberal Unionist Party, which had brought him many valuable contacts. His well-turned walrus moustaches had become a familiar feature in Dublin: he was Senior Presbyterian Education Commissioner on the Irish National Education Board, a Justice of the Peace, Deputy Lieutenant of the County of Dublin, and an energetic organiser of a number of charities, in particular Queen Victoria's Jubilee Nurses Fund, which had proved to be extremely successful. For his public services, he had been given a knighthood.

This did not, however, impress John Redmond Blood; still less his wife Sophie. Dublin gossip had it that Malcolm's father had found three of his sons too incompetent in business to stay in Scotland, or even to have any prospect of succeeding in England; but they might just – he hoped – get on in Ireland. One of them had stopped off in Belfast, there to found the firm which for many years was to be Belfast's leading bakery (its vans would occasionally be seen on television in the 1970s, requisitioned as barricades in the street fighting, burning away in the background). The other two had gone on to Dublin, where James had married a Catholic; in consequence he was never spoken to (and rarely, about) again by Malcolm and his side of the family.

Malcolm had found a lowly job in Thomas Heiton and Company, working his way up until he had become Chairman. But the firm had only become a limited company as late as 1895. Until then, Malcolm had been 'in trade'. Worse, it was the coal trade, which had an unenviable reputation. Everybody assumed that coal merchants lavishly watered the 'slack' which accompanied the coal, and was used in households to keep the fires in overnight. The fact that Malcolm had become Chairman, as well as holding several director-ships in other firms and being vice-President of the Dublin Chamber of Commerce, could not break down the social barriers erected against a parvenu.

John Redmond Blood – Jack, to close friends – had also worked his way up from humble beginnings. His father had taken him from school at the age of sixteen to put him into the family business. But there was a significant difference: the business was the Findlater's Mountjoy Brewery, owned by Jack's mother's family. 'I do not know why it should be a crack thing to be a brewer,' Herbert Pocket remarks to Pip in *Great Expectations*, 'but it is indisputable that while you cannot possibly be genteel and bake, you can be as genteel as never was and brew. You see it every day.' The Bloods prided themselves on their gentility – or, rather, on being of the gentry: 'the quality', as they were known in Ireland. The Bloods could trace their ancestry back to settlers who had been awarded estates in the West of Ireland in the seventeenth century. Since that time they had helped to maintain the Protestant Ascendancy as landowners, or had served the Empire as soldiers and administrators.

Sophie had become even more proud of the Blood escutcheon than her husband. Her family, like Malcolm's, had come from Scotland to Dublin, where her father had set up in business manufacturing envelopes. But it had been a limited liability company; even more important, it dealt only in wholesale. If people found something the matter with a packet of envelopes they blamed the retailer: the name of Armstrong did not appear. Sophie, keenly alive to social nuances, did not approve of the Inglis family.

She had another reason to mistrust young Claude. He had grown up as the pampered youngest son of Malcolm's family in Donny-brook – well into the countryside south of Dublin, in those days – on Montrose, an estate large enough to contain a private nine-hole golf course. Malcolm's eldest son, Johnstone, had made something of a reputation on them by playing scratch golf equally well left-handed or right-handed. He had also been elected to the Royal Hibernian Academy – the youngest painter ever to have achieved that honour, his family claimed. But through drink and dissipation, he had become so notorious in Dublin that he had been compelled to emigrate to America, where he sank to be 'the lowest of the low', in Sophie's terms: a dock worker. Of Malcolm's other sons, three had taken a similar course and been compelled to emigrate. Another had died young. Sir Malcolm had himself died in 1902, the family fortunes squandered. Young Claude was no catch, financially. And might not he, too, follow his older brothers' disreputable ways?

As it happened, Claude was determined not to follow them. He was a keen golfer – one year he reached the semi-finals of the Irish Amateur Championship at Portmarnock – but he was also an uncommonly hard worker at his studies in Trinity College, Dublin. There, he had been fortunate enough to study under the remarkable John Joly, a Fellow of the Royal Society. Joly still secures an entry in *Chambers' Biographical Dictionary* for inventing the photometer, making the first precise calculation of the age of the earth, pioneering colour photography and initiating a technique of radiotherapy. He was also an inspiring teacher, setting Claude on the course in which he was to make his career. As well as being a model student, Claude played a useful modest role in the life of the college as Registrar of the Choral Society, and cellist in the orchestra. There was nothing against him personally except the collapse of the family fortunes.

Montrose had been sold (the house still stands, self-consciously, in front of the brash Radio Telefis Eireann studio buildings which now cover the ground where he learned to play golf), so he had no home to offer. Still, he had a job with, by the standards of the time, quite good

5

prospects, as he was able to claim in the letter which he wrote in reply to Jack Blood's order to stop corresponding with Vera.

> Dear Mr Blood
> As you know, before I left home Vera and I saw a good deal of each other and as a result became very great friends. At that time Vera was fully aware that I was not in a position to even think about becoming engaged, and for this reason she was all the more friendly and natural with me.
> In spite of this, and in spite of her always treating me as a boy chum, I soon realised that my feelings towards her were something more than those of a friend; and knowing this and the hopelessness of my position I made up my mind to hide my feelings as much as possible.
> That I did not succeed in this as well as I had intended was perhaps natural. Be that as it may, before leaving home I had fully realised that Vera's friendship was my most treasured possession; and wishing to continue that friendship, and believing that she did, too, I asked her to write to me as often as she could and felt inclined . . .

Claude then went into detail about his post and his prospects. His salary, he explained, brought him in £500 a year. For somebody only just starting on his career, this was satisfactory. (Roger Casement, in his far more responsible consular posts, was being paid only £300 a year.) It was all the better in that living costs in India were low; and the job was pensionable, after twenty years service, at £350 a year. As Claude would not be back at the earliest before 1908, there was no need for an immediate answer, but – he concluded –

> I need scarcely repeat how much my future happiness depends on that answer and Vera's feelings towards me.
> I dont wish to talk about myself or my own doings, but I do wish to say that I honestly believe I have no tendency towards any of what are generally understood as the vices, and up to the present I have lived a straight, hard and clean life.
> > Yours sincerely
> > Claude Inglis

Claude made a copy of Blood's letter and his reply, and sent it to Vera with a note to say that although it might come as a shock to her, he thought it was the best thing to do. 'Mind you,' he added, 'although I have more or less tied myself down, I don't expect or want you to do likewise, and I have asked your father not to talk to you, so as to leave you absolutely free; and also, of course, I don't . . .' – at which point the page ended, and Vera, who kept the letter thus far, did not keep the rest.

Claude did not, in fact, return until 1911, as he was promoted twice in between. In the meantime, Vera must have made it clear – though this was the only letter that passed between them before his return which I found after her death in 1972 – that she would wait for him, but that she was not going to sit around with a candle in the window.

Vera Blood was bright; so bright that her parents had allowed themselves to be persuaded to send her to Cheltenham Ladies College. There, she impressed the formidable headmistress, Miss Beale, who recommended that she should try for a scholarship to Oxford or Cambridge. Her mother put her foot down; girls who went to university, she feared, became bluestockings, frightening off eligible young men.

By Dublin standards, she became a bluestocking anyway. By the time she was out of her teens she was an avid reader of the plays and prefaces of Bernard Shaw, *John Bull's Other Island*, *Major Barbara*, *The Doctor's Dilemma* and, in particular, *Man and Superman*, in which I suspect she saw herself as Ann. And although *Man and Superman* was beyond the limited resources of the Trinity Players, they happened to be in a flourishing state at the time and Vera was brought in to become one of their guest stars, sometimes as an *ingénue* but for preference in comedy parts, occasionally playing them in Dublin's leading theatre, the Gaiety.

That her mother disapproved went without saying; but Vera was in luck. Although Sophie Blood had been an attractive girl she had not attracted a husband until – as she put it, in a letter to a friend at the time – she was beginning to feel she was an Old Maid. This made her passionately grateful to her husband, and also violently jealous of anybody who disputed her priority as, she had found, Vera and Joan, her daughters, began to do. When Jack came back from work he liked to be with them until their bedtime; Sophie became as adept as one of Saki's aunts in finding excuses to thwart him, by instancing examples of bad behaviour on the girls' – usually Vera's – part during the day.

Little though she liked the idea of Vera becoming stage-struck, at least performing with the Players kept her out of the house for much of the time; and any fears that she might misbehave were allayed by the knowledge that her constant companion was her cousin Charlie Armstrong, who had brought her into the Players. Charlie was a born comedian; it was impossible to think of him as a potential seducer, and Vera could use the Armstrong home, with its three boys and three girls of about her own age, as if it were her own. Egged on by Sophie, Jack once felt compelled to warn her that she might become known as 'Charlie's hack'; but on the whole they were relieved.

Vera had admirers who would have been delighted to step into Claude's shoes, but they received no encouragement. Some were to be killed in the war; one, of whom she had particularly fond memories, survived the trenches only to fall victim to the flu epidemic the day after he was demobbed. But another who remained a friend for his lifetime was W. F. Casey, a South African who was to become a journalist and to end his career as editor of *The Times*. 'W.F.' was to play a decisive part in my life, as a result of his choice of career; but at the time he was fascinated by the theatre, in which he hoped to make his name – as, for a time, he did. The Abbey, where Yeats's Irish National Theatre Society was presenting its plays from 1904, accepted his *The Man Who Missed The Tide* and *The Suburban Groove* and produced both of them in 1908.

They were potboilers, which worried Yeats; but as the *Irish Times* critic, Andrew Malone, was to insist years later, 'Casey deserves to be remembered because he found humour in the Dublin suburbs, and made a Dublin audience laugh at itself.' For a time, Casey acted as Secretary to the Society; later, he used to tell gently entertaining stories about Yeats ('Mr Casey', the Abbey's bank clerk asked him, 'Why does your director sign his cheques "Yours sincerely, W. B. Yeats"?'). But there was little money in it; his plays did not become a steady part of the Abbey's repertory; and he went to England to try his hand at journalism. 'A comedy writer of some power,' Malone felt, 'was lost in Casey'; for many years he remained the only Abbey playwright to explore the way of life, eventually to be mocked by Jimmy O'Dea and other comedians, of the denizens of Rathmines and Rathgar in south Dublin where social climbers with 'refeened' accents congregated.

I do not recall Vera reminiscing about *The Countess Cathleen*, or the plays of Lady Gregory – or even *The Playboy*; but she saw *The Shewing Up of Blanco Posnet*, the first Shaw play to be produced at the Abbey. Whenever a conversation led to discussion of some moral issue she was likely to quote Blanco: 'There's no good and bad; but by Jiminy, gents, there's a rotten game, and there's a great game. I played the rotten game; but the great game was played on me; and now I'm for the great game every time.'

Vera left only one other letter from this period. It was written by Claude after his return from India in 1912. He had gone to stay in Howth to await the verdict of Vera's parents:

> Dear Vera
> I can't write! I can't think! I can scarcely believe my own eyes! I have read and read your letter, and can't believe it is true. I am so perfectly happy that I dont know how to contain myself till tomorrow . . .

Details followed of where and when to meet, more after the manner of the Claude I was to know – as was his perfunctory closure:

> Goodbye – till tomorrow
> Yours
> Claude

To the best of my recollection I never saw or heard him in *any* emotional state, happy or unhappy, until his death in 1974.

Claude and Vera were married in Dublin, honeymooned briefly in Venice, and arrived by P. & O. in Bombay to find that he had another promotion, to the Poona Irrigation District. They were to make their home in Poona, apart from leaves, for the next thirty years. When Vera became pregnant in 1915, though, they judged it less hazardous for her to risk the German U boats than to have her confinement in India; I was born in Dublin. It had been fashionable to give the eldest boy, for his second Christian name, his mother's family name; but Brian Blood Inglis was thought unsuitable – fortunately for me: I can imagine what mirth the second 'B' would have given rise to at school, when somebody found out what it stood for.

Vera for her second name had been given St John, as she was born on 24 June; she decided I should have it, too. It was quite a popular choice in Ireland; the dramatist St John Ervine wore it proudly; the popular novelist Donn Byrne gave it to his son. I used to style myself 'B. StJ. Inglis', in journalism, until finding that initials were going out of fashion. 'Brian' it had to be; 'St John Inglis' would have sounded pretentious.

Vera determined to get back to India as soon as the war ended, only to find that there was no chance of a passage for months. But she was in luck. 'Haggie' Campbell, Lord Glenavy's daughter, used to play golf at the Island, the club across the estuary from Malahide which my grandfather had founded, and of which he was Hon. Secretary. Haggie had the reputation of being a little cracked, an embarrassment to her family; but she told Vera to take a chance and call on her brother Gordon, who had been working in a wartime ministry under Beaverbrook, and might have 'pull'. As Gordon himself was later to tell me, he found Vera ravishing (according to Paddy, his son, he adored the company of pretty women); 'pull' was exerted, and a passage secured.

I was two years old. We were in India for a couple of years, a period of which I have only the haziest of recollections. The Anglo–Indians, as the expatriates working there still called themselves, believed that it was unsafe for children – boys, in particular – to stay out there after they reached the age of five or six. The reason usually given was the risk of catching some tropical disease – my closest playmate, Marcel Richards, caught smallpox. But my father once admitted that his chief fear was that my being so much with the Indian servants – an ayah, Francheese the cook, the puttee-wallah, and sundry hangers-on – would induce bad habits, especially as I could speak their dialect fluently. Before my fifth birthday, my mother took me back to Ireland.

For some years, her father had rented a house in Malahide, nine miles north of Dublin but still very much a country village. On his retirement he had gone to live there in 'Ballykilty', named after the home of a senior Blood line in County Clare. It was a happy time;

Sophie, now that she had her husband around all day, was less jealous of her daughter. But the convention which obliged Anglo–Indian parents to send their children home when they reached school age also demanded that the mothers should return to their husbands in India. My mother did not feel it was fair to her father to leave me in Malahide, nor had she any trust in her mother. One of the few clear pictures I have from that time is walking with her along a windy promenade in Bexhill, Sussex, before she left me at St Catherine's School.

2

Bexhill

What was it like, I have often been asked, to be left at a boarding school at the age of five, never having been separated for more than a few days from my mother? Was it traumatic?

I do not know. Such recollections as there are suggest vague unhappiness, but not the misery some Anglo–Indian children (as we were called), such as Kipling, had suffered.

St Catherine's was specifically designed to cater for us. The Misses O'Sullivan, co-headmistresses, had themselves been Anglo–Indians. When at meals they wished to discuss something which was not for our ears they would apologise to any adults who were present and converse in Hindustani (not the Marathi I had picked up in Poona, which in any case I quickly forgot). They tried to make us feel at home; we called them 'Auntie Aga' and 'Auntie Kate'. Although they were quite strict disciplinarians, this was chiefly to teach us habits and manners which would impress our parents, when they came home on leave. I was only whacked a couple of times; once for doing something naughty in the bath; once for failing, in spite of a reminder, to put away my outdoor shoes. In those days of spare the rod, spoil the child, this was unusual.

The method must have worked. When I went to stay with cousin Ida in Dublin, little more than a year later, she wrote to my parents to express her astonishment that I did not have to be told to brush my teeth; that I was 'ready to answer when spoken to, but not putting in my word all the time, as most children do'; and that I refused to start to eat at meals until she had said grace, which was not something she ordinarily thought of doing.

Discipline of this kind was chiefly inculcated by means of deprivations for defaulters, and rewards for the well-behaved. Marks were awarded for clean teeth, subtracted for plaque – which old Sheridan, the family dentist in Dublin, wrote to the O'Sullivans to tell them was unfair. Sweets, cakes and goodies which came in for our birthdays were taken and divided up between us, roughly in proportion to our level of marks. And every day, some child would feel the weight of one of the aunts' displeasure: no jam for tea!

It was in any case necessary to eat two slices of thick bread and thin butter to qualify for a slice of bread and jam. Memory of the food stands second on my list of loathings at St Catherine's – going for walks in 'crocodiles' being the first. The food was plentiful enough, but stodgy, and the same, week in, week out – dinner in the middle of the day on Tuesday would be the same the next Tuesday, and the next. Along with potatoes, there were always certain root vegetables which soon nauseated me, parsnips, turnips, carrots; followed by certain equally-hated stewed fruit, figs, apricots, dates. And, of course, roly-poly pudding, 'spotted dick' and suet in various guises.

The prospectus for St Catherine's had an ominous entry: 'Complete charge taken if required'. There were some Anglo–Indian children who had nowhere to go in the holidays. Easter, summer, and Christmas, they stayed with the 'aunts', the routine (and the food) unchanged, except that there were no lessons. This was not, however, to apply to me, as I would be welcome at Ballykilty. But then the blow fell; grandfather died.

My only recollection of him is of his giving me, every morning, the sliced-off top of his boiled egg for breakfast. He had been quite a remarkable man, I was later to discover. His father had joined Findlater's Mountjoy Brewery to run its business side; grandfather, without any qualifications, was expected on joining the firm to supervise the brewing side. Soon, he was buying the ingredients and monitoring their course through the various stages until they were ready for consumption as ale or 'Mountjoy Nourishing Stout'. This entailed getting up at four a.m., three days a week, to supervise the 'mash' – as my mother used to recall; sometimes she would be woken by the bell which the night watchman, still around in Dublin at the end of the century, rang to rouse him.

Their Dublin home was beside the Mountjoy Brewery in North Dublin; a district then still fashionable, soon to go downhill (my mother was to be delighted to find that Brendan Behan's family, when he was growing up between the wars, lived in the house next door; by which time, according to Brendan's account, it was one of North Dublin's slums). Even when the Blood family were in Malahide, grandfather would return to Russell Street for mash mornings.

His conscience was allowed to relax only in connection with sport. He had been a keen rugby footballer, playing for Wanderers and Leinster under the alias 'J. R. Gore' to disguise his absences from his father. And when he and some friends took a lease on the sandhills which lay across the estuary from Malahide, and constructed the golf course which they called 'the Island' (it was in fact a peninsula, but the contrast between the sandhills and the fields behind made it look like an island, from the south), he still entered competitions as 'J. R. Gore', in case he should do well enough for his name to appear in the sports reports in the *Irish Times*.

By people in business and in sport, by the brewery workers and by the members of the Island, grandfather was both respected and loved. For my mother, devoted to him, his death was a double blow. He was still in his early sixties, and she would have expected to return several times on leave while he lived, as well as leaving me in his charge for holidays. But, grandmother in charge? My mother did not care for the idea. Yet if the alternative was leaving me at St Catherine's . . . ? Grandmother, sounded out, was willing. There was a tried and trusted cook-general, Mary Brophy, at Ballykilty; we had got on well, in spite of my plying her with endless questions; she would keep an eye on me when grandmother was playing golf or bridge. It was a risk, my mother decided, but worth taking.

Malahide lies on a hillside, overlooking the Swords River estuary and on the far side, Donabate and Portrane, with the mountains of Mourne in the dim distance (if they could be seen clearly, in the local view, it was bound soon to rain; wits would add that if they could not be seen, it was already raining). In Victorian times an attempt had been made to promote the village into a spa; the pungent ozone which was wafted up from the seaweed at low tide was irrationally believed to have therapeutic properties, as was the sea water, available to non-swimmers at baths which lay behind the Grand Hotel, automatically refilled with each rising tide.

But another tide, of fashion, was gradually to scupper the project. The Georgian houses on the north side of Dublin began to fall into disrepair; their owners moved south, or gave up having a town house. The once proud Mountjoy Square began to decay into tenements, prompting the professional classes who lived there and in the neighbourhood to move their families and their consulting rooms to Merrion Square and its neighbourhood, south of the Liffey; and when they went to the country at week-ends they tended to go still further south, to Delgany or Foxrock or Greystones, for their golf and tennis, rather than north to Malahide. The Great War finished off Malahide's pretensions to spa-dom; when I began to explore, and climbed the crumbling wall of the baths, the stagnant water was covered with green slime. Even the hotel, though it continued to fill up in summer, had a seedy look, its stucco peeling so that its façade looked like a miscalculated sun tan; we called it 'the Pink Hotel'.

Facing it, across a small park and some tennis courts, was another dilapidated testimony to the earlier optimism: St James's Terrace, a row of substantial houses built in the style commonly found along the sea front in British coastal towns. Grandfather had rented one of them when he came to Malahide for holidays – that it was for rent itself indicating the first stages of downgrading in the social register. For a time the Bloods were looked on with suspicion – as one of the residents of the terrace, Win Knowles, was to recall in a letter she wrote to me after reading *West Briton*.

Win was of the generation between my parents and me. Born in No. 5 St James's Terrace in 1898, she could remember the Bloods coming to stay 'and being looked on as "foreigners" for a long time!' Her family's predecessor had been a marquis; their next door neighbour was a niece of 'Buck' Whaley, the celebrated Regency rake, whom she was just old enough to remember. Another terrace resident never left his house without putting on his stovepipe hat. Some of the families lived all the year round in their houses; some used them only for their holidays; but that a St James's Terrace house could be rented was threatening.

By the time of the setting up of the Irish Free State in 1921 St James's Terrace was losing its gentry; and its social status was irretrievably undermined by the sale of Nos 1 and 2. They had been owned by Charlie Dillon, soon to become a cousin by marriage of the Bloods, to the Free State government, which converted them into a barracks for the Garda Siochana. No. 12 had long been the residence of the Captain of the Coast Guards, who were stationed beyond the north of the estuary; as he was usually a retired naval commander, he was socially acceptable. But a barracks! And for the 'Civic Guard', as grandmother called them!

Under the Union the Royal Irish Constabulary had been thought of, at least in Malahide, much as English country bobbies were thought of; genial fellows who bicycled around keeping an eye out for rough village lads who might be tempted to scrump apples or strawberries out of gardens. The Malahide RIC had been housed on the Diamond, in the middle of the village; their relations with the Protestant community had been good; and there had been no trouble with the nationalists. But with the coming of Sinn Fein after the Easter Rising in 1916, the constabulary had been forced more and more into confrontation with the guerrillas, who retaliated whenever the opportunity arose. One night the Malahide force was herded out at gunpoint, to watch the barracks go up in flames.

They remained a gutted ruin for a time after the Treaty; then the Gardai moved into St James's Terrace. Its residents could hardly have been more perturbed if a 'nigger' (as they would have called him; or, facetiously, 'a coloured gentleman') had bought the houses. Inevitably, worse followed. The house next door went the melancholy way of its elders and betters in Mountjoy Square. Unable to find a buyer, or to continue letting it in the summer holiday period, the owner turned it into a tenement, with a family to each floor and, in some cases, to each room. To get the children out of their hair, the mothers used to tell them to go and play on the terrace. The mark of Cain, indicating tenemency, was the ever-open – or, sometimes, missing – front door.

Later, there were to be few days when I did not come down the hill to the terrace. It was on the way to the Island boat; and my closest friend, Tony Robertson, lived in no. 10, at the still respectable end. But there was to be a gap in the holidays spent in Malahide. Grandmother began to find Ballykilty depressing, after grandfather's death. Sometimes she was away, staying with friends or relations, in my holidays; and when she decided to have a smaller house built for her, she did not want to have me around while she moved out and settled in. The 'complete charge taken if desired' in the prospectus was invoked, and I spent one whole summer holiday at St Catherine's.

Paradoxically I remember it for the only event in the four years I was there that still fills me with gratitude. Our small group of Anglo–Indians, aged between five and nine, was joined by Philip, who had left to enter a prep school, but had nowhere to go for his holidays and had to come back to Bexhill. He can hardly have been more than ten, but to us he was wonderfully grown-up. After lights out he told us stories; among them a long serial, in which he related from memory the whole story of *King Solomon's Mines*. Learning to read need no longer be just another boring school lesson, I realised, if it would enable me to follow so gripping a tale. It came easily; somebody gave me *The Coral Island*, and the rest of Ballantyne followed.

In the spring of 1923 my mother came back for six weeks from India. Men in the Public Works Department had nine months off, every four years; convention allowed their wives to leave them in the middle of their tour, to find out how their children were faring. I had been writing to 'Dear Mummy and Daddy' every week; my mother, who ordinarily kept everything written by me or about me, mercifully disposed of all except for two, one reporting the loss of both front teeth at tea, the other describing the end of term Christmas feast. But when the Mummy of the letters arrived in person it was difficult to accept her tentative caresses. Something of the blue-stocking had sunk in; she was not a naturally cuddly person. It was like being with just another aunt, to be welcomed for giving me treats, like going to see a Charlie Chaplin film, but not really close.

By this time the new Ballykilty was ready. The architect was 'Pa' Hicks, who had made his name by converting a Martello Tower, originally erected to defy Napoleon, into his family home. His speciality was homely homes; he made quite a reputation with them in and around Dublin – Samuel Beckett grew up in one of them in Foxrock. Ballykilty proved to be chronically damp and in winter petrifyingly cold, but my mother was reassured by what she found.

From that time on the holiday's routine scarcely varied. Sometimes I would stay briefly with my mother's sister Joan, but she had four young girls to look after; usually I would be met at Victoria by my father's sister Jean ('Pa' Hicks, when I mentioned her years later, rapturously recalled 'Jeannie with the light brown hair' as one of the most attractive girls he had ever met) and her husband Hugh Geoghegan. They lived with their teen-age daughter Barbara in Golders Green, which he hated, but for some reason would not leave; and for a couple of days Uncle Hugh would put himself out to fall in with my wishes for entertainment. Then, he would put me on the 'Irish Mail', which left morning and evening – always from platform 13 at Euston, which I suspect worried Aunt Jean; she was meticulous about observing the rituals used to ward off Fate, from touching wood to saying, if I sneezed, 'God bless you and keep you from the fairies', repeated after each and every sneeze.

One of the cousinhood would meet me off the boat at Kingstown: Ida, or Charlie Armstrong, who had been made my godfather, would be there to pass me on to the stopping train to Malahide where, in the early 1920s, there was still a horse-drawn cab meeting passenger trains. It took me up the hill from the Diamond, past the Church to the new Ballykilty, which from this time on until the war I regarded as home.

The domestic routine hardly varied. Before breakfast I would collect the *Irish Times* from Roseneath, across the lane, where the Franks lived. It was brought up from the station each morning by the Franks' gardener, Paddy, almost the stock stage Irishman, with that long upper lip made familiar to the British in *Punch* cartoons, though by this time mysteriously vanishing (as Frank O'Connor was later to observe, puzzled at the rapidity of its disappearance). Then, the milkman would arrive. Joe's cows grazed in the field beside Ballykilty; we could have had the milk jugs filled by handing them through the fence. As it was, they came in a cart whose back seat had been removed to be replaced by two milk 'churns', as we called them, though they were simply containers, with polished brass taps sticking out through the tailboard, from which the jugs left outside by householders were filled. The jugs could be seen every morning, in all shapes and sizes, outside Malahide's front doors.

The bread vans followed. There were two rival firms, both Dublin-based, Kennedy's and Boland's; I would be sent to select whatever loaves were required. On their way out from Dublin the weight of the load at the back of the van was sufficient to lift the shafts until the horse's hooves barely touched the road; on the way back the rear of the van would be so far up in the air that the shafts appeared to be pressing the horse down. Nobody, though, in Malahide would have dared to be cruel to a horse. 'Ma' Mitchell, who lived further up the road from us, was a powerful-looking woman who did not hesitate to belabour anybody she saw thrashing a horse to speed its progress up the hill. To thrash dogs was all right; horses – except race-horses – no!

Every morning, grandmother would walk down the village to shop, but mainly to gossip; better still, to hear and pass on scandal. Scandal was the life-support of the old ladies – as I thought of them, though grandmother herself was still in her early fifties. If there was no current scandal, she would seize the opportunity to drag up some dirt from the past.

A charming woman, Charlotte Thornhill, used to come and stay in Malahide occasionally, still carrying a mildly disreputable aura because, as Ellen O'Malley, she had been an actress. Impressed by her performance as Nora in *John Bull's Other Island*, Bernard Shaw had determined that she should play Ellie Dunn in *Heartbreak House*; when the producer tried to insist on the part being given to another actress, Shaw took it out of his hands and had it produced in another theatre. 'I wrote the part for her; and it fits her like a glove,' he wrote to tell St John Ervine; no other actress, except two who were too old, could do it. He had known her before the war, and it had irritated him that she was given only *ingénue* parts, in which she had been 'about as interesting as a steam hammer closing licked envelopes'; but before he could extricate her, she had married 'a very good sort of man (they really deserved one another and were an ideal couple).'

When Thornhill died on war service abroad, Shaw had seized the opportunity to rehabilitate 'that most forlorn of actresses, a dud *ingénue*'; and she had played Ellie. But her run of bad luck continued: *Heartbreak House*, which today would probably run *St Joan* close as a contender for the award of Shaw's most impressive contribution to the theatre, was a flop. Later, she found she could no longer memorise the kind of parts she was being offered. She turned to teaching diction; I can recall her saying, in the late 1920s, that the young actor to keep an eye on was Ralph Richardson. I found her delightful; but grandmother, though she fawned on her if they met in the village, resented her. If her name came up in conversation, and somebody recalled that she had been 'Ellen O'Malley', grandmother would invariably interject 'Queenie Jones', in a cross between a snigger and sneer. (It had been the first stage name which Charlotte had used.) Inevitably this would be relayed back to her, to her annoyance, as she had hoped her later achievement as Ellen O'Malley had led to its being forgotten. She would never come to Ballykilty.

The other talking point, on those shopping encounters, was the civil war which had broken out after the Treaty of 1921. The fighting which had led up to the Treaty had been traumatic enough; the Unionists had come to mistrust and fear the 'Black and Tans' as much as they detested the rebels. The decision of some of the rebels to hold out for a Republic, though, proved even more destructive. In general Anglo–Irish families were assumed to be on the side of the Free State, and were consequently a target for the IRA.

Gordon Campbell, who had used his influence in London to get my mother back to India, had returned to work in Dublin. One night he and his family were roused by masked men and told to leave the house, but not the grounds. In his wife Beatrice's recollection they were courteous, even a little apologetic, helping to get the children's toys – it was shortly before Christmas – out of the house. Beatrice, who despised possessions, found the occasion exhilarating, telling the masked men what they could do, and what they must not do; but the revolvers they carried so frightened the gangling nine-year-old Paddy that his knees began to knock together. His mother stuffed a pillow between them; when a raider ordered 'Hands Up!' it fell, and his knees began to rattle again 'like castanets', leaving them painfully bruised.

Nobody was likely to bother to burn down Ballykilty; but grandmother's sister, my great-aunt Maggie, and her husband and daughter went through the same experience in County Meath. He had been known as a 'good' landlord, who had not pressed for his rents when times were bad; but this afforded no protection. He was still a landlord, an enemy of the people. Disgusted, he moved to England, where he died soon after – of grief, we were told. Aunt Maggie lived on in London in a tiny flat where I was to see and hear a wireless for the first time: a crystal set.

In between the gossip about 'the Troubles' there was the shopping at Hogan's general store. It took time, as few of the goods in those days came packaged. Sugar was taken from a sugar loaf of pyramid shape; butter was scooped out of a tub and patted into the 'brick' that remains the standard shape to this day. At first Hogan's had only two rivals, one of them a small, dirty huckster's shop of the kind still occasionally found in Ireland, with a wretched collection of tired vegetables, a few tins of food and drink, and assorted sweets. Its owner, Maggie Winnett, had been a local 'character'; she was bedridden, and once each holidays I had to visit her – much as the young Guy Crouchback, in Waugh's *Officers and Gentlemen*, had to visit Mrs Barnett because his mother felt Mrs Barnett would miss it if he did not come. Unlike Mrs Barnett, Maggie Winnett was embarrassingly, effusively, garrulously thankful for the appearances of her 'young dochther'; Grandmother hoped this might excuse her failure to patronise the shop.

The other store was in the Post Office, presided over by Mrs Holton, who sold everything from lamp oil to bottled stout. She had four rounds of different types of butter, fresh from their tubs, on the counter; Win Knowles remembered watching fascinated when customers found it hard to make up their minds, as Mrs Holton would 'deftly remove the pencil which reposed in her ginger-coloured bun of hair and, scooping the blunt end into the mound of butter, tender it for tasting'. But when the telephone reached Malahide – grandfather was one of the earliest customers; Ballykilty was Malahide 4 – it became difficult enough to dispense stamps and deal with telegrams as well as selling groceries. The Post Office ceased to be a store, though it held its own as a place to linger in. Mrs Holton's daughter, with her rich but penetrating voice, could be heard making the connections and, often, chatting with the subscribers as she connected them.

The store was to be replaced by Findlater's, one of a new chain. This was another embarrassment to grandmother. She felt bound to patronise it, as the owners were cousins. This was not something to be proud of, certainly not to boast about; but grandfather, she felt, would have liked her to shop there, because his mother had been a Findlater. On the other hand, he would not have wanted her to leave Hogan's. She compromised by dividing her shopping between them, often with confusing results; she would forget what she had bought in one after pausing for chats on the way to the other.

It did not occur to me then to try to understand the contradictions firmly established in her character: on the one hand, a lack of sensibility accompanied by a disposition towards malice; on the other, a determination to fulfil certain social obligations, and to make sure I did, too. Once each holiday I also had to call on Mary Brophy, who had been her cook-general for years, but had left on the excuse that the hill would be too much for her. A few months later she had taken a job at a house even further up the hill. She had found grandmother, without grandfather, too tiresome to deal with. Although grandmother was hurt by the defection, she still insisted I must do what well-behaved children were expected to do, and visit her as an old family retainer.

Grandmother, in fact, was guided by the social mores instilled into her; partly as a child, but still more through her passionate admiration for her husband. Whatever he did, and thought, *must* have been right. In spite of the continuing hostility of Archdeacon Lindsay – the 'archdemon', as she would call him – she managed to have a memorial stained glass window installed in the church, portraying the good Samaritan; she took her seat in the pew beside it every Sunday morning. She was not a religious woman; morning service, for her, was welcome mainly for the opportunity it provided afterwards to talk to people who, since grandfather's death, were less inclined to visit her, or have her round. But in general, her ways continued to follow the courses mapped out for her by what grandfather would have approved.

In one respect, this was fortunate for me. Even more than the church, the Island Golf Club was a shrine to his memory. The first time I came back to Malahide on holiday I was presented with one of grandfather's old clubs, cut down to fit my size, along with a battered golf ball, and shown how to play.

At first, grandmother took me to the Island as a duty; soon, as a habit; and it was not long before she let me go there on my own. What harm could possibly come to me? The two boatmen who ferried golfers over the estuary, 'Vincie' and Hatch, had both been employed by grandfather, and were treasured as if they were family retainers on an estate. The artful Vincie O'Brien, one eye closed as if in a protracted wink, was one of those characters with which Anglo–Irish recollections, in memoirs and in fiction, abound. If invited to play a round of golf at the Island, he would ask to be given 'hoops', instead of the strokes which, with his high handicap, he would ordinarily take. Innocents would agree, assuming it was some local custom; only to find that this meant he was entitled to shout 'whoops' as they reached the top of their backswing; an unnerving prospect well-calculated to put them off their stroke. It was characteristic that he should be known to all of us by his Christian name. I never heard the dour but reliable Hatch, who rarely spoke, called anything but Hatch.

In the clubhouse were Mary Jane, who did the catering and the cooking – years before, she had been the cook at Ballykilty – and Mary Molly, who helped and did the cleaning. They, too, could be regarded as family retainers. Soon, I was collecting other golf clubs, and carrying them in a 'ladies' bag hardly bigger than the sheath in which pictures of Robin Hood showed where he stowed his arrows; playing matches with Tony Robertson over the full eighteen holes, often joined by Frank Cave, the son of the new rector. Going shopping with grandmother almost ceased; on fine days, the Island took precedence.

On one appointed day each holidays, however, wet or fine, grandmother took me to Dublin to shop for St Catherine's needs. The day had to be arranged in advance because there was an appointment with Sheridan the dentist in his elegant consulting rooms near the Shelbourne Hotel on St Stephen's Green; a dreaded occasion, as he did not like to use anaesthetics during 'stoppings'. Yet he was gentle by the standards of the time. Then, we crossed at Dawson Street to Stephens and Bourke for new shoes, always examined with the help of the X-ray machine the shop had proudly installed, to find if there was room for the toes to wiggle. Next, there was Jules, the hairdresser, with his huge brushes descending from the ceiling on ropes, twirling round to sweep away loose hairs. Not until years later were the X-rays banished as dangerous, and the brushes as unhygienic.

Coffee and buns would follow at Bewley's Oriental Café in Grafton Street, one of the few landmarks to survive into the 1980s; afterwards, a visit to Charlie Armstrong or Cousin Ida; then, back to Aston's Quay to catch the Malahide bus. Until the red 'pirate' buses were outlawed, there would usually be one of them waiting to take off a few minutes before the scheduled service. Grandmother never took it; grandfather would have disapproved. Even when it was raining, we waited on that windswept quay for the company's bus, with grandmother expressing her contempt for those who succumbed to the lure of the pirates.

She had no wireless at Ballykilty, until cousin Mungo Park came back from the East with a present of one; but *The Coral Island*, *Ungava* and other Ballantyne's, reinforced by Ernest Thomson Seton's animal stories, read and re-read, sufficed. And the next day, unless it was too stormy for the boat to brave the estuary, there would again be the Island. For a golf and adventure story addict, it was an idyllic existence, on which 'the Troubles' rarely impinged. There was only the occasional scare locally. Rumour on one occasion had it that the rebels planned to blow up the railway bridge which carried the main line to Belfast across the estuary. A posse of volunteers went out to defend it, among them 'Pa' Hicks who took the precaution of bringing a tea-cosy to keep his head and ears warm; but no rebel force arrived.

Only once did I become directly aware of what was happening, as distinct from hearing grandmother's lamentations whenever friends and acquaintances were reported in the *Irish Times* as the rebels' targets. We had gone over to the Island, and from the first tee, looking out over the point between Malahide and Portmarnock, we could see black smoke being carried out to sea from the coastguard station, which had been burned down the night before. Grandmother and the other golfers who had come on the boat stood looking at it, for a while, and castigating the perpetrators, before driving off. I could not help recalling the episode, years later, when somebody presented me with a copy of Harry Graham's *Ruthless Rhymes for Heartless Homes*,

I was playing golf the day that the Germans landed,
All our troops had run away, all our ships were stranded
And the thought of England's shame, altogether spoilt my game.

My parents came back from Poona on leave in 1925. But for some photographs of my father at Ballykilty, I would have entirely forgotten him; yet it proved easier to come to terms with him than with my mother because he played golf, and could give me lessons. He also had a car, a Fiat, shaped like an old-fashioned bathtub. Best of all, he had decided he would like to have a few days trout fishing in the West of Ireland. A group of us went down to stay at the Butler Arms in Waterville, County Kerry. As the car was full of fishing gear, my mother and I went by train on one of the romantic lines that were soon to be closed, along the coast to Cahirciveen. At some point, coming out of a tunnel onto a mountainside, it provided a spectacular view over the sea of a kind I had not encountered before, capturing me for the West there and then. I was to become a fly-fishing addict to the point of willingly sacrificing even golf when the opportunity occurred.

The convention was that Anglo–Indian children, and indeed most boys destined by their parents to go to public schools, would have four years at a prep school – usually a boarding school – on the principle that it would provide the necessary hardening to enable them to face the rigours of public school life. I was already hardened, up to a point; my mother must have noticed the streak of insensitivity it had induced, observing my undisguised preference for the company of my father. Only once, though, did it prompt a worried rebuke.

Mary Brophy had been succeeded as grandmother's cook-general by Bridget, a young woman who, most unusually for those times in Ireland, was six foot tall. We got on well, and I would often be in and out of the kitchen. As we were leaving Ballykilty – my parents to return to India, I to school – she stooped down to kiss me. I slapped her face. 'You shouldn't have done that,' they said, as soon as we were in the car. 'She's only a servant,' I replied. Both of them then muttered something to the effect that I shouldn't think things like that, let alone say them; but they must have realised that this was what I had been conditioned to accept. A nanny could kiss; not a servant.

My mother could not bring herself, even later, to regret the convention that had compelled her to leave me at St Catherine's at the age of five. 'Compelled' is hardly too strong a term; mothers who preferred to come back with their children were ostracised – as Mrs Russell, soon to come to live in Malahide with her son Beano, found herself. The only hint that my mother felt a little defensive about it came years later, when she recalled in a letter how she had been careful to ensure that I was not a mother's darling, while in India. I would stay contentedly with her friends the Richards', or with Aunt Joan when she was out there, a reassurance that I would be self-reliant and get on well with other children. But there must have been many occasions, on that leave, when she would have felt disturbed by the loss of the emotional tie which most mothers had with their sons.

3

Dragons

There are four grades of school, Mr Levy of Church and Gargoyle, scholastic agents, told Paul Pennyfeather in Waugh's *Decline and Fall*: 'Leading School, First-rate School, Good School, and School. Frankly, School is pretty bad.' In the 1920s there were a great many in the grade 'School'; my mother had made inquiries among her friends in India who had children at preparatory schools to find if theirs could confidently be recommended. The one which had emerged in the 'leading' category had been the Dragon School, Oxford; I had been put down for it; and I was taken there shortly before she and Claude left for India.

My mother watched me play my first game of rugby football; she was amused to see that the second row forward whose buttocks I was shoving from the back row was Crystal, daughter of A. P. Herbert, already admired for his *Punch* articles and soon to enjoy his first success as a writer of lyrics for the theatre. 'The Dragon', as it was generally called – except by those who had known it when it was 'Lynams', the name of the two brothers who had founded it around the turn of the century – was co-educational, unusual at the time; but as there were only 25 or so girls to nearly 300 boys, they did not attract much attention until the time came for them to appear in school plays, or impending adolescence made us look at them with different eyes. For me, it was a boys' school. I enjoyed rugger that term; soccer, and hockey, which we played in the Lent term; and, in summer, cricket and swimming in the still unpolluted Cherwell, which ran along the far side of the playing fields.

We had to work. 'Hum' Lynam, the headmaster – his brother, 'the

Skipper', had retired to sail the seven seas in his yacht, the *Blue Dragon* – was under no illusions that the curriculum could be geared to anything except the Common Entrance examination for public schools. If it looked possible that one or other of us, by making a greater effort, could win a scholarship, Hum was scrupulously careful to ask the parents if for financial reasons they needed the boy to be helped (the word 'crammed', which was implied, was avoided); if they did not, would they wish him to be helped anyway, as they might like the idea that he could achieve the distinction. For the rest of us, all but a handful would need to pass the Common Entrance. Unless parents specifically said they did not care whether their boy passed it or not we were made to work for it.

As well as the work, though, and the games there were facilities for a range of activities from carpentry to playing the violin. And, more importantly, there was encouragement to develop whatever talents we might have, outside those fostered by the curriculum. In *Surprised by Joy* C. S. Lewis recalled that among the 'new bugs' in his year at his public school there were two who had come from the Dragon, 'and from them I got an impression that there was a world I had never dreamed of, a world in which poetry, say, was a thing public and accepted, just as Games and Gallantry.' And in *Summoned by Bells* John Betjeman recalled the days he and others whose tastes ran to botany or architecture had found them catered for by one of the older masters, Gerald Haynes

> Much do I owe this formidable man
> (Harrow and Keble): from his shambling height
> Over his spectacles he nodded down
> We called him 'Tortoise' . . .

Ten years later, so did we; not to his face, even if he was in a good humour, as he was growing crotchety. Yet it was characteristic of the school that we thought of most of the masters as friends, and although it might be yes sir, no sir in class, outside class we called many of them, and called to them, by their Christian names.

It was at the Dragon that I first became aware of my Irish identity. One of my contemporaries was Bryan Gahan, from Kilkenny; we became friends, soon to be known as 'I' and 'Y' as a convenient distinction. Neither of us had an Irish accent; individually we might have passed for English, but as a pair, both from Ireland, we tended to be the butt of mild teasing – not, as has happened since, for being simpletons, but for 'Irish bate' – hot temper. Neither of us was in the least belligerent, or hot-tempered, but we found the implications useful. Together we formed an alliance proof against bullying, so long as we gave the impression that we would be dangerous adversaries.

One winter when we were both playing for the school rugger side, which was in danger of defeat, our history master 'Bruno' called to us from the touchline, 'Remember Cromwell!' History was my star subject, but Ireland scarcely figured in the books we used; I had no idea what he was talking about. It was clear, though, that the Irish must have suffered at Cromwell's hands. Both of us tried to take it out of the other side with renewed ferocity. For a time, I was to begin to feel Irish in England more than I felt Irish in Ireland, where the 'Anglo' element prevailed.

The Anglo–Irish Protestant minority, Yeats told the Irish Senate in 1925 in his speech against the Cosgrave government's legislation abolishing divorce in the Free State,

> are no petty people. We are one of the great stocks of Europe. We are the people of Burke; we are the people of Grattan; we are the people of Swift, the people of Emmet, the people of Parnell. We have created most of the modern literature of this country. We have created the best of its political intelligence . . .

I doubt whether any of the men he cited would have meant anything to me, except Swift; we had been set *Gulliver's Travels* to read as a holiday task, as Hum was a believer that every boy in the school should at least to try to read, during the holidays, one of the classics of English literature.

When I thought of myself as Irish, though, it was with the assumption of Anglo-Irish superiority, reinforced by the fact that my heroes tended to be from the predominantly Anglo–Irish rugger teams. There was the great forward 'Jemmy' Clinch, immortalised by a sports reporter who described him as crossing the line for a try 'festooned with Saxons'; and the crafty full-back Ernie Crawford who, seeing two English three-quarters bearing down on him with nobody else between them and the line, shouted 'pass' out of the corner of his mouth before diving to tackle the one who, with luck, would (and did) receive the pass. A passion for rugby football, even as a spectator, was a much more effective inculcator of patriotism than any political indoctrination – and still is. How else could the Irish rugger side have for so long surmounted the problems presented by partition, and remained chosen from both sides of the Border?

My friend Tony Robertson was a born rugby footballer – he was to get into Portora's first XV in his first term there; and on one of what had now become our frequent visits to the Island he produced a miniature rugby football which he had managed to save up to buy. Between us we invented a one-a-side game, played on the beach after the tide went out so that a pitch could be marked on the hard, damp sand. How we played it, I forget; but one of Tony's tries was scored by the remarkable feat of 'selling me a dummy' – so remarkable that the story got around, in rugby-playing circles. Thirty years later one of Fleet Street's advertising executives came up to me in a pub to ask, 'Are you the Brian Inglis who . . . ?' When I told him I was, he fell about laughing; he had been dining out on the tale of my discomfiture, he claimed, for years.

Tony and Frank enjoyed golf; I was infatuated with the game. Partly this was the consequence of the lure of the Island – the boat-crossing as preliminary, followed by the descent, at the second hole, into the valleys among the sandhills. Apart from the summit of the third – the notorious Andes – there was no further glimpse of the outside world until the ninth. Even the names of the holes were romantic: Stoneybatter, Valhalla – and Cricketfield; so-called, we were assured, because W. G. Grace had once played there, and been bowled for a duck; an even more improbable tale than the scores of others in which he featured, and still does, because the springy turf surface ruled out any possibility that cricket could ever have been played there.

The Island had its silences, but not many. From the sandhills closer to the beach came the soothing sound of the surf and the raucous sound of terns; there were curlews, and numerous larks. Bracken beside one part of the course and rushes by others provided us with the opportunity to construct an alternative game; one of us would take up a position while the other two, sometimes joined by friends, tried to get as close to him as possible without being detected. Even on stormy days when I could not go, I still could use the putting course I had laid out on the lawn at Ballykilty, lavishing care and Brasso on my motley collection of clubs – their names, too, romantic: driver, brassie, spoon, cleek, mid-iron, jigger, mashie, mashie-niblick, niblick, putter. No wonder that golf was so addictive, when the implements – unlike the matched sets which were soon to cast a numbered pall over the game – each had a personal history, some dating back to grandfather's early visits to the Island.

Although I no longer went shopping with grandmother, she would greet me on my return from the Island with whatever scraps of scandal there might be; and in 1926 there was a ninety-nine days' wonder in which Malahide for once became the most written-about village in the country. 'A house in flames, and six dead bodies lying on the lawn!' – Judge Kenneth Deale set the scene in his *Memorable Irish Trials* in 1960 – 'This dreadful happening on the 31st March 1926 at Malahide, a village near Dublin, is still remembered there.'

La Mancha was a substantial house half a mile or so from the village. It had been owned by Tony Robertson's father; but on his death his widow found he had left hardly any money, and the family, three girls and two boys, had to move to St James's Terrace. The brothers McDonnell, retired merchants, had bought the house and lived there with two sisters and two servants, 'all wiped out in one awful stroke', as Deale put it. The fire brigade arrived in time to pull out the bodies from the burning house, but not to save the house itself, which was gutted.

The McDonnell's gardener, Henry McCabe, fell under suspicion; his lies and prevarications quickly turned it into the near-certainty that he was the criminal. Brought to trial in November, he made a sorry showing; the jury took less than an hour to find him guilty. The prosecution's case, though, was not watertight, and there was some feeling that he ought not to be hanged – certainly not by Pierrepoint, the British executioner, who had hanged Sir Roger Casement, and who would have to be brought over, as there was nobody qualified in the Free State to undertake the task. In *More Kicks that Pricks*

Samuel Beckett was to recall the campaign for a reprieve: 'Belacqua', collecting lobster for lunch, heard from 'the tragic voice across the counter' that the petition for mercy, 'signed by half the land, having been rejected, the man must swing at dawn in Mountjoy'. With Pierrepoint officiating, McCabe duly did.

Deale called it 'the Malahide mystery', partly because it was hard to see how McCabe could have committed all the murders, one by one; partly because valuables which the McDonnells were known to possess had disappeared, and could not be traced to McCabe or anybody else. A possibility was that he – or the real murderer – might have buried them in the grounds. The temptation was to go prospecting with a spade; but it would have to be at night, and the fear of ghosts was an effective deterrent. Frank and I went once to see what remained of La Mancha; the steps up to the hall door, and the gutted ruin were as they had been after the fire, as nobody had cared to re-build. Even when the property was sold, and the remains demolished, it was left for years undeveloped; but eventually, as the commuters began to flow in, along with executives from the new airport nearby at Collinstown, La Mancha was submerged under what the older residents disgustedly described as a bungaloid growth.

On one other occasion, Malahide was again to be in the news – and internationally. In 1930 it was reported that a collection of Boswell manuscripts had been found in a box originally used for storing croquet materials. The interest in Malahide was largely centred on how the papers had been found; it was typical, the gossips told each other, of poor old Lord Talbot that they should have been stuffed into the box – he might have done it himself. The only surprise was that they had not been used to light the Castle fires with.

As that genial, now forgotten, author George A. Birmingham – in public life, Canon Hannay – once observed, peers are not taken so seriously in Ireland as they are in Britain. We were not impressed by the fact that Lord Talbot's ancestors had come over to Ireland with Strongbow in the twelfth century; he seemed to us a sadly downtrodden little man, obviously henpecked by his formidable-looking wife. Soon after the war began she formed a committee to make preparations in case Ireland was invaded, and my cousin Hilda Park was a member. One of its meetings happened to be held the morning it was announced that the Italians had invaded Eritrea.

'Who owns Eritrea?' somebody asked. After a moment's pause, as nobody felt quite sure of the answer, Lord Talbot was heard to ask 'Who trains her?'

Ancestry did not interest me – not even my own, with a single exception, thanks to the way Uncle Hugh used patiently to take me to see the sights, whenever I stayed a night or two in Golders Green. In the Tower of London there was an engraving of Colonel Thomas Blood, who in 1671 had tried to steal the Crown Jewels – and very nearly succeeded; he had actually got hold of the Crown and Orb and was leaving the Tower when he was caught.

For a schoolboy, Blood was an ancestor worth boasting about. There was a portrait of him at Ballykilty, looking suitably sinister. A mystery remains about him which, so far as I know, has never been fully explained. He was one of the most unscrupulous and dangerous rogues in Irish history, with a long record of violent crime. In 1663 he had tried to capture Dublin Castle; as a former Cromwellian soldier, he was aggrieved by the Lord Lieutenant's liberal policies after the restoration of Charles II, in particular Ormonde's conciliatory attitude to Catholics. Thwarted, he tried in 1670 to kidnap Ormonde in St James's Street in London, intending to hang him at Tyburn; but, again, Ormonde escaped. Then came Blood's attempt to steal the Crown Jewels. Yet Charles II pardoned him, even awarding him land in Ireland. Why? The most plausible explanation has been that the theft was conducted on the King's behalf; the jewels would have been taken to the Continent and pawned.

Otherwise the Bloods were an undistinguished lot. Many of them had been army officers: one, Sir Bindon Blood, a general. His *Four Score Years and Ten*, published in 1933, reads today like a parody, with its tone of glib self-satisfaction about the occasions he arranged tiger-shoots, with elephants and beaters; one tigress 'gave me a good galloping shot at about 30 yards, which I took successfully, killing her with one bullet so that she went head over heels. Quite a pretty shot, though I say it!'

My mother was proud of the fact that Fanny Blood had been the cherished companion of Mary Wollstonecraft, whom she greatly admired; but she was inclined to poke fun at those members of her family who took their ancestry seriously. Shortly before she died she was sent the proofs of a proposed new edition of *Burke's Irish Family Records*, with the request that she would check the information on her own family. To her astonishment there were fifteen packed pages of branches of the Bloods. Many of them were people she had known – 'such cod!' One entry particularly amused her, listing one of her uncles as Francis Johnston Corscadden Blood 'of Hampstead, Glasnevin, Co. Dublin', which to the uninitiated could have passed as an estate. 'Hampstead' had in fact been a private nursing home for members of 'good' families who had to be put away, usually because of alcoholism.

Ascendancy society was notorious for the high incidence of alcoholics, among them two of Bernard Shaw's uncles who, he recalled, 'died in the family retreat, Dr Eustace's, in the north of Dublin'. 'Dr Eustace's' also took in two of grandmother's sisters, my great-aunts; both were cured, but Aunt Jessie had decided it was best to stay on there. She used to come to Ballykilty for Christmas; a gentle creature, it was impossible to visualise her drunk. She had been put into 'Dr Eustace's' before the turn of the century, the family contributing to a capital sum which paid for her at the established rate, £3 a week. As the staff became fond of her, and she caused no trouble, no attempt was made to charge any more until after the Second World War, when inflation compelled Dr Eustace – who must have been the son, or grandson, of the one who admitted her – to put up the rate. The capital, from which it had to be taken, rapidly dwindled. Charlie Armstrong, who had been left in charge of her affairs, began to get worried; but Aunt Jessie died as she had lived, unobtrusively, just as the money ran out.

Grandmother was losing her memory, which was becoming exasperating; she would ask the same question two, three, four times an evening after I returned from the Island. But she had one more good turn to do me. As a young woman she had fallen in love with Leenane, on the Killary estuary – a small-scale replica of a Norwegian fjord – and took me down there on two summer holidays, between my parents' leaves.

Trains then still ran between Galway and Clifden, another of the lines which tourists would now flock to use in the West if they could be reconstituted, running as it did though Connemara, along the flank of the Twelve Pins. 'The best guide-book ever written cannot set the view before the mind's eye of the reader,' Thackeray wrote in his description of them, admitting that he could not hope to conjure up the picture 'of those wild mountains, over which the clouds as they passed, or the sunshine as it went and came, cast every variety of tint, light and shadow'. All he could do was 'lay down my pen and ruminate, and cry "Beautiful" once more, and to the reader say, "come and see"'.

We were joined at Leenane by my cousin Cecil Park, his wife Hilda, and their son Johnny, four years younger than me but just old enough to be put into the care of Meehan the ghillie, who showed us how to catch trout in Joyce's river. Meehan had only one arm – the other had been 'bit off be a pig' when he was a child – but he could tie tiny trout flies onto the finest '4 X' gut casts quicker than I was ever able to do, and he was the ghillie most in demand when his services were not already booked by the tall, commanding Mr Punch, managing director of a firm in Cork, who used to bring back catches on days when nobody else had even 'risen' a fish.

A Manchester businessman who had grown up in Leenane was to write to me after reading *West Briton* to recall his affection for Meehan, whose cottage was on the family estate. Jimmy Meehan made a living in the summer, but found the winters hard; and he would not accept charity. So he had to be asked for advice on which variety of potato, or cabbage, was keeping best that year, before accepting a bagful. He inspired immediate trust; although Johnny, an only son, was seven at the time, Hilda had no hesitation in leaving us with Meehan. His face and his calm confidence are still with me.

I longed to go back to Leenane when my parents returned on leave in 1929; but my mother had written to say they had other plans for the summer. I was at school when they came to Oxford to take me out for the day (it was close to the end of term, but that meant it was exam time, and there could be no question of starting the holidays earlier). They rang from the station to say they were on their way, and Hum himself brought me from my class room to meet them at the school gates. The taxi drew up on the other side of the road, and as they got out Hum whispered, 'Go on. Go on over!' and, as I hesitated, 'Go on, kiss them!'

I had never kissed my father; the idea of kissing a man had not even occurred to me. Greeting Ida, or Aunt Jean, I submitted to the ritual peck, and could expect it from my mother. But to hug them, as Hum clearly expected, was inconceivable. I had written to them regularly, every week, and her letters had been as regular; but it was as a letter-writer that I knew her. As flesh and blood, she was a stranger. The encounter was acutely embarrassing.

In *Goodbye to All That* Robert Graves recalled that a twelve-year-old boy at his prep school had to be told that his parents in India had died of cholera. He was watched, initially with sympathy, but it turned to disgust when he continued to fool around as he had before. 'He could not have been expected to do otherwise,' Graves felt. 'He had not seen his parents for two years. And Preparatory schoolboys live in a world completely dissociated from home life.' In such circumstances, school became the reality, 'and home life the illusion'. Had I heard that I had been orphaned in the same way, I am sure that the St Catherine's conditioning would have led me to behave in the prescribed fashion; a few tears would have been shed, followed by a stiff upper lip and a day or two of occasional abstraction; but I doubt whether there would have been any real feeling.

Once again, I was to find my father the easier of the two to get on with when the holidays came. Not that we had much in common except golf; but he had greater self-confidence owing to his success in the PWD. This was the result of a combination of fruitful new ideas, such as that time could be saved in preparing land for drainage by studying the weeds on it (making it possible to assess the condition of the subsoil accurately, and thereby to reduce the need for boreholes), and impressive results, vindicating theories which had often been scoffed at by his superiors. He had no diplomacy; my mother used to cite one of his colleagues as saying that 'The trouble with Inglis is that he can't be content with showing a man is a fool; he must show he is a bloody fool.' If any of his recommendations had proved to be unsound, he would have been in trouble. As things were, when the Irrigation Development and Research Circle was set up in 1927, he was put in charge. As it was exactly the post he wanted this eased his mind, leaving him more placid.

My mother did her best to come to terms with the young Philistine she had to deal with; this cannot have been easy, as my holiday diary that summer reveals. 'The Skipper' had established that we Dragons should all keep diaries, rather than read a classic, in the summer holidays. Mine recorded that within an hour of reaching Malahide I was on the boat to the Island, and thereafter went to play golf there every day except Sunday, when boys and women were not permitted, or when it poured.

'Y' and I had been made prefects for our last year. This, too, was valuable, as Hum insisted that their role was to make themselves useful, to look after the school – from turning out the lights at night, to breaking up fights which broke out on the playground. The aim was to try to instil a sense of responsibility to the community before they went on to their public schools. The two of us had won our colours as forwards in the school rugger team, and were in line to win them for cricket, when the news came in 1929 from Uncle Hugh that I would have to leave a term early, to be sure of a place in Oldham's House at Shrewsbury.

Hugh, like my father, had been at Shrewsbury, and as he knew Oldham had put me down for his house. As Hugh was formally my guardian, in the absence of my parents, Oldham had written to him to tell him that an unexpected vacancy had occurred; if I wanted to be certain to go to Oldham's, it would be wise for me to step into it. Hum was annoyed. Public schools, he used to complain, tended to regard prep schools as having no function except to get boys through the common infectious diseases – measles, mumps and scarlet fever – and the Common Entrance. In a letter to my mother expressing his disappointment, he suggested that the public schools were feeling the pinch of the Great Crash of 1929. Several of them were collecting boys earlier than planned. 'We shall miss the "two B's" a good deal,' he claimed. 'Your Brian has been going along his rather comfortable way, with no signs of overwork, and his usual very pleasant demeanour.'

Report after report had been making the same point, sometimes less politely. 'A little inclined to be charmingly ineffective,' Hum had written the term before, 'an inclination which he must strenuously resist.' He had asked my mother if she thought I needed to be pushed, from her point of view, as a scholarship would have been a faint possibility; she had said no; so there had been no pressure. A sense of duty made Hum give the group of leavers a brief lecture on the problems we would encounter at puberty; all I can remember of it is that we were not to worry if we woke up to find our pyjama trousers damp. Bryan and I left the Dragon with genuine regret, but tempered with the feeling that our next schools would be surely even more enjoyable.

4

Salopian

There cannot be many public school housemasters who have been the subject of a full-scale biography; but Michael Charlesworth's *J. B. Oldham*, published in 1986, is a sympathetic account of a man who led a life which 'whatever its importance, was extraordinary'. Charlesworth only came to Oldham's Hall as a new boy the term after Oldham retired; but when he returned to Shrewsbury to teach he found Oldham still school Librarian, and came to know him well. The fact he was not in the house under Oldham has helped him to present a more balanced view of this character than any of us who were under his charge could have hoped to give.

James Basil Oldham had entered Shrewsbury at the same time as my father, though neither of them had any recollection of the other. An elder brother had acquired the nickname of 'the Gash'; Basil – perhaps because of a certain slurring of his voice – became 'the Gush'. He was to find it had stuck to him when, after Oxford and a scaled-down version of the 'Grand Tour', he had an invitation from the headmaster to return to Shrewsbury for one term to teach history, a subject then held in such little esteem that in the History Side, formed from boys specialising in the subject, he had only three pupils.

The temporary appointment, however, was renewed, term by term; and when the number of boys began to increase following the arrival of the polymath C. A. Alington as Headmaster, he was not merely brought in to the permanent staff but encouraged to build the new house that was needed, out of his own pocket – on his terms: he would be the housemaster, and have the lease for ninety-nine years.

This appeared to ensure he would remain housemaster until he retired. In the meantime, he determined to make his house outstanding not in terms of sporting or scholastic achievement (though he would have welcomed that, too), but in producing the Right Type of Boy.

Godliness and manliness were the qualities to be sought after, 'along with Loyalty and a sense of Duty', Charlesworth recalls; 'team spirit' summed up all these qualities. This, Oldham believed, required a degree of intimacy with those boys whom he was prepared to trust, far closer than most housemasters would have approved. He actually described himself as homosexual. The term had only come into use in the 1890s; he employed it in its initial sense of preferring male to female. In his case, this was an understatement; he would occasionally show signs of having a physical aversion to women. When it became clear that certain boys were likely to provide him with suitable material, he would take them on trips abroad where, to facilitate the process of getting to know them, he behaved as one of them, while still imposing his rules; a cold bath, or shower, first thing every morning, after which he would put on socks and boots and then shave, before finishing dressing. A heavy drinker of whisky himself, he let his boys drink what they wanted to; we would occasionally be invited to a formal dinner in his section of the house, and given sherry before, and wine with, the meal.

If this system was going to work, Oldham decided, he must show that he could leave the day-to-day running of the house to those in whom he had decided to place his trust. He went to great lengths to avoid interference; if he wanted something, or someone, he would open the door which led from his section and wait there until a boy appeared, before asking him to do whatever was required. He would not even call out, if no boy happened to appear for a time. Only last thing at night, by which time everybody would be in bed, did he come round for a ritual 'lights out'.

As a result, Oldham had little idea what was happening in his house. He did not realise – not, at least, until it began to dawn on him after his retirement – that the loyalty and team spirit which he inculcated were interpreted by his chosen few as being not to him, but to them. For any of us to tell 'the Gush' about what was going on in the House illicitly, because of his misplaced trust, would have been as unthinkable as telling our parents. This conditioning was startlingly effective; I would not have dreamed of telling my parents that after the Dragon School, Shrewsbury for the first couple of years was a hell for anybody who was not an exceptionally gifted footballer or cricketer.

In one respect it was the worse for me, through arriving in the summer term as the only new boy in the house. Oldham benevolently invited me to arrive a day early, to get used to the feel of the place before the rest of the forty-five-odd members of the house arrived; but, being busy, he despatched me to wander round 'the Site', the area enclosed by the school's bounds. Beside the school hall, named after Alington, I encountered another new boy from Riggs Hall – Haydon's House; we fell into conversation, and it turned out he came from Dublin. Ball had an agreeably friendly way with him; how lucky, I thought, to fall in with a likely friend from the start.

During the time we shared at Shrewsbury, I was never to speak to Ball again – except on the mail boat back to Ireland; and when I took to returning on the B & I boats from Liverpool even that connection was lost. There were few more rigorously enforced conventions than that the boys from different houses must not be seen together, however close friends they might be from their prep school or in the holidays.

When we ran a 'John Bull's Schooldays' series in the *Spectator*, from 1958 to 1961, it was the recollection of the first day, and the first term which followed, which I used for my contribution. This prompted Oldham, who was meticulous in corresponding with 'his' boys, as he still thought of them whenever he saw their names in print, to protest that the housemasters could not be held responsible for the 'taboo' as he called it; it came from the boys, and had been there when he himself arrived at Shrewsbury. He had not himself approved, he insisted, 'but as you know as well as I do, it is hopeless to try to break a rule boys have set up for themselves.'

There could hardly have been a more abject admission of failure; yet clearly Oldham still did not realise it. Housemasters in fact condoned the taboo, partly because the general system of letting the boys make their own rules meant that the housemaster would not be required to keep discipline himself; partly because if two boys from different houses consorted together, it might be for, or lead to, sex. By the time I arrived Oldham's had developed into the most boy-controlled house in the school; and this was particularly unfortunate for those boys who had come just before me and those who came just after. We had Watney to fear.

Watney was a house monitor, with ample scope for indulging his appetite for beating younger boys with a 'swagger cane' or, in his bedroom, a slipper. Every Saturday night he would conduct what were known as 'colour exams' in his bedroom, asking what 'colours' footballers or rowers were entitled to wear (the First VIII had no less than nine varieties) and going on to ask esoteric questions about the school and its jargon until enough victims were lined up for his satisfaction.

In Oldham's, though beatings were frequent, only Watney was feared. He even had a cruel face, with a cruel look on it. I have never loathed anybody as much as I loathed him, and I doubt whether there was any other boy in the house, younger than Watney, who did not feel the same. We would fantasise what we would do to him if, by some quirk of Fate, revenge became possible. As it happened, one who suffered under Watney, and for longer than I did, was to have the opportunity to obtain some sort of revenge. 'I hated Watney,' John Malins told me some thirty years after he had left Shrewsbury. By that time he had become a consultant, and one day Watney had been wheeled into his hospital with terminal cancer. It would have been difficult to pity anybody so pitiless; but John had wryly to admit 'He made a good death'.

Yet, in retrospect, I can see that Watney looms too large in memory; he was the exception in Oldham's. The recollections of writers who were at Eton, say, at the same time, or Marlborough, suggests that we were relatively lucky. As for schools in Ireland, the evidence is that boys there were far worse off, with the masters as the tyrants. In English public schools there were very few Wackford Squeers left in action. The Headmaster of Shrewsbury, Canon H. A. P. Sawyer, plied the birch rod occasionally, and house-masters were allowed to beat their boys, though they seldom did. At Irish schools the pandybat was still being wielded as freely and as savagely as it was by the prefect of studies at Clongowes in *A Portrait of the Artist as a Young Man*.

More soul-destroying than the licensed bullying at Shrewsbury was the regimentation. At the Dragon, our free time could be used largely in any way we liked to use it. At Shrewsbury, particularly in the first two years, our time was never our own. Games were compulsory, at least once a day, except on Sundays; and at other times all 'douls' – as fags were known, from the Greek for slaves – had to hang around the house in case they should be called upon to carry out some chore. The school library stood next door to the house, and Oldham was the Librarian, but he would have been surprised to find any doul from his house using it. If challenged on this, he fell back on the excuse that the system was enforced by the boys themselves – as indeed it was; the other douls would have taken it out of any boy who tried to escape by skulking in the library.

Oldham also affected to believe that the derivation from the Greek lent the douling system some sanction. When it was put to him that the term doul was retained only because it was easier for monitors to shout when they needed one, and that in fact for their first two years boys were known as scum, he actually tried to maintain that the term was a corruption of *adsum*, the Latin for 'Present', which earlier in the school's history had been used by the boys at call-overs; a curious example of etymology in its common role as the harlot of the sciences.

Enjoying games as I did, they were one of the two pleasures of Shrewsbury, the other being sex. I was later to be surprised to find that some boys managed to go through their public schools from start to finish without being aware of the prevalence of covert homosexual activities. In Oldham's, homosexual encounters, or the fantasies they conjured up, were pervasive, welcome as lending colour and life to an otherwise drab emotional existence. Public displays of feeling were not encouraged, except for the enthusiasm generated by watching a school or house side storming to victory. Laughter was allowed, but tears were taboo – girlish. Privately, orgasm was the peak experience.

My introduction to the facts of life as met with in a public school was provided by Oldham soon after my arrival. The system he had adopted was to leave a message with the new boy's bedroom monitor that after lights out, the new boy was to be sent down in pyjamas and dressing-gown to Oldham's study. The summons was greeted with glee; the new boy would be told what to expect, and how best to answer leading questions designed to elicit embarrassing information. Oldham would be waiting in his study, also in pyjamas and a dressing-gown which, he explained, was intended to make the new boy feel at ease. Inevitably it had the opposite effect.

As a boy, Oldham had been told that masturbation led inexorably to insanity. He had seen no reason to change this view. It was also 'bad for training', inducing lassitude and poor performance in football or cricket. Mutual masturbation with another boy, he warned, would lead to the immediate expulsion of both. I might find, though – Oldham continued, relaxing – that an older boy would be taking an excessive interest in me, without actually making any physical advances. Affection of this kind was common enough and could be tolerated unless it began to look ridiculous, in which case when he came to hear about it he would tell both boys gently not to be silly. He would get them together for this purpose, he explained, visibly relishing the idea, as if it had given him vicarious delight to intervene in this way in the past.

Becoming serious again, Oldham concluded the lecture with a warning about possible encounters in the holidays. He actually told me, as I had been assured he would, 'never touch a woman' – by which he meant picking up a prostitute; the consequence would be a painful venereal disease followed by madness and death. He then settled himself comfortably back in his chair; did I have any questions? Of the various possibilities that the dormitory wits had supplied, the safest seemed to me to ask about the mystery of the voice breaking at puberty. Visibly disappointed, Oldham brushed it aside and I was allowed to escape back to bed, there to regale the others with a report of what he had said.

What he had said about masturbation meant nothing to me, a state of innocence that was soon remedied. One of the boys who had come to the house two terms earlier was a member of the species I was later to encounter when working in newspapers as 'the office bicycle'. He enjoyed mutual masturbation, and he liked variety. He, and those of us who accepted his advances, took hair-raising risks, retiring to the tiny room where boots and shoes were cleaned, or even the cupboard where top hats were stowed during the week. In a few cases sex was openly indulged in; Watney had a boy who would be ordered into his bed. But nobody in my time was caught; or if anybody was, it was not reported to Oldham.

My recollection of the douling years is of boredom and frustration punctuated by periods of 'wazz', the only piece of Salopian slang that I can recall which does not have an everyday equivalent. 'Wazz' was what we did, or felt, when a monitor some time during the day used the dreaded formula 'see me after dicks' – 'dicks' being the formal prayers which Oldham, reeking of whisky and with the red blotch on his forehead which emerged when he had drink taken, came in to say to us before we went up to the bedrooms. It was characteristic that the beatings – almost every night in Watney's time – were conducted immediately after prayers, during which the collective wazz could almost be felt.

At Shrewsbury in the 1930s all new boys were given a classical education. In the lower school, when I joined it, this meant that the main subject each day was Latin. At the Dragon under Tortoise I had reached the stage of being able to convert Latin prose into passable Latin verse. By my second term under W. D. Haydon my Latin marks were so poor that he reported me to Oldham, who held out the threat of a beating and 'superannuation' if they did not improve.

There was a double reason. I had developed a block, so that even the simplest passage from Caesar or Livy seemed abstruse; and the system of marking was calculated to keep me at or around the bottom of the form. Haydon had been a master at the school for nearly half a century, and he was growing deaf and blind. He would read out questions which we would answer on slips of paper; we would then exchange our slips with other boys; and he would read out the answers. The boys at the back did not bother to exchange their slips. They kept their own, and where necessary corrected, or filled in, the answers. At the end of the week the seating was arranged so that the boys with the highest marks sat at the back. Those with the lowest continued to sit at the front, too near to Haydon to cheat.

At the beginning of my third term we were told of a decision which, trivial though it sounds, was to transform my school existence. In view of the need to get us through the Schools Certificate, the 1930s equivalent of O-Levels, the slip system was to be suspended so that we could have more practice in taking examinations. We would still be called upon to prepare, night after night, to translate Caesar, or whatever Latin text was being studied, and it would still be laboriously construed verbally the following mornings; but there would be no slips. Instead, every fortnight the exam papers would be collected and marked by Haydon. It would still be possible for a boy at the back to consult a crib, but extremely dangerous; possession of the English text, if discovered, could lead not just to a flogging but to expulsion.

Even better, from my point of view, it was possible to jot down each day's correct translations so that at the end of the fortnight, the evening before the examination, I could go through it, sorting out and memorising the tricky bits. The first exam results confirmed that the method worked. When we moved to our new desks, in order of precedence, I was among the new elite in the back row. Convinced that his critical report the previous term must have been responsible for my reformation, Haydon was pleased; Oldham was reassured; renewed self-confidence lifted the 'block'. When, the following term, we heard that Watney was not returning, the worst was over.

A year later, Fate was to make an even more important intervention. When the summer term began in 1932, Oldham was a worried man; after a few days he left for a 'rest cure'. One of the boys in the house, John Vaisey, had not appeared at the beginning of the term; now he returned. Gradually, rumour had it that the two events were connected. What exactly had happened between Oldham and Vaisey has never been made known; but, at a stroke, it ended Oldham's career as housemaster.

He had become fascinated by book bindings, and occasionally he would ask boys from the house whom he was grooming for positions of trust to come and stay in a hotel with him, wherever he was conducting his investigations. When he asked Vaisey to come to stay in London, his homosexual feelings had got the worse of him – not, in all probability, leading to anything more serious than kissing the boy, but it was enough to appal Vaisey, whose chief interest at the time was football. Vaisey's father had been killed in the First World War (as John was to be in the Second); but, unluckily for Oldham, John's uncle was a leading Q.C. Told what had happened by John's mother, he had written to the Headmaster to say that John could not return while Oldham remained in charge of the house. Sawyer, realising what a scandal there would be if Oldham stayed and the story got around, told him he must go. Oldham was shattered. Charlesworth recalls how the night before he left he asked Rowley Hill, who was head of the school as well as of the house, to come to his study; according to Hill, 'the breaking point had come and the last shred of his restraint vanished. He threw his arms around my neck, buried his head against my shoulder, and wept as I have never seen anyone weep.' Only when Vaisey returned did Hill learn why.

Oldham still had a powerful card in hand; the lease of his house. The compromise was reached by which he could continue to be the school Librarian; he would be given a capital sum, and an annuity in return for the surrender of the lease. He came back to the house for the annual 'Bumpers' celebration, at the end of the house rowing races on the Severn; a tense occasion for all of us, but it passed off successfully.

Oldham's successor as housemaster, S. S. Sopwith, was a quiet, shrewd English teacher, in almost every respect Oldham's antithesis. The atmosphere of the house immediately changed. The substitution of fortnightly exams for the slip system, too, had helped to lift me into the Upper School, there to prepare for the Schools Certificate under the genial D. J. V. Bevan, also an admirable teacher. No longer a doul, I was in the house football and cricket teams. And in the holidays I was old enough to be able to leave my grandmother to go to church alone, while I joined Charlie Armstrong and his friends on the Island, still 'men only' on Sundays.

They might have been the originals for Wodehouse's 'wrecking crew' in *The Heart of A Goof*. Charlie was 'Old Father Time, the Man with a Hoe'; he spent an interminable time fanning the ball before stroking it up the fairway for a hundred yards or so. Norman Chance was 'the Gravedigger'; he stabbed at the ball as if killing a snake. A burly character, he had been in a Trinity rowing VIII in which the crew were given the names of the characters in *Peter Pan*; the comically inappropriate 'Wendy' had stuck to him. When he connected with the ball, it would shoot off for long distances in unpredictable directions.

As Tommy Hughes, who had succeeded grandfather as Hon. Secretary, was in the group, they enjoyed immunity from the usual conventions, often being joined by friends or relations, some of whom could be described as golfers only out of courtesy, in five-balls or six-balls. I once saw Gordon Armstrong, Charlie's brother, shave the ball so finely off the toe of the club that it went off at a right-angle, hitting the tee-box and bouncing back almost to where he had struck at it – a feat matched only by David Fitzgerald, Paddy Campbell's friend, who according to Paddy once stroked a ball so finely off the heel of his driver that it shot out between his legs, while the club, detaching itself from his grip, sailed up into the branches of a nearby tree.

The news in the summer of 1933 that I had passed the School Certificate meant that I would be allowed to specialise when the school reassembled for the Michaelmas term, and to concentrate upon what had always been my favourite subject, history. The departure of Oldham had meant that the History Side was now being taken by J. R. M. Senior; he was transforming it, attracting talent which he described in my first report as 'well above the average' – a tactful way of explaining why my position in the list was so undistinguished. The Side included Richard Wainwright, baby-faced but with the keen political sense that was to make him, as M.P. for Colne Valley, one of the mainstays of the Liberal Party; the sardonic David Gieve, scion of the celebrated London tailoring firm; and the formidably knowledgeable Richard Cobb, destined forty years later to become Professor of Modern History at Oxford.

In *A Sense of Place* Richard has recalled that he has had a great deal of luck in his life, 'but the greatest stroke of luck came my way in a typically accidental manner, in my second year at Shrewsbury' – the departure of Oldham, and the succession of Senior. 'I still think that the first time I found myself securely seated on the History Side was the happiest day I have ever spent.'

Senior introduced a system which he had encountered as a university student: each week, two by two, we would take our essays round to read to him in his rooms. Richard regards his pairing with me as an example of Senior's intelligent coupling; I had more ideas, but he made up for it by 'having read more than Brian'. For me, Richard's erudition was awe-inspiring, and most of my ideas must have been naive; but Senior, as Richard recalls, was sympathetic and tolerant, which 'made of a History Side of eight boys a permanent, exciting and endlessly rewarding centre of debate and wonder'.

Senior's political views were well to the Left. They were stimulated when he first arrived at Shrewsbury by having to share a House with Major West, who ran the OTC and was notoriously reactionary; and then by moving with relief to share with a newcomer, Frank McEachran, who turned out to be a disciple of

Henry George, the advocate of a Land Tax as the cure-all economic measure.

Georgism is a seductively simple creed. As a method of raising the money the State requires there has never been a better; but Bernard Shaw and others who thought like him, though attracted to it, became more interested in what the State should do with its revenue than how it might be raised. By 1933, however, the hopes of the Fabians had been dashed by the Labour government's inability to deal with the economic slump after the great crash, and the defection of Ramsay MacDonald, Snowden and Thomas. McEachran, a forceful advocate of the need to return to George's ideas, impressed Senior with his arguments; and in a form which included Cobb, already an apolitical anarchist, Wainwright, who then had strong Communist leanings, and Gieve, ready to uphold capitalism, there was a constant ferment of controversy which turned history from a school subject into a protracted and, for me, fascinating series of debates.

It took time to catch up with this alarming trio. 'He has developed very slowly,' Senior comented in my report after my second term, prompting H. H. Hardy, who had succeeded Sawyer as Headmaster, to add 'I begin to doubt if I ought to have agreed to his specialising.' Even after the summer term, when Senior noted some improvement, Hardy was unimpressed: 'He cannot hope to be up to a scholarship'. There would have been no question of my even trying for one, at Oxford or Cambridge, had it not been for the kind of surge which occurs when passionate interest is aroused, not merely making work a pleasure, but sealing what is heard and read into the memory and stimulating the flow of ideas in much the same way as the imagination can start the saliva flowing.

Senior admitted himself astonished by the change. Even so, I would not have been allowed to go up for an Oxford scholarship had it not been for the system whereby a college could accept entrants even if they did not reach scholarship standard, thereby removing the need to take the Higher Certificate ordinarily required. I secured a place at Hertford; and over Hardy's objections, Senior insisted I should have a try for a scholarship in the second round of examinations, in the Lent term. 'If he has produced of his best', he wrote in my term's report before the results were known, 'I think he will have made the examiners consider his claims very seriously.'

Nobody else did; certainly I did not, regarding the days in Oxford simply as a chance to escape from the boring Lent term at Shrewsbury. But when I opened the main history paper it included three questions which might have been designed for me. I had written an essay on one of them – Stanhope's foreign policy in the reign of George I – a few days before. Shortly before the end of term Sopwith was informed that I had won a scholarship to Magdalen. When he rang the headmaster to give him the news, Hardy told him that somebody must be pulling his leg.

My last term at Shrewsbury ended, as such terms traditionally end in school stories, in an agreeably golden haze. Oldham's Hall, as we were now called, had won the house cups for football and for fives; if we won the cup for cricket the most coveted trophy of all, for the house with the best all-round sporting record, would be ours for the first time. To be top scorer in the match, narrowly won, induced a greater glow of satisfaction than a mere scholarship could provide.

It was not long, though, before disenchantment set in. The oppressiveness, even more than the oppression, of the doul years, returned to haunt me when I renewed acquaintance with the Dragon School. Douls in my last year did not, I hope, feel so oppressed. Certainly they had less need to wazz. Beatings by monitors had almost ceased; colour exams were abandoned; there was less segregation between the age groups, so that friendships could be formed without incurring suspicion. But the code, Done and Not Done, remained in force; sport remained king; Lower School teaching remained wretched. It was to be many years before new brooms and new attitudes swept the basically Victorian principles and practices away.

In *A Sense of Place* Richard has presented a rather more favourable picture of Shrewsbury than mine – to my surprise; he had not been so charitable earlier. He had a hateful time as a doul, and detested his housemaster; but his tributes to Sopwith as a teacher of English, and to Senior, leave me with the uneasy feeling that I did not sufficiently appreciate them. Sopwith for him was 'inspiring', a 'master of rhythm, sound, and evocation of place and season'. I can see – or, rather, hear – what Richard means: Sopwith read poetry with heroic self-effacement, so that we could each of us read into it what our own imaginations conjured up – much as we form pictures in our minds of characters in a book or a radio play. Anthony and Cleopatra emerged for me more vividly and movingly than they have ever done in the theatre.

When, in December 1934, Richard found that he had won a scholarship to Merton, it did not occur to him to return to Shrewsbury. He simply sent a wire to his housemaster to announce he was leaving, and his housemaster was probably delighted to see the last of so intractable a non-conformer. When I heard of my scholarship, at the end of the following term, it never crossed my mind that I could, and should, leave. Sopwith's House, Richard recalls, was 'one of the happiest in the school'. It was *the* happiest, I would think. It had enfolded me. I did not want to escape from our collectivity.

Besides, I was in love with a younger boy. For a monitor to be 'crashed' on a doul was fashionable. There was rarely any sexual consummation, but this did not prevent the affairs, while they lasted, being highly emotionally charged; pleasurably, though gooily, romantic.

5

Magdalen

'You'll find you spend half your second year shaking off the undesirable friends you made in your first,' Charles Ryder's cousin Jasper warned him in the course of his first week as an undergraduate at Oxford. Magdalen in the late 1930s contained some of the undesirable types Jasper had in mind, 'God-botherers' chiefly – Buchmanites in particular – but no one of the kind Ryder fell in with in *Brideshead Revisited*. I can recall no Sebastian Flyte, no Anthony Blanche – nor any character in the university who left the kind of impression Ken Tynan was to make when he came up to Magdalen ten years later. Even the office-holders at the Union were unimpressive compared to the post-war intake. One of them was later to succeed, for a while, in politics; but at that time Edward Heath looked like, as Philip Toynbee put it, 'a cuddly teddy-bear'.

On my second evening, waiting at the bottom of the stairs leading up to Hall for dinner and envying those around me who were talking animatedly to old and new friends, I saw to my relief a familiar face. Michael Jefferson had been in Tortoise's form at the Dragon with me in our last year there. After 'Aren't you Jefferson?', 'Aren't you Inglis?', we set off up the steps and sat down together at the end of one of the tables which freshmen occupied. Michael turned out to be a medical student, and we were joined by another, Charles Phillips. There was to be no need for 'shaking off the undesirable friends' in our second, or any, year; we were still sitting together in Hall when the time came to take our finals, with other friends we had made in the meantime.

Magdalen, and the university in general, encouraged a division between the Hearties, who continued to devote most of their time to sport, and the Intellectuals. I was custom-built to join the Hearties. In Lent terms at Shrewsbury some rugger was played, and this had whetted my appetite to take it up again; after a trial, I found myself picked for the college X V. It soon transpired, though, that there were only two of us that year who had come up from soccer schools, and were ready to continue playing, so I was roped into the college X I as well. Magdalen had no fives courts, but it had squash courts; before long I was using them, too. And there was golf. With a handicap down to single figures, there was the prospect of getting into the university side.

Michael and Charles were the antidote. It was difficult, in Michael's company, not to feel abashed at the depth and the width of my ignorance of what the Intellectuals – not that he would have used the term about himself – regarded as an irreducible cultural minimum; a measure of acquaintanceship with certain novelists, such as Forster, Joyce and Proust, and certain poets such as Eliot and Yeats. Some younger poets also needed to be read so that their respective merits could be argued about, notably Auden, Isherwood, Spender and MacNeice. And although it was not essential actually to have read the works of, say, Freud, it was desirable to have a rough idea of his theory of the unconscious, Ego, Superego and Id, and of his views on dreams.

It was also considered desirable to have some acquaintanceship with the works of the great composers. Here, Shrewsbury had done its worst, with a music master who believed that compulsory attendance at recitals was the best way to instruct us. The light-hearted concerts with topical songs which had occasionally been organised were replaced by formal performances of the classics; I sat bored and resentful through a recital by the great Schnabel, wishing I could get back to listen to Ambrose and his band, who broadcast on Saturday evenings, on the wireless in the monitors' study. Charles eased me out of this ingrained hostility with the help of *Till Eulenspiegel*, *Eine Kleine Nachtmusik* and other such pieces until by 1938 I was fancying myself as a critic, commenting in my diary that in the London Philharmonic's rendering of the *Freischütz* overture 'the strings were rather stringy' but that Brahms Third was 'excellent, especially the last movement'. This was the first time I had heard that symphony; it was to complete the process of getting through the layers of prejudice against the classics.

The Modern History tutor at Magdalen, J. M. Thompson, had had the rare distinction of being formally un-frocked by the Anglican Church on account of a book he had written denying the divine nature of the miracles of the New Testament. For this he was to feature in Ronnie Knox's poem 'Absolute and a bit of hell' as 'Magdala'

> Who, setting out the Gospel Truths t'explain
> Thought all that was not German, not germane:
> Whose queasy stomach, while it tried in vain
> Recorded Miracles to entertain,
> Eschewing Luke, John, Matthew and the rest
> Read Mark, but could not inwardly digest.

To the general surprise of his colleagues the kindly 'Thompy', who had been given his job as a kind of consolation prize for his treatment at the hands of the Church authorities, proceeded to write commentaries on the French Revolution which established him as a leading authority on the subject. This sounded promising; but first, it was necessary to devote a year or more to medieval history, under K. B. McFarlane.

Bruce McFarlane was 'a man of great austerity and singleness of mind', Alan Bennett has recalled, 'shy, very kind; the most impressive teacher, and in some ways the most impressive man, I have ever come across.' Bennett at that time – the late 1950s – was a research student, preparing to become a don; not, as he soon realised, a vocation to which he would have been suited, but he was to be rescued from it by the success of *Beyond the Fringe*. To some extent his admiration must have been coloured by the fact that the research project on which he was engaged concerned the retinue of Richard II in the period from 1388 to 1399, an era about which Bruce could be regarded as the greatest living authority. Bruce, too, was particularly good at holding the balance between encouraging research for research's sake – the smaller the target area, the more fascinating the details – and discouraging expectations built on the finished product. This even applied to his own life's work. He always referred to medieval history, according to Bennett, as 'a branch of the entertainment business'.

He would not have called it that twenty years before, when I suspect he was still a little embarrassed at not having produced published work by which to assess whether his high reputation was justified. Oxford was awash with dons reluctant to complete whatever projects they were engaged on for fear that other dons, deep in 'that state of resentful coma which the academics call research', as Harold Laski described it, would pounce gleefully on errors and omissions. Bruce was indeed 'shy, very kind' and an impressive teacher in his own field, but it happened not to be mine, and I could not wait to move on to modern – post-Wars of the Roses – history.

I had to wait, nevertheless, owing to the institution of Pass Mods, an exam we had to sit at the end of our first term. It represented the university's concession to those who feared the ill-effects of specialisation; we had to endure what could best be described as brain-washing by specialists in economics and in philosophy. The economists of the time were obsessed by theories, formulae and graphs; they had convinced themselves that the human element need not be considered in their equations. The philosophers were succumbing to logical positivism and linguistics. I was also startled to find that in two years on the History Side I had managed to forget all but the simplest Latin. It came as no surprise to hear that I had failed, and would have to squander another term on a second try.

Only one clear-cut memory remains from that Lent term at Oxford. Reading *The Times* in the Junior Common Room one morning I came across a news story about the disappearance of a well-known Dublin doctor's wife. Mrs Ball's abandoned car had been found, blood-stained; it was suspected that she had been murdered.

I had not seen Edward Ball after he left Shrewsbury, a year earlier. The only mark he had made there was when he and his friend Clover shook tambourines three times whenever the line 'Three French Hens' was reached in a carol concert (to while away the seemingly endless *Magnificat*, when it was sung in chapel, some of us invented new verses; John Malins' contribution was

> O ye Riggs Hall, Clover and Ball
> Praise Him and magnify Him for ever).

I had been kept abreast of what Edward was up to, however, by Richard Cobb, at Merton, whom I continued to see from time to time.

Edward had begun to perform as a spear carrier at the Gate Theatre, where Michael MacLiammoir and Hilton Edwards had established their partnership; his mother, with whom he lived, regarded him as a ne'er-do-well; he called her Medea (his father, who lived apart from her, was Moloch); they had fierce rows. Richard, when he went to stay with them, in her home in Booterstown, just south of Dublin, thought her both cruel and cunning; and he had left after watching them hurl cups of tea, a teapot, a pot of strawberry jam and a vase of flowers at each other. Sooner or later, he thought, something more serious was bound to happen.

What had happened was narrated by Kenneth Deale in 'Danse Macabre', in his *Celebrated Irish Trials*. After another ferocious row, Edward had taken an axe to his mother. In a statement he made after his arrest on a charge of murdering her, he maintained that she had committed suicide by cutting her throat. Hoping to conceal what she had done he had dragged her corpse down to her car and driven it to a nearby beach, where he planned to tip it over into the sea. There were still some people around when he arrived, so he had got into the back of the car and sat with the corpse – according to a witness at the trial, as if they were a courting couple – until they had all departed. The car then stuck on the path down to the sea. Edward pulled the body out and dragged it down into the water; then managed to get a lift home, where he tried to clean up the worst of the bloodstains before the maid arrived in the morning.

'How much of Ball's story was true?' Deale asked at this point in his narrative. The answer was 'all of it', except that Mrs Ball had not committed suicide by slitting her throat with a razor blade. Bloodstains found on the axe belied Edward's tale. He could hardly have escaped hanging, but for the fact that his mother's body was never found. Edward's father, giving evidence, revealed that Mrs Ball had been eccentric, a pathological liar and a kleptomaniac; perhaps this had driven Edward temporarily out of his mind. The jury found him guilty, but insane; and he was sentenced to detention during the pleasure of the Governor-General in Dundrum Criminal Lunatic Asylum.

Richard Cobb has since given his version of the story in *A Classical Education*. He and Edward had not been really close friends in Riggs' Hall; but they enjoyed playing practical jokes together, particularly when the target was the school chaplain – he preferred to be addressed as 'Padre' – the future Bishop, Rev. A. L. E. Hoskyns-Abrahall. He had joined the staff in that capacity after Canon Sawyer's retirement, introducing 'juicy new prayers that seemed to run with treacle', as Richard puts it. He delighted in ritual, which only the headmaster's disapproval kept in check. At first we called him 'Oilskins-Overall'; later, when his unctuousness provoked irritation, 'Foreskins-Urinal'. Richard and Edward would ring him up from a phone-box, pretending to be the Bishop of Matabeleland or some such dignitary, for the pleasure of watching him rush off on a fruitless errand. The two of them had little in common except the companionship of risk-taking.

In the Preface to *A Classical Education* Richard claims that he has been more concerned with readability than accuracy: 'I am not always sure at what stages fictional inventiveness takes over from the chronicle of memory'. His memory was certainly at fault in accepting Edward's fantasies about driving the car with his mother's corpse through Dublin, and in attributing to me knowledge of the Ball household which I did not possess, except through hearing Richard's colourful version of his stay there. For a while we made light of the events; but when Edward was charged with matricide, Richard recalled that he had written letters to him which might be interpreted as incitement to get rid of his mother. And a few weeks later, Richard was informed that Chief Inspector Fox of the Oxford C.I.D. wanted to question him.

Oxford colleges were traditionally 'sanctuary'; the police did not enter them except by invitation. Merton's law tutor promptly told Richard on no account to leave the college; and for the next five days he was in effect 'gated' while the law tutor and the Chief Inspector decided what to do. At this point my own memory was at fault; I had a mental picture of the questions being asked through the window of the front lodge, with the Chief Inspector on the pavement and Richard inside. Richard says that a compromise was reached; the Chief Inspector was allowed in, but the law tutor was present while the questions were put, and could advise Richard not to answer them, if necessary. It was not necessary. The Chief Inspector dismissed the 'incitement to murder' letters which had put the Dublin police on to Richard's trail as 'kid's stuff'; he would report back to Dublin that the C.I.D. proposed to take no further action.

Just before he left, the Chief Inspector asked Richard where he intended to spend the next vacation. Richard said, Paris; only to be warned, 'Go to Brussels'. The French, Fox explained, had an extradition treaty with the Irish Free State; the Irish police would slap a subpoena on him to appear at the trial. Richard, safely unextraditable, read the reports of the trial in the *Continental Daily Mail* in a café near the Place Brouckère.

Some of Richard's narrative, as he warned, is indeed simply fictional invention, either his own or more probably Edward's; notably the description of Edward doing a detour through Dublin before reaching the coast, running out of petrol in the middle of O'Connell Street, and accepting a man's offer to push the car, with corpse in the back, to a petrol station. Edward had never driven a car; how he got it even as far as the coast remains a mystery – and there he stuck because he did not know how to put the car into reverse. But the episode which gives Richard's book its title is surely no invention.

Released from Dundrum at the Governor-General's pleasure (or, rather, the President's – the former Irish Free State had become the Republic of Ireland), Edward went in 1950 to France, where Richard was waiting to meet him at the Gare St Lazare. His first words to Richard, after they had greeted each other, were 'What a pity that we went to a classical school.' Richard asked why; Edward explained that he had tried to wash off the blood from the axe in hot water, instead of cold, which would have left no trace. Edward 'seemed quite genuinely aggrieved about this gap in our education', Richard recalls, 'as if Shrewsbury had let him down personally'. He then proceeded to treat Richard and the customers of the restaurant where they had dinner to 'a blow-by-blow account, in happy ringing tones', of the murder – Richard falling back into his old role of fellow-conspirator, 'shaking with gust after gust of irresistible adolescent laughter'. Some other diners, picking up the gist, nervously called for their bills and left.

I had myself seen Edward when he was released from Dundrum. He came in to the *Irish Times* to ask me whether I could help him get tickets for a cycle of the Ring at Bayreuth. Wagner had become his obsession, along with the novels of Charles Morgan. I introduced him to the paper's music critic, and saw him no more until, some time in the 1960s, I was in the Automobile Association's offices in

London and went to a counter to pick up some document. 'Inglis?' the clerk asked; and, when I nodded, said 'Ball'. I would not have recognised him, so thin and depressed-looking had he become, and I could not think of anything to talk about. He was still alive when Richard's book came out in 1985; he had even joined the Old Salopian Club, doubtless for sly amusement. But the first reference to him in its journal was the announcement that he had died.

To fail Pass Mods once was not considered a disgrace. It could even be taken as an indication of a mind above such mundane considerations as study, in much the same way as getting a Fourth in Finals. To fail twice, however, would have been considered reprehensible. I worked at the subjects, and the Sunday before the exam took Holy Communion under the amiable Canon Adam Fox in Magdalen chapel, praying for a safe passage. It was the last prayer I made, apart from joining in those used on formal occasions such as weddings and funerals. Like Father Rivas in Graham Greene's *The Honorary Consul*, 'I never knew how to pray'. Rivas knew many prayers by heart, but they should really, he thought, be called petitions 'if you want to give that mumbo-jumbo a name. You might just as well write them down in a letter and get your neighbours to sign it too, and stick it in a postbox addressed to the Lord Almighty'. The news that I had passed was celebrated not on my knees, but legless.

In an otherwise uneventful second year two things happened which were to prove decisive, later. One was an invitation to teach two afternoons a week at the Dragon. I had thought of making my career there; confronted with a class of ten-year-olds, I could not even keep order. It needed only a term to convince me that a career in teaching was no longer an option.

The other event was the publication of the subject for that year's Gladstone Essay Prize: 'The Influence of Irish Economic Problems on English Domestic Politics, 1815–1848'. It could be presented as a thesis in the history finals, Bruce pointed out, and was ideal for me as much of the research could be conducted in Dublin during the long vacation.

It was even more suitable than he realised. Every summer Professor George O'Brien of University College and his friend Professor Edmund Curtis of Trinity College used to come to

Malahide to stay in the hotel; and from time to time they would be joined by Jimmy Montgomery, the Irish Film Censor. Montgomery had the reputation of being the wittiest member of Dublin's troupe of wits; it was he who, asked by an American visitor what was the difference between MacLiammoir and Edwards' Gate Theatre and Yeats's Abbey Theatre, had replied 'the difference between Sodom and Begorrah'. He liked to make fun of his job, which he described as a sinemacure watching Californication; Frank Cave and I found him delightful company, and he would let us sit in on his censoring when we were in Dublin. I was later to find that rival wits, such as Oliver Gogarty, were notorious for appropriating Montgomery's cracks for use in London and New York as their own.

Frank and I went often to the hotel, as Mrs Forbes Russell, who had disgraced herself in Anglo–Indian eyes by preferring to come back to Ireland with her son Beano while her husband stayed on working in India, was living there. Beano, at school in England, was one of our gradually widening circle of friends during the holidays. Through them and through Montgomery, I had come to know and admire the taciturn Curtis, author of the then standard history of Ireland, and the nervous but friendly O'Brien, whose economic histories of Ireland had established his reputation. As one of O'Brien's covered the period from the Union of 1800 to the great famine of the 1840s, I had the advantage of, in effect, an additional tutor – very necessary, as I had learned no more Irish history than was provided in English history books, which was superficial and, as I soon found, misleading.

Armed with George's list of recommended works I obtained a reader's ticket at the National Library, adjoining Dail Eireann, and began for the first time to enjoy that curiously addictive drug, historical research. The addiction, I was eventually to realise, takes hold because the introductory works, such as George's, point to original sources which in turn open up the prospect of fresh discoveries. Missing links have to be tracked down; like the missing letter in crosswords, they nag at the mind, assuming an importance out of all proportion to their intrinsic worth. Easy though it was to sidle off on trails of this kind, though, I was held to the main subject by sheer astonishment, at first amounting almost to incredulity, at what I was reading, and its implications.

I knew about the Great Famine of the Hungry Forties. It had left its mark on Ireland, particularly in the West; scores of ruined cottages littered Connemara, emptied by death or emigration. It had also featured in history at school as a classical example of the unwisdom of a peasant population coming to rely too exclusively on the potato as its staple; the blight which destroyed the crop left the foolish Irish with no alternative food. Nevertheless Sir Robert Peel, out of the generosity of his spirit, had sacrificed his political career by repealing the Corn Laws, which his Tory party was pledged to maintain, to enable cheap grain to flow into Ireland to try to save the peasantry from starvation. His decision had split his party and let in the Whigs; but it had been a noble deed.

What I had not known, and was now compelled to recognise, was that the Irish peasants had not chosen to subsist on potatoes. They had been compelled to by the system of rack-renting which enabled a landlord to push up rents to the level where his tenants had no option but to subsist on the cheapest available food. Nor had I known that Peel's excuse for Repeal – to provide corn for the starving Irish – was spurious; having no money, they could not buy it. There was no shortage of food in Ireland, apart from the potatoes; but it was owned by the landlords, who had to sell it to the British to maintain their properties. The aged Duke of Wellington, clear-headed as usual, warned Peel of the consequences of his policy, but Peel declined to listen; so four million foodless Irish had to battle with starvation, as one commentator put it, 'until the Premier had matured and carried his measure for securing cheap food for the artisans of England; and further, those same famishing millions had, day by day, to submit to be insulted by the false and hollow assertions that all this was done for them.'

Peel's duplicity was the ugliest of the injustices perpetrated by British governments of the period, but it was far from being isolated. The record of the Whig governments in the 1830s, too, was of procrastination linked to deviousness, glossed over with cant. Day after day, in the National Library, I found myself becoming as steamed up about the dishonesty of English politicians as if they still were alive and cheating a century later. Until then I had thought myself a Unionist – as an essay I wrote as a sixteen-year-old for Bevan at Shrewsbury, which my mother kept, still reveals. The subject was taken from *HMS Pinafore*: 'Do I prefer to "remain an Englishman"?' It had allowed me to castigate the English for some failings – stand-offishness, snobbery and xenophobia; but I admired their sportsmanship, their 'respect for the weaker sex' and their patriotism: 'Yes!', I had concluded, 'I would like to "remain an Englishman".' No longer; from time to time I was tempted to go out into the street, grab two passing English tourists and knock their silly heads together for the wrongs which their forefathers had done.

At Shrewsbury I had not been regarded as Irish; now, I wanted to be. I was later to find that such conversions were not uncommon. Cyril Connolly's mother had been one of the Vernons of Clontarf, just north of Dublin – distant cousins of the Blood family; and when he went to stay with them one holidays, he was delighted with what he found. Becoming intrigued by Brian Boru, who had defeated the Danes in the Battle of Clontarf in AD 1014 but was himself slain, Connolly decided to cultivate his Irishness – the Connollys, after all, had come from Ireland. He contemplated learning Gaelic, and devoured books about the heroes of the nationalist movement, from Shane O'Neill to Wolfe Tone and Lord Edward Fitzgerald. For a time he regarded the Anglo–Irish as a superior people, better-born than their English equivalents but less snobbish; poorer, but this only brought their natural aristocratic temperament into relief. They were also much loved 'by about four million devoted bog-trotters, who served them as grooms, comic footmen, gardeners and huntsmen'. He even fantasised himself as heir to the former Connolly estate at Castletown.

It only occurred to him later that his Anglo–Irish Vernon grandfather was one of the landowners – with a thousand acres of suburban Dublin, and a shoot in the country – against whom the patriots had fought; 'that the Anglo–Irish were themselves a possessor class', and that their resentment against the English arose mainly out of fear that an English government might decide to desert them – as the Lloyd George government was eventually to do. The reaction was then painful. The Vernons, Cyril decided, had no real Irish blood; the Connolly family had not been in Ireland for two centuries. 'Now, despite my early infatuation', he admitted in *Enemies of Promise* in 1938, 'nothing infuriates me more than being treated as an Irishman.'

My own research left the very different impression that the blame lay almost entirely with English governments. I continued to think of my Anglo–Irish forbears as genuinely Irish – the best class of Irish, in fact, looking after the bog-trotters, and fully justifying the devotion of their servants. Of course there were exceptions, but these were mainly the absentee landlords, who left an agent to squeeze every penny out of every tenant in order that they might be able to indulge their appetite for wine, women or the gambling tables, in England or on the Continent.

The Preface to *John Bull's Other Island* confirmed this impression. My mother's attempts to convert me into a Shavian had made little impression until I began to see performances of his works at the Oxford Playhouse, where they were staged every four months or so. Prompted to buy the Collected Prefaces, I found them riveting; *John Bull's Other Island*'s in particular, with Shaw's entertaining passages contrasting the gullibility of the English, as portrayed in the play by Broadbent, and the illusion-free Irishman, Larry Doyle. By 'The Irish', Shaw left no doubt he had the Anglo–Irish in mind; his own stock. He liked the English better than the Irish, he admitted, but he would never think of an Englishman as his countryman. Nor, from that time, would I.

One thing disconcerted me: Shaw's crack that the Irishman 'may be a gentleman (a species extinct in England, and nobody a penny the worse)'. I had had a succession of models, all gentlemen, which I would hope to emulate when I grew up. First it had been Rider Haggard's Sir Henry Curtis; then Dornford Yates' Berry Pleydell. By this time, though, it had become Major Yeates, the Irish R.M. in the Somerville and Ross stories, an exemplary Anglo–Irishman, tolerant, good-humoured, honest, incorruptible, who employed or jailed the bog Irish with fine impartiality; who was a keen, but not too accomplished, sportsman; and who knew how to distinguish between members of his own class and those who longed to join it, but could not be allowed to cross what Somerville and Ross called 'the bounder-y line' without mockery.

Our class snobbery was different from the one I occasionally encountered in England, but there were many features in common, notably the still powerful prejudice against accepting socially anybody in trade. The justification was that he, and his family, would not feel at ease with us – which was often true enough. We certainly would not have known how to put them at their ease, and would have been unlikely to try. If accused of snobbery, we would have indignantly denied the charge, pointing out that in 'our set' there were no barriers between the richest and 'the poorest of the poor', as grandmother called them, some of whom had no income but were cared for, like my godmother Janie Ramsay, in homes for distressed gentlefolk.

Malahide in this respect was like Mrs Gaskell's *Cranford*: 'We none of us spoke of money, because that subject savoured of commerce and trade, and though some might be poor, we were all aristocratic.' The Robertson family fortunes had vanished with the death of Tony's father; two of his elder sisters were working as poorly paid secretaries in Dublin firms, and Tony had to get a job with a Dublin manufacturer, but they were not 'in trade' because they came from a 'good' family.

The same applied to Catholics, or 'R.C.s', as we called them. They would not have stood a chance of becoming members of the Island, or the tennis club, unless from a 'good' family, which meant either descent from one of the aristocratic Anglo–Irish who had refused to convert to Protestantism (or had only pretended conversion); or the outcome of a mixed marriage, usually a Protestant falling for some girl who 'dug with the wrong foot', as Francis Jameson had done when he married a Miss Tobin.

The Jameson family, Ireland's leading whiskey distillers, had never broken into the peerage as the Guinnesses had managed to. But John George Jameson of Seamount, just the other side of Malahide hill, looking across the Howth and the Dublin mountains, had become the trend-setter in the village, owing to the Talbots' retiring ways. His children and my mother had grown up together. Hilda had proudly used her new car to bring Vera to marry Claude; Vera was to introduce Hilda to our cousin Cecil Park, whom she married. In grandmother's eyes the Jamesons could do no wrong; Vera had been allowed, and encouraged, to let Francis take her out sailing, although Francis had acquired a reputation as a Don Juan. Perhaps grandmother hoped that he would distract her daughter from Claude. When Cecil took early retirement from his job as a Hooghly pilot in India, he came with Hilda to live at Seamount, and although Johnny was four years my junior, and his sisters younger still, Seamount became a second home. I went there every Sunday for lunch and games and tea, as well as for Christmas and birthdays.

Seamount provided my direct experience of Anglo–Irish manners, habits, conventions, dos and don'ts. In one respect it was not representative; although it had a gate lodge, a walled garden, greenhouses and other standard trappings, the stables were no longer occupied by horses and ponies. I never knew 'the Big House' as portrayed in thinly-disguised reality by Somerville and Ross, or in David Thomson's marvellously evocative *Woodbrook*: though, as it happened, Woodbrook's owner, Major Kirkwood, was a frequent visitor to Seamount in the years leading up to the Second World War – the time when Thomson was a member of his household, brought in as a tutor and staying on, as tended to happen in Ireland's Chekovian households, as part of the family. My social responses in mixed company were moulded by Seamount. As my cousins were younger than I was, we went through the range of children's games from 'Oranges and Lemons' – Tony and I were always the last left in to be 'pulled away': he always won – to, eventually, bridge, poker and 'Murder', with its agreeable opportunities to locate and kiss one of the attractive girls who came to the parties. Very attractive they were, too, particularly Rachel Blair White, though annoyingly she appeared committed, at the age of fifteen, to a Cambridge under-graduate: worse, a double Blue. Fortunately Donald lived in Dublin, and was not always around.

For Christmas in 1938 my mother sent me a five-years-to-a-page diary, which I began to fill fairly regularly not with great thoughts – there was too little space – but with what had been done each day. The Island still featured, but less obsessively, as few of the girls played golf; there was a round of parties, cinemas, dances, dinners, day after day. How did we afford them? The boy always paid. It was calf love time, passionate but without a thought of intercourse. The contrast between behaviour with boys at Shrewsbury and girls in Malahide had not struck me as odd, at the time. They were two forms of pleasurable experience, not to be regarded as in any way inconsistent. But gradually girls were beginning to be the pre-occupation.

Francis Jameson's children, Patrick and Biddy, were in the party round, and came to Seamount every Sunday. We had felt a little patronising about their having to attend Mass at Malahide chapel (as we called the Catholic church; 'chapel' applied to any edifice used for Christian, but not for Church of Ireland, services). We had envied them, though; if they went to an early Mass they were free for the rest of the day, whereas our morning service did not start until 11.30 and

63

was more protracted than theirs, especially if the Rector chose to deliver one of his more boring sermons. Even when I escaped attendance, Frank had to continue to read the lessons -- in a sepulchral voice, totally out of character.

Otherwise, apart from the Chance family encountered at the Island, there were no Catholics in our Malahide set; and no Jews. Nevertheless 'Jew' had picked up a distinctly pejorative sense, in spite of the fact that we never encountered any. Ireland was the only country which had never persecuted the Jews, Mr Deasy told Stephen Daedalus, 'and do you know why?' Stephen asked why: 'Because she never let them in.' That would have amused us, if we had read *Ulysses*. Our mind's eye picture was of Shylock, or the type of parvenu often portrayed in *Punch* and the stories of Dornford Yates. It was to come as a surprise to find there was a flourishing Jewish community in Dublin, among them one who sat in the Dail as a member of de Valera's party.

It also came as a surprise to find that there was a middle class of Protestants. We knew there was a lower (as we described it) class, because we saw the children who went to the local national school. When the Leask family bought a house in Malahide they were acceptable, as Protestants and not 'in trade'; the daughters, too, were attractive and good fun. But when they invited me to have tea with them, I was astonished to hear that it would be at six o'clock rather than four, the established hour at Seamount and, of course, at Ballykilty. This must be the 'high tea' which I had heard about, I realised; and so it turned out to be. Betty Leask was engaged to Ken Donald, a doctor and a hockey international; but he was pursuing higher medical qualifications in England, so she could join our set and I could take her to dances, enjoying the feeling of superiority that the temporary possession of so attractive a partner provided. That her family declined to change their timetable to conform to our set's ways eventually established itself as a point in their favour, not least because their teas were decidedly more interesting than grandmother's dinners – roast joint on Sunday, cold slices on Monday, minced remains on Tuesday.

I was even slower to grasp that there was also a burgeoning Catholic middle class in Malahide; 'artisans', as grandmother called them. In the 1920s the sandhills on the Malahide side of the estuary had stretched out into the sea; a nine-hole golf course, the Shore links had been laid out on them. We used to play over them occasionally, as a change from the Island, driving off from a tee beside 'Pa' Hicks' tower, with a fine view out towards Lambay Island. But by the 1930s the sandhills had all but disappeared, eroded by the tide that raced through the Short Deeps. The sandhills grew up again on the Island side, eventually making it possible to extend the course over them; but the unfortunate Shore golfers had to buy fields inland, on Malahide hill, for their club to continue; it consequently ceased to be a 'links' becoming 'inland' and – to our way of thinking – boring. 'The Shore' had been as socially select as the Island; to survive, it had to admit the artisans.

I had made no social distinction between the contractors who built and repaired houses in and around Malahide and the labourers who worked for them. They were the equivalent, I assumed, of sergeants and privates in the army; non-commissioned officers from the same class as the other ranks. But one day Frank, who as the Rector's son was better-informed about the ways of people not in our set, told me he had to drop in to give a message to one of the contractors on our way to the Island. We were brought in to the living room; I was astonished to find it was comfortably and tastefully furnished, with decidedly more attractive pictures on the walls than we had at Ballykilty.

The contractor was a product of the new Ireland which the 1921 Treaty establishing the Free State had brought into being, but which we in Malahide were slow to recognise – slower, I would guess, than anywhere else in the country. Where it impinged on us was chiefly in the form of minor irritations, such as the proliferation of signs in 'Erse', as we derisively called the Irish language. As time was to show, the campaign to restore the language by imposing it, particularly by insistence on teaching through the medium of Irish, was misguided; and unluckily it was in the hands of pedants. When it was decided that Kingstown, so-called after George IV landed there on his visit to Ireland, should revert to its former name, Dunleary, the version decided upon was Dun Laoghaire – now with the spelling modernised with Dun Laoire.

So far as our set were concerned, it remained Kingstown; and if we were buying tram tickets to go there to meet some friend off the mailboat, we would say 'Kingstown' without a thought – until the new Ireland began to catch up on us. If we were unlucky, the conductor would profess ignorance of such a place, perhaps appealing to the other travellers, asking whether *they* knew of such a place; and they would join in the game. In Malahide, though, we remained largely insulated from such teasing. The men and women who worked for us were loyal to us and respected our conventions – or were sacked.

We 'loved' the people who worked for us – slaved, in some cases. Maura Murtagh, the last in the line of grandmother's cook-generals, earned £29 a year for a six-and-a-half day week. During her working hours, which effectively meant whenever she was not in her bed at night, she had to be ready at any time to answer the front door bell, or grandmother's calls – usually to look for lost keys. Maura did the cooking and the cleaning, made the beds and emptied the chamber pots. Her diet consisted mainly of bread and butter, with a teapot kept refilled throughout the day. As a member of the Third Order of St Francis, she also had her devotions and her obligations. Grandmother, her memory getting progressively worse, must have been a constant source of irritation; but I never saw Maura show any sign of impatience.

Murphy the gardener, Christie the postman, we looked on as family retainers in much the same way as we looked on Vincie the boatman and Mary Jane at the Island. They were our friends – so long as they knew to keep their place. To our surprise, in the late 1930s Mary Jane announced that she would be leaving, as she was going to marry Hogan the grocer. By this time she must have been about fifty – typical of one common type of Irish marriage (the other being undertaken young and followed by a string of children with barely a year between them). We felt a little sorry for her, as marriage to Hogan meant that she sat all day in the shop, made out his customers' bills, took their money, and gave them their change. Then, to grandmother's astonishment – all the greater as Mary Jane had once been her cook – Mary Jane arrived at Ballykilty on what, it soon transpired, was a social call.

The visit gave grandmother and her friends material for gossip for days afterwards. Would those she visited be expected to return her call? Unthinkable! What, in future, should she be called? Those who had known her had continued to call her 'Mary Jane'; must it now be 'Mrs Hogan'? Perhaps because she sensed grandmother's manifest embarrassment, inadequately disguised while she was in the Ballykilty drawing-room, she abandoned the projected visits; but not before Hogan's lost custom to Findlater's, from shoppers not caring to face her.

We were fearful snobs, in short, without being aware of it. And even the influence of Senior in the last two years at Shrewsbury, which had led me to become what was derisively called a 'parlour pink' by Communists and 'fellow-traveller' by Conservatives, had little effect upon my attitudes in Ireland. In some ways Oxford actually reinforced social conformism. I fell readily into the accepted convention of not paying tradesmen until they threatened to give no more credit – particularly hard on tailors, as often they could not get their money before the undergraduate customer graduated, which made him all the harder to dun. During my first term the tailor whose premises lay just opposite the Magdalen library came round to my rooms with a bunch of patterns, and measured me for the one I chose; it never appeared, because, as he explained when I inquired, the cloth had not reached him. I thought it odd that he should put up with the delay, but the explanation came a few days later; the tailor went out of business. The wholesalers had refused to supply him with any more cloth until he paid off his debt to them, and he had not been able to extract the money owed to him by a generation of undergraduates.

The bilking of tradesmen appears to have been endemic throughout Europe – and in Russia, to judge from *Anna Karenina*. With the Anglo–Irish it was an ingrained habit, almost a compulsion, indulged in by rich and poor alike, and described by writers from Maria Edgeworth to Molly Keane. It would no more have occurred to me to condemn it than it occurred to me to question the right of the syndicate which governed the Island to deny membership to anybody who was not in our set. But shortly before the Second World War, which was effectively to terminate the power of the old Ascendancy in Malahide, my complacency was a little shaken.

'What did Bloom do?', Joyce asked in his account of the return of Leopold and Stephen to Eccles Street. He laid the fire with paper, sticks, and 'irregular polygons of best Abram coal at twenty-one shillings a ton from the yard of Messrs Flower and McDonald of 14 D'Olier Street'. Flower and McDonald were, like grandfather Inglis's Heitons, an old-established firm, with premises at Malahide and other distribution centres along the coast. A scruffy coaster would come up the estuary at high tide, settle itself on the sand close to the slip which the Island boats used, and begin noisily to discharge coal into carts. They would take their contents through a gate in a wall which proudly proclaimed its owners' names – all too visible from the Island boats.

One of the owners, Howard McDonald, had bought a country house to the south of Malahide, where he lived with his wife and four children. They were Protestants, and regular churchgoers – though as Mrs McDonald was a little scatter-brained, they were invariably late. The children went to 'good' schools, and to university. When Olive became captain of the Trinity College Ladies golf team, she decided she would like to join the Island. The syndicate turned her down, even my tolerant godfather concurring. *She* might be all right, but it would create a dangerous precedent.

I thought this unfair, but not to the point of making any serious protest. It was not until much later that the full force of the prejudice about 'in trade' came home to me. There was a shop in Dublin which I had always badgered grandmother to take me to, and later had taken myself to; Elvery's 'Elephant House,' an Aladdin's cave full of a jumble of all kinds of sports goods. There were golf bags with a range of accessories from sponges for cleaning balls, to racks for a variety of artificial tees; there were fishing rods, reels and wonderfully-coloured salmon flies. And presiding over the shop was a benevolent character who seemed clearly to be one of our set, likely to be encountered at the Island, or on one of the trout lakes in the West.

Patrick Campbell's mother Beatrice was an Elvery. In *Today We Will Only Gossip* she was to recall that when her parents moved to Carrickmines, in the heart of Dublin's equivalent of a stockbroker belt, she could not make friends there. 'We are not allowed to play with you,' a girl at Sunday School told her, 'because your father has a shop.' Beatrice was fortunate in that when young Gordon Campbell proposed to her, he was working in London. 'When his family heard of our plans that bogy of my father's shop made one faint effort to put in an appearance, but quickly faded away.'

That fade was by no means quick, according to Patrick in his autobiography. In the 1920s his grandfather, the first Lord Glenavy, used to give glittering tennis parties every time his second son, Cecil – a Wimbledon star – came over from England. Gordon, although he was back working in Ireland, was not invited; neither Glenavy nor Cecil 'could overlook the fact that my mother's family were in trade'. And just as Flower and McDonald's name on the sea front at Malahide underlined the connection, so the model elephant outside Elvery's loomed over the members of the Kildare Street Club in the 1930s as they walked to and from Jammet's restaurant, a reminder of the misalliance which Gordon – by this time, the second Lord Glenavy – had contracted.

I did not realise it until after the war, but the reason I had not met my cousin Dermot Findlater was that he owned and ran the chain of grocery shops which spread out of Dublin in the 1930s. Grandmother was proud of her husband's Findlater connection, and the branch of the family in the wine business was socially acceptable, as part of The Trade. Besides, theirs was basically a wholesale business. Retail was a different matter – and as for groceries! Dermot, I was to find, had a massive chip on his shoulder as a result of the rebuffs he had had to endure.

We Anglo–Irish, in short, had a curious confusion of loyalties. The most important one, in our daily lives, was to the standards accepted in 'our set'. The Anglo–Irishman, H. M. Pim – an observant Ulster Protestant – had written, 'dwells in a social attic with one skylight'. He believed himself superior to the natives, whom he observed with a tolerant smile expressing honesty, good-nature and common sense – or so he thought; in fact all it expressed was 'sheer bovine contentment'.

We were also loyal to an abstraction – 'the Crown'. Again, this could be confused. I saw nothing strange in holding, at the same time, the nationalist anti-English sentiments which research for the Gladstone Prize had bred, with a determination to preserve what remained of the Union. At private dances, hunt balls and such, we all insisted that the band finished up not with the Irish national anthem, 'The Soldiers Song', but with 'God Save The King'. The band did, its members knowing that if they refused they would not be asked to any Anglo–Irish dominated function again.

Early in 1938 a letter came from my father – an unusual event. He had been back on his annual leave with my mother the summer before and all had gone smoothly; it had included a visit to the Falls

Hotel near Lahinch, in County Clare, run at the time by the father-in-law-to-be of Dylan Thomas, Francis Macnamara – a remarkable character, by all accounts, but not by mine, as I was too busy playing golf to notice. I had entered for the South of Ireland golf championship and reached the last eight, only to be defeated by a diabolical stymie, through which the eventual winner blocked my path to the semi-finals. As things turned out this was to be the summit of my career as a golfer. Becoming captain, that winter, of the Magdalen football XI – the secretary of the previous year automatically became captain – and needing to prepare the Gladstone Essay, I had to let my ambition to play golf for Oxford fade.

A letter from my father usually meant trouble of some kind. He had shown no concern about my future while he was on leave; now he – or more probably, my mother – had realised that it was only a matter of months until Finals. I would then have to begin to earn my living. What, then, did I propose to do?

I had no notion. If the Finals produced a first, it would probably suffice to land some postgraduate post, but that could not be relied upon. The immediate problem was solved; although the thesis did not win the Gladstone Essay Prize, its merits and the time it took was considered sufficient to justify giving me a further year before Finals. But what then? A history degree would have given a safe passage into the Dragon, but this was no longer an option. Would it not be wise to use the Long Vac to revive and improve upon the languages I had learned at Shrewsbury?

It happened that Patrick Jameson had just been in Germany for a similar reason. Jameson's were not prepared to take him in, in spite of the fact that his father was in the firm; at the executive level, Catholics were not welcomed in the Protestant-dominated Distillery. Instead, he was joining Palgrave Murphy, a shipping firm (shipping, for some reason was not regarded as in trade). Patrick had to go to Germany to learn the language; he had stayed with a Herr Professor and his family in Heidelberg, and warmly recommended them. In July, I went there and spent the month with the Schencks.

From the point of view of learning the language the stay was a success. The Professor's method was boring, but very effective. It consisted of endless questions on trivia, ranging from the weather to the breakfast food, repetition after repetition gradually making it possible for me to talk casually without taking thought. Heidelberg, too, and its surroundings were attractive. Schenck, his wife and daughter were congenial company. For most of the time the threat of a second world war, which had arisen when Hitler's forces had entered Austria a few months earlier, seemed remote. But one day we went on an excursion into the countryside, calling on a friend of the Schenck's who was a schoolmaster there; a whole wall of the main schoolroom, I found, was covered by a map which purported to show the distribution through Europe of the Aryan race. Its message was that Aryans were to be found throughout Europe, and that Germany's destiny was to reunite them.

Another map was designed to warn that enemy bombers could reach the heart of Germany from Czechoslovakia; and although there was no anti-semitic propaganda in the school, the village café had a sign outside, 'Jews not wanted' and inside, a board covered with press cuttings denouncing Jews, and cartoons of long-nosed men and women stealing money-bags. Before the end of my Heidelberg stay the tension began to grow, with the propaganda campaign for the return of the Czech Sudetenland. Even the Herr Professor and his friends, uneasy though they were about the Nazis, were nevertheless convinced that the Sudeten Germans were being cruelly oppressed, and that they should be reunited with the Reich, by force if necessary.

I was sufficiently under the influence of the stock Marxist line to assume that the basic motive was capitalist expansion; that German arms manufacturers were exploiting Hitler and nationalism for their own ends, and that if the expansion process threatened the British Empire, England would fight to preserve her gains, however ill-gotten. 'But the fact that England's motive for fighting might be discreditable,' I concluded in the dogmatic style which my letters to India displayed at the time, 'does not mean that she should not fight; if it destroys militarism, any motive is justifiable.'

It seemed inconceivable, though, that there would be another war while memories of the Great War were still so clear. Perhaps if Czechoslovakia, reputed to be well-armed, stood firm, and Britain and France, who had little to gain from a militarily-defeated Germany, stood by her, Hitler would have to climb down. There is no evidence in my diary during August, spent in Malahide, of any uneasiness about the deteriorating international situation; and when, in September, the second stage of my mother's languages project was due to start, I looked forward to it as the chance to stay with a family in Paris, see the sights, and convert my school French into the vernacular.

The outcome was farcical. Madame Esterlin lived in a sizeable flat into which she had evidently decided to cram all the furniture she could from the house she had had to leave when her husband had died: heavy tables, looming cupboards, knick-knacks everywhere. I was always relieved to escape from its suffocating atmosphere. Her son Jean, a French army reservist, was quite good company but spoke a curious fluent English, which he wanted to air, derived from listening to Radio Luxembourg. He liked to combine its commercials with the anti-English jokes then circulating in Paris. Through his policy of appeasement, the Prime Minister had come to be called 'Monsieur j'aime Berlin'; and Jean assured me that Chamberlain was expected to launch a new Radio Luxembourg commercial for the Nazis: 'Don't be Vague – Ask for Prague'. Although I duly 'did' the galleries, I spoke hardly any French, spending part of the time going to the cinema with an English girl, and part seeing life in Paris with Richard Cobb.

Richard had set himself to discover, live in, and become identified with the real Paris, as a prelude to becoming the greatest living authority on modern French history – as he indeed was to become. This took us one evening to a café where he demonstrated how, on his meagre income, he was able to enjoy the night life. At that time Paris had become notorious for its 'Apaches', reputedly sinister at the best of times, and extremely dangerous when under the influence of their favourite tipple, absinthe. 'Apaches', consequently, were one of the sights which Americans on the 'Paris by Night' bus tours expected to see. The tour operators felt compelled to include a glimpse of them in the itinerary.

As it happened, Maurice Chevalier had a song 'I'm an Apache' which had been widely seen, as well as heard, in cinemas through the United States. As he had worn an off-white roll-necked sweater and a cap at a rakish angle, this was what the tourists expected. It was what they were given, Richard found, when he went to a café near where he was staying. Following a telephone call to the proprietor to say that the 'Paris by Night' bus was on its way, half-a-dozen of the customers would get up and put on Apache outfits. When the tourists filed in, they were asked to sit down at tables a safe distance away, each being presented with a glass of wine. The Apaches would look suitably menacing, and make as if to beat up their women, while the guide reassured anybody who felt nervous; soon the bus-load would be off to the next stop. The rest, as Richard demonstrated as soon as they had left, was easy. We simply treated ourselves to the wine they had left unfinished, and often untasted, while we watched the Apaches getting back into their ordinary clothes. The evening cost nothing except, in my case, an agonising hangover.

A week later the diary, which I had dutifully been keeping in French, reverted to English: 'Chamberlain at Godesburg'. When it became clear that the visit had been fruitless, and the French reservists were called up, Jean among them, I seized the excuse to leave by the night ferry – the train which brought passengers in their sleeping cars from the Gare du Nord to Victoria without the need to leave them – Richard seeing me off in a Pernod-induced haze.

On the way through London, and in Oxford when I got back, trenches were being dug in the parks and gas masks distributed; the prevailing feeling was of unpreparedness for war, and a longing for the appearance of some excuse, any excuse, to avoid it. Nobody caught the mood better than Louis MacNeice in his *Autumn Journal*:

> We who have been brought up to think of 'Gallant Belgium'
>   As so much blague
> Are now preparing again to essay good through evil
>   For the sake of Prague.

The fact that it would be difficult to stick to pacifism, in view of the threat which the Nazis plans posed, made the Munich agreement a few days later come as a heartfelt relief, even to those of us who knew it was an unforgivable betrayal:

> We feel negotiation is not in vain –
>   Save my skin and damn my conscience
> And negotiation wins,
>   If you can call it winning
> And here we are – just as before – safe in our skins;
>   Glory to God for Munich.

73

It had been thought that the university term just due to begin would have to be postponed. Now it was on again, and I found I had a new tutor to deal with – a brash young man from Manchester University, A. J. P. Taylor. Curiously, he made little impression on me. Less curiously, I made none on him. The head of steam which had accumulated in Ireland in the research for the Gladstone Essay Prize had evaporated. It was becoming clear, even to me, that I was trundling along towards a respectable second, which only a fluke could turn into a first.

It did not seem to matter. The Oxford by-election, held less than a month after Munich, showed that many people who had welcomed Munich were now, even if not regretting appeasement, ready to cry 'Hold, enough!' Quintin Hogg won the seat, but the calibre of the signatures of university men and women who came out for his opponent, A. D. Lindsay, suggested that the relief felt at the time of the settlement was not going to sustain Chamberlain for long. His 'Peace in Our Time' speech could be relied upon to haunt him as soon as Hitler resumed the campaign which the map in the village school had imprinted on my memory.

In the meantime, though, things could go on much as before. The cares of the football captaincy over, and with the prospect of golf blue vanished, I was free to play other games as well: squash for the college, even on occasion to turn out for its hockey team as well as for the Old Dragons. That term, too, I was cast as one of the black slaves in the college's annual Gothic play – 'Monk' Lewis's *The Castle Spectre*, dating from 1797. We had no actor of the ability of Michael Denison, the previous year's lead; but we had the benefit as our Producer of Nevill Coghill – nephew of Edith Somerville (of the Somerville and Ross partnership) and the shrewd translator into modern English of Chaucer's *Canterbury Tales*. The *Oxford Mail* called the slaves 'astonishingly good'. They were two quite meaty parts, and playing one of them introduced me to Robert Kee, who was the other. He had come up to Magdalen two years after me; our careers have sporadically and agreeably intersected in journalism and television ever since.

Otherwise the diary entries might have been for the year before, so little did life at Malahide and Oxford change. But in my penultimate term an entry, 'A v.g. party, but it's let me in for something!' signalled a break. Discussing the indications that a second was now in prospect, Bruce McFarlane had intimated, gently but bluntly, that my continuing 'hearty' self, enjoying whatever games happened to be available, day after day, was responsible. What was required, he suggested, was another shake-up of the kind the Gladstone Essay Prize had provided. I needed to fall in love . . .

The 'something' the party let me in for, ten days after he had given this advice, was meeting Jean. Attractive though the Malahide girls were, none of them had any pretensions to scholarship. Jean, as attractive, was about to take her Finals in Politics, Philosophy and Economics. Michael Jefferson introduced us; we joined a party going to a St Valentine's Day dance; and for the next month we saw each other almost every day, going to the theatre or the cinema or to romantic dinners in restaurants in the Oxford countryside. This, I thought, was falling in love.

Then, she backed away. I found this incomprehensible; we had been getting on so well. The explanation came a few days later when she sent me a folder of hand-written pages. She had been jotting down her thoughts and feelings while reading for her Finals, expressing irritation with her work – 'God – I'm fed up with Kant!' – and on occasion with me – 'you were a little pleasanter today than yesterday – when you were *quite* insufferable (And don't you like to be told that?).' But she had not showed me what she had written, and I had remained blithely unaware of her feelings. She saw that our mutual attraction, strong though it was, was on my part shallow, easily dispersed. She hated, too, my parlour pink dogmatism, deriding emotional commitments as bourgeois sentimentality; and my 'brilliant glib way of dismissing everything – and not so brilliant, always; just unpleasant – does it mean that there is literally nothing you care anything about?'

When eventually Jean showed me what she had written, pages of it, it was a revelation of painful sensitivity on her part and self-satisfied insensitivity on mine. She had been in love before; when she became demonstrative, her lover had been frightened off. The same thing, she feared, would happen with me. I only thought I was in love; it was the thought of it that I had fallen for, not her. She had known it would not work, 'but one always hopes'. The hope had made her more involved than she cared to be, longing as she did for a secure relationship; 'So I don't very much want to see you again.'

It would be pleasant to recall that I was chastened, as indeed I was to be when I found the letter again, many years later. At the time I thought she was just being silly. We got on well, didn't we? We had common interests, and tastes, and could continue to enjoy each other's company without getting too involved. In any case, term was ending in a couple of days; we could pick up again, I felt sure, when we got back to Oxford after Easter. Reluctantly, Jean agreed to meet for tea, and to see how things would go in the summer.

Punch that week carried a typical Bernard Partridge cartoon, 'The Ides of March'. John Bull is waking up under a calendar showing 15 March. An ugly wraith, 'War Scare', is flying out of the window; John Bull is saying 'Thank goodness that's over'; and a note underneath recalls that 'pessimists predicted "another major crisis" in the middle of this month.' *Punch* went to press on 14 March; on the day it appeared, the wireless and newspaper headlines announced that Hitler's armies had invaded Czechoslovakia.

In a way, this came as a relief. In the next war, it had become clear, air power would be decisive. Baldwin had been reported as admitting there could be no defence against bombing; and the film of H. G. Wells's *The Shape of Things to Come*, with its warning of devastation, did not appear to be a far-fetched portrait of the immediate future. It was pointless to worry about the results of Finals, or indeed about a future career. I went back to Malahide when the Ides of March had come and gone, to resume going to the Island and to Seamount, seeing as much as I could of Rachel, and generally carrying on as of old.

My expectation that Jean would come to her senses – as I thought of it – when the summer term began was not fulfilled. She had her looming Finals to worry about, which provided an excuse to ease out of the relationship; soon I heard she had been seen around with another man, whom she later married. We did not meet again until years later, when she was with a second husband and we could look back to 1939 with some ironic detachment. In that last term, though, I felt bound also to use the excuse of Finals to account for seeing little of her. The impending war meant that there was little need to worry about failure to get a first, but it would have been gratifying to do well enough at least to be given a 'viva'. The papers, when I sat down to them, left me with no illusions. Unless the thesis carried weight, which was unlikely as it had not been the prizewinner, a second was all I could expect.

When, a few weeks later, I had the viva it was a short one, too perfunctory to hold out any hope of a first. A second it turned out to be. But there was a curious postscript. Charles Phillips wrote to me from Oxford to say he had run into Bruce McFarlane, who had been on the examining board. When I had left the viva room the chairman, G. N. Clark, had turned to Bruce and said, apparently on the strength of the thesis, that in his view I was the only candidate that year who 'had the makings of a historian'.

I left Magdalen with few regrets. Its beauty had impressed but never grabbed me, as it has grabbed so many others, and later I tended to blame it for my own failure to grow up. The main mistake was not doing something entirely different between school and university – or living in Paris, as Richard Cobb had done, not in the company of English speakers.

It was to be company of this kind which made a second spell in France, of my mother's arranging, almost as farcical as the one the year before. It was to take a course at the university of Grenoble. At my pension there was another graduate from Oxford, an attractive Swedish girl, a young Nazi from Germany, and a harp-playing Jewess from Austria, a refugee; the explosive arguments would have provided fascinating instruction had they been conducted in French, but English was our common language. The university course, too, had hardly got under way when we heard the ominous news of Hitler's pact with Stalin. Each day, the number of students dwindled, until the news of the German invasion of Poland on September 1 drove the last three of us who were from Britain to catch a train to Paris, an interminable journey through lines choked with trains full of troops and weapons moving up to the positions behind the Maginot Line.

My pacifism had been finally routed by the occupation of Czechoslovakia; and any notion that fear of the Russians might deter Hitler, had been banished by the pact. I did not, though, like the idea of returning to England and perhaps being conscripted. I would go through to Ireland. At Holyhead we were told that Britain and France had declared war on Germany. Passengers of an age which suggested they might be seeking to avoid military service were questioned before we were allowed to board the mail boat, but no attempt was made to check whether those of us who said we were Irish were telling the truth. There were a few bystanders on the jetty, when we sailed. We could just hear them, booing.

6

The Irish Times

Grandmother's closest friends in Malahide had been the Franks, across the lane in Roseneath. Their two sons had both joined the Royal Air Force. They were ten years or so older than I was, and I had seen little of them until Gerry, coming on leave with his new wife Jess, was in need of somebody to join him in occasional rounds of golf at the Island. He had laughed at my pacifism, and on one of his leaves he had brought me a present of a practice bomb – emptied of the contents, which would have provided the puff of smoke when it hit the ground on bombing practice run – painted to look as if it were silver; making it a surprisingly attractive chimneypiece ornament, in spite of the associations. It would be a reminder, he suggested, that if I did decide to join one of the services, it should be the RAF.

Volunteers from Dublin had to present themselves at a recruiting station in Belfast, where we were given a preliminary medical test. If I wanted to train as a pilot, I was told, there would be a further and stiffer test and an interview in England; and as there was a long waiting list, prospective pilots were being advised to go back to their homes and their jobs. It might be weeks before we were summoned. I had no home, and no job. The home problem presented no difficulty; Mungo Park was moving into digs in Dublin, pending his decision which of the services to join, and I moved in with him. But how to find a job?

When she was back on leave, my mother had brought her old friend from her Trinity Players' time, W. F. Casey, to lunch with us. He was in charge of the foreign desk at *The Times*, and on her last visit she had sounded him out on the prospects of my joining it, in

79

some capacity. He had not been encouraging: it was an unhealthy and unrewarding career, he had found, which he would not recommend. Yet he was unable to disguise the fact that his had been an interesting life, for all the stresses it had brought. Journalism in Ireland had not occurred to me as a career possibility, but to get a job on *The Times* would be a very different matter. Foreign correspondents, as 'W.F.' described them, could achieve almost diplomatic status – some virtually had, as the *History of the Times* was later to show. Perhaps after the war . . . In any case, it would be useful if I could gain some experience, while waiting for the call from the RAF.

The Sunday golfers at the Island had been joined by a threesome: the French Minister, the Polish Consul-General – deprived of his job by Hitler – and a short, burly man whose clothes looked as if they were disreputable not because they were originally of quality and had seen long service, which was acceptable, but because he had got them 'off the peg'. This, I was told, was the editor of the *Irish Times*, Bertie Smyllie. The diplomatic corps had quite a high social standing in Dublin, and it would have been embarrassing to turn down their regular playing companion on the ground of his despised profession. Besides, the *Irish Times*, though we thought it devoted too much space to the Dail and to Gaelic games, had at least remained faithful to the Crown. Smyllie had been admitted as a member.

Seeing him in the club house the Sunday after I came back, Charlie Armstrong went over to have a word with him. We were introduced, and Smyllie suggested I should come in to see him at the *Irish Times*. I have no recollection of the occasion, or whether it was in the office or the 'branch office' – the Palace Bar, across Westmoreland Street. But the outcome was that I would become unofficially a member of the staff, beginning in the reporters' room, where I should report for duty the following morning. I would not, of course, be paid, but I could expect 'reasonable' expenses for fares and meals.

If journalists were not highly regarded in our set, reporters were considered to be an even lower species. Lionel Fleming, the son of a Church of Ireland clergyman, recalled in his autobiography *Head or Harp* that when he became a reporter on the *Irish Times* in the early 1930s he found there was a stigma on the profession; an assumption 'that reporters are all seedy and rather unscrupulous men, with a taste for drink, an ignorance of grammar, and a capacity for never getting the facts quite right.' His parents, who had been impressed when he told them he had been asked to write some articles for the *Irish Times*, were disconcerted when he became a reporter; 'not quite the thing', they thought.

This, he found, was the general impression among his friends. When he was asked to cover an event in Trinity, where he had been a student, people who had known him and expressed pleasure at seeing him again were taken aback when he explained why he was there. Sent to do interviews, he had sometimes been turned away from the door by servants who felt they could be as rude as they liked. On other occasions he had interviewed men who, with conscious offensiveness, had 'spelt out simple words' to help him take his notes. His worst moment came when his cousin, old Admiral Somerville, was murdered by the I R A. Naturally he had not wanted to cover the story, but from the *Irish Times*'s point of view there was nobody else who could. His embarrassment was made worse when he found that his relations were unaware of what he was doing – possibly because his parents had not cared to tell them. 'Oh, Lionel, how kind of you to visit us in our trouble. We've been so bothered by those dreadful reporters.'

I had myself encountered reporters only as seedy, scruffy creatures who would turn up at funerals and weddings, wanting lists of people who attended, scribbling down names on the backs of envelopes, and invariably, to judge from the next day's *Irish Times*, getting them down wrong. The presumption was that the reporters from the *Irish Independent* were no better, but as its coverage was largely of Catholic events we did not read it; still less were we likely to read de Valera's paper, the *Irish Press*. It had not occurred to me that I would be pitchforked into reporting. Entering the *Irish Times* the next morning, I felt as if I were going back to school; a new school, with menacing lower-class boys of the kind that at Shrewsbury we would have called oicks.

The office consisted of three houses facing on to three streets which formed a triangle: Westmoreland, Fleet and D'Olier. Between them a network of passages had been constructed, the more confusing in that there were no signs showing which way to go. The editorial staff in those days went in through the main Westmoreland Street door by the counter where people were putting in advertisements, or collecting replies; up the main staircase; past the

Manager's office, on the left, and the editor's, on the right, before switching direction to reach the D'Olier Street house, where two rooms had been knocked together for the reporters. Nobody was in any of the upstairs offices when I arrived at nine. They were all dark, dusty, dingy and depressing. The reporters' room, when I found it, at least had large Georgian windows overlooking the street; but I had a long nervous wait there before the chief reporter, John Molloy, came in.

He did not look my idea of a chief reporter, acquired from Hollywood films. A gentle, quiet man, he must have been told to expect me – in itself surprising, as I was to find; Smyllie's snap decisions did not always filter down to those they affected. He wasted no time on formalities before presenting me with a couple of tickets for the trade showing of *Three Smart Girls Grow up*, a vehicle for the talents of Deanna Durbin, then at the peak of her career as the nice-girl-next-door who happens also to have a mellifluous voice. I had seen it a few days earlier in London, but refrained from mentioning the fact.

There were refreshments afterwards, in the cinema manager's office. I knew nobody; most of the small audience turned out to be men and women who would be connected with the distribution of the film through Irish cinemas. One of them was bemoaning the failure of Disney's *Snow White*; he feared it had been above the heads of country audiences.

No more work was required of me that day, but the next morning my name was in the 'Markings' book, at the foot of the list of reporters, as 'Day Town' – the full job description being 'Day Town, Coast, Accidents, Funerals, Hospitals, Fires, Police etc.' – in other words, anything which might happen unexpectedly in and around Dublin. This was the most junior reporter's daily lot, as James Pettigrew, who had been 'marked' for it until my arrival, explained. It entailed telephoning around police stations, hospitals and other likely sources of information, informing the chief reporter of anything newsworthy, and answering the telephone – there was only one, at that time. As it appeared to be permanently in use by reporters ringing out, this was not likely to occupy much of my time; but hospitals? There were dozens. Where should I begin? James in those days was uncommunicative, very unlike the Fleet Street figure he became in later years, full of Irish blarney. He was not disposed to act as nanny; so I began to call up Dublin hospitals.

82

It soon became clear that hospitals did not care to confide in reporters. Neither did Fire Stations, nor the police. At first 'Coast' was puzzling, but another reporter explained that it was a relic of the days when there had been coastguard stations; they had gone the way of the one at Malahide in the Troubles. I grew more and more nervous, as the reporters' occupation of the telephone meant that if anything newsworthy had happened I would be unlikely to hear of it. But nobody called me to account; and the Dublin evening papers carried no stories of the kind I would have been blamed for missing. And that evening, Alan Montgomery arrived in the reporters' room, to come to the rescue.

Alan was a son of 'Lynn C. Doyle' – the pseudonym adopted by Leslie Montgomery on the strength of an ad for linseed oil in a shop. Leslie was an Ulster boy who had become a bank clerk at the age of sixteen, but later had made his name with his 'Ballygullion' stories, light-hearted tales about a fictional Ulster village which were eventually collected and published by Penguin. On his retirement he had come to live in Malahide, and to play golf at the Island. I had met Alan occasionally and knew he was on the *Irish Times*, but not that he was a reporter. It turned out that he was on Night Town, a 'marking' which entailed staying in the office until the paper was finally put to bed in the small hours, taking telephone calls and if necessary going to the scene of an accident or a fire. Often, though, the hours passed with nothing to do; and Alan that night typed out a junior reporter's *Vade Mecum*.

I kept it for years, dining out on it; but at some stage, alas, it disappeared. Essentially it consisted of a commentary upon what a junior reporter was expected to do, in theory, and how he would eventually find himself doing it, in practice. The presupposition was that if anything newsworthy happened in and around the capital on a weekday before midday it would be reported in the evening papers, – the *Herald* and the *Mail*, which newsboys, still barefoot, would bring onto the streets early in the afternoon. It would be time enough, then, to put through a quick call or two – not to the scene of the event, but to one of the reporters who had covered it, to check whether there might be some particular *Irish Times* angle. There was rivalry for circulation between the newspaper owners, and up to a point between their editors and the higher ranking staff writers, but very little between the reporters. If for any reason one of them arrived late for some briefing – by, say, a minister, in which the hand-out happened to be accompanied by some unforeseen but important off-the-cuff remarks – he could usually rely on obtaining a 'black', a carbon copy of what one of the other reporters would put in to his newspaper, or failing that a telephoned run-down of the other man's notes.

A serious accident or fire was unlikely to be missed. It had become known that newspapers paid for a tip-off, and there was no shortage of men ready to qualify for half-a-crown. Dublin was unusual in that there were few residential squares and streets in the city centre without slum areas immediately adjacent to them, wealth and extreme poverty existing back-to-back. The unemployed – in country villages as well as in the towns – habitually stood in a row outside a pub, along the pub wall as if propping it up. They were well placed to see, or hear of, anything unusual which could be relayed to a newspaper – or newspapers; there was rarely any way of knowing whether the informant might have passed it on to the others too.

Some of the time on 'Day Town' was spent reporting minor functions of the kind which had little news value, but which space had always been found for because they were attended by *Irish Times* readers, or the kind of people the management hoped would become *Irish Times* readers when they saw their names in the paper as having won a prize for the best sponge cake at a local fête. I loathed having to find out who had won such competitions, and to ask how they spelled their names in case there was some catch (I was once caught out by hearing that the name was Hogan, which seemed safe; he turned out to be of Canadian descent, and spelled it Haugen; while the Irish version of 'John' might be spelled 'Sean' or 'Shaun', as well as 'Shane'). The smallest error in a report, too, could be guaranteed to bring in an angry correction; pointing out, for example, that the prize was for the best seed cake, not sponge cake. Local jealousy in such matters was often intense.

Reporters were indeed a despised species, I found; all the more because we were needed, if the functions were to be accorded the space their organisers considered they deserved in the paper the next morning. We would also be invited to formal dinners, ranging from the celebrations of centenaries to the annual 'thrash' of rugby football clubs; the convention was that we were expected to wear whatever the guests were wearing, a dinner jacket if necessary and even, on some occasions tails and a white tie, the suits hired from Ging's the theatrical outfitters. Usually, though, we did not sit down with the guests; a side table was provided where we had our chicken-and-ham and St Emilion, the standard dinner fare. We would be expected to stay for the speeches, and then leave before the remains of the bread rolls began to be put to their traditional club dinner purpose.

In more than one sense we were a class apart, detached from whatever station in life we had grown up into. A few of the *Irish Times* reporters could have been in 'our set' in Malahide; as Alan Montgomery was, on the strength of Lynn Doyle being a bank manager – not on account of his popularity as a writer, as writers were not taken seriously if they chose frivolous subjects such as the goings-on in an Irish village. James Pettigrew too owed his job to his Sligo background, Smyllie being an admirer of the Ascendancy families in that county. For the rest, it would have been difficult to tell what their background was, or their religion. Even when their accents proclaimed them to be Ulstermen, or Scots, or English, they seemed to have taken on a form of protective colouring, identifying themselves as newspapermen.

Not that this meant uniformity. A few of the reporters – and of the sub-editors who, in their dark windowless room, took our copy and re-fashioned it before it went to the compositors – seemed Victorian in their manner. James Wright, responsible for the proceedings in the High Court, was clearly the kind of man to whom the judges would pay glowing and sincere tributes when he retired. Matthew Bunyan, whom I remember as looking remarkably like the Phiz drawings of Mr Micawber, always came to the Subs' room in a stiff collar. In contrast there was John Collins, whose first journalistic assignment, or so he claimed, had been covering the Franco–Prussian war of 1870, and who looked as if he had not changed his suit since. He suffered from prostate trouble; if the single squalid jakes which reporters and subs used happened to be occupied, he would piss into the fire-bucket beside it.

There was no retirement age; most reporters stayed at their work, unless rescued by a legacy, until chronic illness or death removed them, because there was no pension scheme. When Bunyan's increasing infirmity prompted the management to encourage him to retire by offering him a pension, it was a guinea a week. Scattered through the building, as a result, were other long-serving employees whom the management – the *Irish Times* was a family firm, owned by the Arnotts – did not have the heart to sack; among them Bill Coyne, batman to Sir Lauriston Arnott in the Great War, who had become a kind of doorman. He had also fought in the Boer War; given half a chance he would describe his experiences in South Africa, culminating with an account of the aftermath of one of the battles when 'Bobs', Lord Roberts of Kandahar, had told him 'Put down your gun, Bill Coyne, you've killed enough.'

It was easy enough to get on with this older generation. The younger reporters were more of a problem. I was lucky that one of them, Edward MacSweeney, had been given the job of producing the *Irish Times Annual*, which kept him much of the time in the reporters' room, available to give advice. Some were less patient, and the reporters from other papers were often markedly less co-operative with me than with the rest of us.

One reason was obvious: I was out of touch with the new Ireland. Almost my only contact with it had been *Dublin Opinion*; grandmother for some reason was a subscriber, though I never saw her read it. The cartoons of 'C.E.K.' – a civil servant, Charlie Kelly – enabled me to identify the leading politicians of the time more easily than their photographs in the papers. Working on 'Day Town', though, brought little contact with politicians; more with individuals who were well-known, or liked to think they were, in the professions and in industry. It was embarrassing to have to admit that I did not recognise them and, worse, that I had no idea who they were even when told their names.

The Irish language also presented difficulties. The main parties, de Valera's Fianna Fail and Cosgrave's Fine Gael, had been competing with each other in enthusiasm for the language revival, and although there were already indications that the campaign was failing, people in public life often decided it was expedient to display some acquaintance with Irish by beginning their speeches in it, as Aer Lingus hostesses do in their announcements to this day. Most reporters had a sufficient smattering of the language at least to know they need not bother to report what was said in it; but they did not care to be asked to translate.

It was humiliating to have to ask what on earth the Secretary to the venerable President, Douglas Hyde, meant when he rang the *Irish Times* to give the names of people who had attended some ceremony at his residence, in Phoenix Park, *Aras an Uachtarain*. He gave me a string of names, most of which were familiar because they were little different in pronunciation from the English version. But some were incomprehensible: Walsh became 'Breathnach'. Interspersed between them, too, from time to time came the repetition of what sounded like 'Argusarborn'. To have to ask Harold Brown, a dour Ulsterman who combined being a reporter with acting as the *Irish Times* motoring correspondent, what it meant, was as embarrassing, as the discovery that all it meant was 'with his wife' – *Proinsias Mac Aogain agus a Bhean* turned out to be the Minister of Defence, Frank Aiken, and Mrs Aiken.

I am not sure it was Harold Brown who did the explaining on the first occasion, but it certainly was Brown who took a call from the front office one morning and called out to me, in my 'Day Town' capacity, that there was a baton charge in West Moreland Street. I started out of the room, trying to think where West Moreland Street might be; and at the door I inquired. Nobody paid any attention, so I went out through the front office to find there was no need to ask the way; the police were dragging some men to a van, just outside the *Irish Times* doors, and thrusting them in – one of them shouting 'Up the Republic' (de Valera had banned the I R A, and although his aim was an all-Ireland republic, he wanted to obtain it by constitutional means). Only then did it dawn on me that the scuffle had been in what I had always pronounced, as our set had always done, as 'Westm'lnd' Street.

I never discovered whether Brown and other reporters who were in the room at the time thought I was joking, or took it to be only another example of silly Ascendancy snobbery; but the episode shook me into the realisation that friendly though most of them were, they might regard me with derision, or even active dislike – as, years later, I was to find that some of them did. I was presenting a television programme in London, and the Director told me it was being watched by members of the commission set up to plan for the introduction of television in Ireland, whom we were to meet in the hospitality room afterwards. Among them was Mrs Stafford, who as Colleen Kivlehan had been the junior reporter on the *Irish Press* – the only woman reporter in Dublin, as I remember, though Barbara Dickson, who was mainly employed on the *Irish Times* on social and fashion subjects, would occasionally be roped in for general duties.

Colleen had been an attractive but, as I thought, shy and tongue-tied girl; she had become an even more attractive and far from tongue-tied woman, who told me good-humouredly but unsparingly just how impossible I had been on those markings we had been sent on, and went on to leave me in no doubt that some of her colleagues had shared her opinion. In particular she recalled that after one job, I had invited her to tea, by which I had meant afternoon tea at some café, and could not understand why she had refused, knowing what kind of 'tea' she would be offered.

Thickness of skin must often have protected me from realising, that Ascendancy manners, to those who had grown up into the new Ireland, could be simply bad manners. 'West Moreland Street' set me on what could be described as a descendancy course, to become a downstart – as Bernard Shaw had described himself in the Preface to his novel *Immaturity*, for taking a job as a clerk. Now, I wanted to be accepted on the paper; to 'talk the same language'.

This was not just a matter of pronunciation, or of accent; it was more a matter of jargon. We did not go to the lavatory, or the toilet, but to the Jacks (or Jakes; it was still spelled, and sometimes pronounced, as it appears to have been by Kent in *King Lear*). Several Dublin terms were Shakespearian; girl-friends were 'mots', a mildly facetious term – about the equivalent of the English 'popsy'.

The first terms which come back to mind from those days constitute a kind of litany of 'bs' and 'gs': bollocks, bosthoon, bowsy; gouger, gurrier, gutty. Some could be traced easily enough: gutty to guttersnipe; some derivations were slightly more fanciful, gurrier to *guerrier*. In his *Dublin*, in the Small Oxford Books series, Ben Kiely has since claimed that gouger is a corruption of gauger, the excise man, 'the evil and official foe of all free spirits who like their spirits free'; in pub terms it meant somebody whom it was wise to placate, when he became drunk, by buying more drink for him. A 'bowsy', according to Ben, was sometimes used in the sense of blackleg or strike-breaker. It had an allied pub implication – somebody who took drinks, but did not stand them.

Ben also cites a Dublin publisher, Gerry O'Flaherty, as claiming not only that gurrier may have been derived from *guerrier*, but that in the 1930s and 1940s it was a term of approbation; 'a Great Little Gurrier' was 'a bosom friend, a fine fellow'. I recall it only in the sense of somebody notorious for spoiling for a fight, when drunk. A 'bollocks' was simply a nuisance, drunk or sober; a 'bosthoon', an ignorant Dubliner – much the same as was implied in the Anglo–Irish term 'jackeen', though that carried a 'jumped up' implication.

I was to be on 'Day Town' for only three months, not long enough to do more than leave a slight crack in the Ascendancy mould; but it was an exhilarating experience. The work, though, tended to be frustrating for somebody who fancied himself as a writer on the strength of school and college testimonials. It quickly became apparent that reporting at the 'Day Town' level followed a rigid formula, the first paragraph containing either a compressed account of the event to be described or, most commonly, a sentence from a speech followed by a description of the man who had made it and the occasion. 'Colour' was discouraged. Only once was I given a running story, and left to get on with it.

Dublin had been hit by a strike of workers distributing milk. As usual their employers made great play with the sufferings of mothers with young children, and patients in hospitals; the strikers duly promised to make special arrangements for both. As a substantial proportion of the male population drank milk only in their tea, there was no great outcry; nobody seemed much the worse off. But then, the telephone rang in the reporters' room, and it was the Curator of the Dublin Zoo. Some of his animals were accustomed to consume quantities of milk every day, little or none was coming through; could the *Irish Times* draw attention to their plight? When a story of this kind fell into a reporter's lap he was not expected to share it with the other papers; the *Irish Times* enjoyed a 'beat' the next morning, all the more satisfactory in that its readers tended to be great ones for preventing cruelty to animals.

I was ineligible for the range of 'markings' which might require shorthand, such as the Dail and the Courts; but 'Day Town' was occasionally marked to attend a Coroner's Court, and on one occasion this presented me with what I thought would be my first real news story. The evidence at an inquest revealed that shortly before the deceased had fallen out of a top floor window and broken his neck, he had been served a summons by a policeman. No inquiry was made whether there was any connection between the two events; the verdict was accidental death. Surely, I complained to the other reporters on the way back into Dublin, this ought to be investigated? They agreed, but shrugged their shoulders; and nobody took any interest in the story back in the reporters' room. The convention at the time, I was to find, was that death was 'accidental' unless it was so clearly suicide as it might be when somebody jumped from the top of Nelson's Pillar with a note on him explaining why, that no other verdict was possible.

I referred to this inquest in *West Briton*, commenting that when subsequently I had seen statistics purporting to compare annual suicide rates, in Europe, with the Swiss near the top and the Irish near the foot of the table, I suspected that they were a reflection not so much of the emotional instability of the Swiss as of the comparative honesty of their statistics; a comment which provoked a rebuke from the Dublin County Coroner, Dr J. P. Brennan. 'The dead man might have slipped,' Dr Brennan pointed out, 'he might have had high blood pressure, he might have had a weakness.' Yet his comment, 'Irish coroners are guided not only by the law of evidence, but also by the law of charity', was in effect a confirmation of my point. Unless there was inescapable proof of suicide, they did not regard it as any part of their function to investigate the cause of a death which *might* have been an accident.

Straight reporting in those days consequently offered few opportunities for originality; and even when it did the *Irish Times*, following the example of *The Times*, did not name the writer. I would be sorry to have missed those weeks, but chiefly for the glimpses they gave of Dublin and its inhabitants at various levels, for the insights into the ways in which local news is garnered, and for the timely warning given by 'West Moreland Street'.

The work entailed no break with my social life. As the *Irish Times* did not run a Sunday edition, Saturday was virtually free even if we were marked to work over the week-end: some major event might need to be attended, but usually it would be safe to rely on the reports from the Sunday papers. I could play golf at the Island, and go to the Gresham five shilling 'hop' in the evening. But the composition of our set was changing. Of the girls who were now in the Gresham parties, three had come to Oxford, at the end of my last term, to attend one of the 'Commem Balls'; it did not occur to me at the time, but Biddy Jameson, Judy Post and Barbara Strickland were all three Catholics.

So were most of the men who came with us to the Gresham. A bunch of them were at Trinity, doing medicine. Some came from the class which grandmother had sneered at as 'Rathminesy', the implication being that the residents of that Dublin suburb were 'jumped up', or seeking to jump up, socially. I had not encountered the species before, and was surprised to find them like us, but much friendlier. With them, to be an *Irish Times* reporter was no disgrace; on the contrary, it sounded intriguing. I was also the source of free admission, on some occasions, to cinemas or other entertainments. And they were all, like me, going to join the forces, as soon as they qualified.

The medical students had nothing to worry about, except their final examinations. I was expecting to be called up for an interview and a medical at any time, and as I had a small allowance, and about £100 in savings certificates which could be cashed – with porter costing 3p a glass, a pound went a long way – I could join them in their pursuit of girls and their round of parties, under the impression that each week might be the last. Besides, this was the Phoney War period. It had become obvious that Hitler was unlikely to make his next move until the spring; and certainly any fear that Ireland might be invaded had passed.

We felt no embarrassment at being out of the war. De Valera had been right, we felt sure, to maintain Ireland's neutrality. It was unfortunate, we thought, that he was refusing to allow the Navy to use the ports which under the 1921 Treaty she would have been allowed to use; but Chamberlain, after all, had handed them back, and if the Navy *were* allowed to use them, Hitler would have the excuse he needed to declare war on Ireland, and bomb them. As a belligerent, Ireland would have been virtually defenceless, needing massive help from Britain to prepare against possible invasion later. And if the RAF was not yet desperate for my services, I might as well enjoy myself.

The RAF was not ready for them because of the appalling winter weather, which held up training. This might give time, Smyllie thought, to try me out in the editor's room. In February, instead of turning left to the reporters' room I turned right into his room – gloomy at the best of times, as its dome had been blacked out. An inner room provided the editor with his sanctum, as it was sometimes facetiously called; the outer room had a desk for the deputy editor, and a chair for visitors; a narrow passage, made still narrower by files of the newspapers, led to a jakes and a tiny office, hardly bigger than a cupboard, where the assistant editor worked. I sat waiting, uncomfortably, in the visitor's chair.

7

Smyllie

'When, in these trying times, it's possible to work on the lower slopes of a national newspaper for several weeks without discovering which of the scurrying executives is the editor,' Patrick Campbell recalled in 1959, in one of the 'Come Here Till I Tell You' series he wrote for the *Spectator*, 'I count myself fortunate to have served under one who wore a green sombrero, weighed twenty-two stone, sang parts of his leading articles in operatic recitative, and grew the nail on his little finger into the shape of a pen nib, like Keats.'

I have since found it extremely difficult to think about Smyllie, let alone write about him, without resorting to Paddy's article; the temptation has always been to quote from it at length. But Paddy was remembering only his years in the office in the mid 1930s. Since then, Lionel Fleming's delightful *Head or Harp* has presented another portrait of Smyllie as he was when he had yet to become editor (and when he took on the job); and Tony Gray has written a study of Smyllie and his impact on the *Irish Times* from 1920 to 1954 which, I trust, will soon be published, and which fills in the background.

Robert Maire Smyllie had been to Sligo Grammar School and Trinity, where he got the job of vacation tutor to an American boy in Germany. It was 1914; he delayed too long before returning; and he spent the war in Ruhleben, a prison camp for enemy aliens. As Tony emphasises, what for many boys would have been a crushing experience was the making of Smyllie. Ruhleben was populated with internees of many different nationalities, talents and political opinions. To keep themselves from growing bored, they had debates and classes and productions of plays – Smyllie being responsible for putting on the works of the Abbey dramatists. As his father had been the editor of the *Sligo Times*, he could also help in the production of the Ruhleben camp journal. He also acquired fluent German, along with passable French and a smattering of other languages.

Returning to Sligo after the Armistice, Smyllie found that the *Sligo Times* had ceased publication. It had been Unionist in its politics; he thought he would try for a job on the *Irish Times*, by this time the established Unionist organ. Its editor, John Healy, was wondering how on earth, let alone among Dublin journalists, he could find somebody who would have a sufficient grasp not only of the necessary languages, but of the complexities of the European scene, to cover the negotiations which were about to begin at Versailles. Here was a young man who, though not a journalist, had acquired some experience, had the necessary languages, and appeared to be considerably better-informed on the issues which would come up than could be expected of any Irish, or even British, newspaperman. Smyllie got the job.

From the point of view of gaining experience, it turned out even better than he could have expected. Woodrow Wilson, Clemenceau, Lloyd George and the rest did their best to ensure that their deliberations were reported only in formal communiqués, which encouraged Smyllie to embellish his reports with descriptions of life in Europe at the time, as well as to present the views of foreign journalists on the Irish question, his excuse being that the Sinn Fein provisional government was seeking to secure a hearing.

When he returned to Dublin Smyllie was brought on to the staff of the *Irish Times*, eventually establishing himself as Healy's successor. How far it was his influence that weaned the paper from die-hard Unionism cannot now be settled, but he was generally credited with the responsibility for making such decisions as accepting that 'Kingstown' was in future to be printed as 'Dun Laoghaire' – decisions of a kind which can lose subscribers who regard the change as the last straw, and which gain no new readers, except in the sense that readers trying out the paper, who would find the survival of 'Kingstown' ridiculous or offensive, are no longer put off. And there are many indications when he took over as editor after Healy's death in 1934 of his shrewdness in refusing to accept what most of his readers accepted; that the Irish, as distinct from the Anglo–Irish and the Ulster Protestants, were hopelessly incompetent and unbusinesslike.

When C.S., 'Todd', Andrews was appointed to run the new State company set up in 1936 to harvest peat by machinery, to try to reduce Ireland's dependence on British coal, the project excited derision. Undrained bog, it was pointed out, consists of 95 per cent water – more than a glass of milk; the cost of machine-won turf would far exceed the price for which it could sell. Smyllie had no reason to trust Todd, a former gunman and a de Valera appointee; but he knew Sir John Purser Griffith, an expert on the subject, and when Sir John expressed his confidence in the scheme, Smyllie gave it the *Irish Times*'s enthusiastic backing. He 'integrated the *Irish Times* and what it stood for with the Irish nation,' Todd commented in *Man of No Property*, the second volume of his perceptive autobiography; making it possible for the civil servants and men in business and the professions who had grown up in the new Ireland to read it without irritation and embarrassment. The *Irish Times* was 'for all the rising lower and middle classes the symbol of "ould dacency" and respectability'; this in turn compelled politicians to take it seriously, and to long for its approbation.

It had been the practice of the *Irish Times* to employ promising young men from Trinity to write leading articles, when required; one of them, Alec Newman, had become Smyllie's second-in-command. Lionel Fleming had been with Alec in Trinity; finding – as I had – that he would make an abysmally incompetent schoolmaster, he had persuaded Alec to introduce him to Smyllie; and after he had sent in a succession of articles about Cork, at Smyllie's bidding, he had been brought in as a reporter, and later transferred to leader-writing. Lionel – Bill, as he was usually then called, having decided that 'Lionel' was too up-stage a name for a journalist – was eventually to become one of BBC radio's most familiar voices as the Corporation's Colonial Correspondent, at a time when one or more of the colonies were constantly in the news, as the wind of change blew through the Empire; a rich, fruity Irish brogue of the kind Bernard Shaw had made familiar, and has since become a commonplace, thanks to the 'Irish Mafia' in television. As Lionel admitted, it was an identity tag. He had not had such an accent while working in Ireland, and he shed it when, after his retirement, he returned to become Foreign Editor of the *Irish Times*.

Lionel was a typical example of Smyllie using his hunch in the selection of newcomers to the staff. The National Union of Journalists objected; as a national newspaper, its officers argued, the *Irish Times* should insist on its recruits going through a couple of years training on one of the provincial papers. From his own experience, Smyllie knew this was nonsense. Far from being a good training ground, the kind of work reporters had to do in the provinces sometimes actively discouraged what he was looking for, flair. A short spell in the *Irish Times* reporters' room, and perhaps another in the sub editors', could be useful; but he liked to recruit people who could write the kind of articles which he could read with pleasure himself, and which friends whose opinions he valued would tell him they had enjoyed. As the N U J had little power at the time, he had no difficulty in getting his way; there were usually several direct-intake men on the staff at any time, (much as there were to be in John Huston's films – notably Seamus Kelly, pulled out of the *Irish Times* to play one of the *Pequod*'s mates in *Moby Dick*). And the next amateur Smyllie tested, after Lionel moved into the editor's room, was to provide the most emphatic justification for Smyllie's method: the Hon. Patrick Gordon Campbell.

Paddy's earlier career had some curious parallels with mine, four years later. He had been to an English public school, and to Oxford, where he had failed Pass Mods, and where his main passion was golf. When he had left – in his case, without a degree – he had to admit to his father that he could not think of anything, any job, he wanted to do, or could do. His father – by this time, Governor of the Bank of Ireland – thought that languages might help. In Germany Paddy had been appalled by the evidence of the effects of the rise of National Socialism, and had moved on to Paris. In three months there he had managed not to learn any French.

There was nothing for it, Glenavy decided, but to beg his old friend Smyllie to come to the rescue. Smyllie saw Paddy, and told him to write a thousand words about a visit to the Dublin zoo. It appeared, unchanged, the following morning. Even Glenavy was impressed: 'You got the chimpanzee with the straw in its mouth exactly. Very good writing.' Paddy knew, immediately, that he had found himself. 'I'd stumbled into the only job that required no degrees, no diplomas, no training and no specialised knowledge of any kind,' as he put it in *My Life and Easy Times*: 'Journalism might have been designed for my special benefit.'

So it proved. Paddy started off in the reporters' room, but his stay there was brief; the stammer which he was later to exploit with such effect on television proved too much of a handicap, fortunately for him, disqualifying him from 'Day Town'. He was put to writing a 'Courts Day by Day' feature, in imitation of one then appearing in a London newspaper. It began to attract attention – 'your son is educating us,' the normally acerbic Sarah Purser told his mother; and he was soon promoted to the editor's office, there to write leaders' to contribute paragraphs to the 'Irishman's Diary', and eventually to become the paper's literary editor.

When the Dail was sitting, too, he wrote a parliamentary sketch. It treated Leinster House as Bernard Levin was later to treat Westminster, as a staged play – sometimes drama, sometimes farce. His column became immensely popular among readers, and extremely unpopular among most Deputies and Senators – to the alarm of his father. It was time, Paddy decided, to move to London, where the fact that Beaverbrook had known and admired his grandfather, the first Baron, would surely secure him a job.

I had not met Paddy before he went, but he had left a formidable reputation. To be asked to join the editor's office encouraged the hope of following in his footsteps. Alec Newman by this time was securely installed as deputy, in charge of the Diary – it consisted of half-a-dozen contributed paragraphs, and editing it constituted his daily first chore. He was not in, that first evening; the editing was done by John Robinson. John was another of Smyllie's intake, a studious-looking young Ulsterman who looked as if he might be taking Holy Orders. I was to find he was less than happy at his promotion from the reporters' room, as it cut grievously into his social life; all that the hours – 9.30 p.m. to 4.30 a.m. – permitted was 'an early snog in the back row of the Savoy Cinema' (he was later to recall), before putting the girl on the tram which would carry her home.

John proved good company. If things were quiet, after the pubs closed we would go to the *Irish Times* Club. It was literally a case of 'ring three times and ask for Charlie', except that it was Charlie himself, from the top floor of a Georgian terrace house, who called out to find who was wanting to get in, and whether we were members. If we passed his scrutiny, he would throw down the key, and we would climb the interminable flights of stairs to the dingy room where Charlie dispensed drinks.

Sometimes, on inspection, he would disapprove of us. He would not allow any journalist he knew was married to arrive with any woman not his wife. Tony Gray was in the club one night when Ben Kiely – it was not necessary to be on the *Irish Times* to be a member – arrived with a friend who happened to be a respectable middle-aged school mistress. If anything or anybody offended Charlie, he was apt to tell everybody in the club to leave, on some pretext. 'I'm serving no more drink,' he announced, 'to any party which includes Mr Ben Kiely and his bubble dancer.'

If Alan Montgomery, escaping for half-an-hour or so from Night Town, was with us, we would slip across instead to the Temperance Hotel beside the *Irish Times* back door, as it then was, in D'Olier Street. Temperance hotels used to come into their own in Dublin after the pubs shut. They were rarely raided, as they were assumed not to sell liquor; nor did they, but their hall porters would keep a cache of whiskey and stout bottles. In emergency, we could be brought back to the office by a call from Harry Sullivan, who at night single-handedly manned the telephone switchboard. If he liked the reporter on Night Town, he would take whatever action might be required himself, passing only urgent messages to us through to the hotel. Reporters whom he disliked had a hard time of it; he did not hesitate to cut off calls when he felt inclined.

The first night I joined the editors' room there were frequent interruptions, as indeed there were to be every night, from people who wanted to know if Smyllie had arrived and, if possible, to get him to attend to their problems before he settled down to write his leader, when there would be no possibility of gaining his ear. The callers ranged from the manager, who had been with the paper for almost half a century, to chance acquaintances of Smyllie's who had submitted contributions and wanted to know why they had not appeared. Smyllie was continually accepting articles, or Diary paragraphs (for which the payment was 3/6d), knowing that they would be unprintable, because he did not want to hurt people's feelings. And as Lionel had found, he would not even allow his juniors to be ruthless on his behalf. Once, when Smyllie had hidden in the jakes to avoid meeting a particularly obnoxious contributor, Lionel told the man his stuff was no good; when he left, Smyllie was furious – 'Have you no thought for other people's feelings?'

Smyllie, when he arrived that first night, was in no mood to pay attention to any of the messages. I might have been working in his office for years; he wanted a 'pup' on after-dinner speeches, he told me, as well as a couple of paragraphs for the Irishman's Diary. A 'pup' was a 500-word, light, if possible funny, leader modelled on the *Times*'s, which Bernard Darwin and Peter Fleming had made popular. John was given his leader subject; Smyllie went into his sanctum; and the three of us got down to work soundlessly, except for the tapping on the typewriters.

Night after night, the same procedure was followed until the leaders were written, and passed to the compositors. Then we could relax until the proofs came back for correction. There was little need for all four of us to stay on, but Smyllie liked company, and we would wait until the second edition was safely in bed before taking off to our homes. In Paddy's time there had been hard-fought games of dominoes; no longer. Mostly we talked, but sometimes Smyllie, who had quite an impressive baritone, and Alec would sing.

Occasionally Smyllie would start up, as Paddy was to recall, while writing his leaders. They were padded out with Latin tags and a variety of cliché space-fillers; if a controversial step taken by the government was being criticised, he would write 'The government, in its wisdom, has decided . . .', and the repetition might prompt him to read it over to himself, and us, in *recitative*. In Paddy's time Alec, Lionel and he had joined in; we simply listened. But I did eventually join in the choruses on occasions when Smyllie, fortified from the noggin of brandy which he kept in his roll-top desk, and Alec back from the *Irish Times* club, felt like singing.

In most ways Smyllie was rather prudish. Sex rarely figured in late night conversations. But Alec while at Trinity had acquired a stock of lewd limericks and scabrous songs, which Smyllie joined in singing with gusto. I can remember only one of the limericks; about the Young Lady from Bray

who invented a rotary spray.
She said, 'Ah! That's better!
Its washed out that letter
That's been there since Armistice Day.

The songs were mostly those which I had occasionally heard after bump suppers at Magdalen, and was soon often to hear in RAF officers' messes. There were some Irish variations: we sang 'The Good Ship Venus' to the tune of the hymn 'For those in peril on the sea' – the good ship sailing from Nigeria

To Rio de Janeri-er
Along our routes, the prostitutes
Grew wearier, and wearier.

Appalled though he would have been at the idea of blasphemy appearing in his newspaper, Smyllie would nevertheless sing the chorus

O hear us when we cry to thee
For us poor fuckers on the sea.

These late night sessions, though, were the least important part of Smyllie's working day. He would come in to the office around five to be set upon, as he had been in Paddy's time, by men and women who wanted to gain his ear before he gained his sanctuary at the top of the stairs. Occasionally he would be trapped; usually he would break through them, on some excuse. At his desk, he saw anybody whom he could not avoid seeing, and answered letters he could not avoid answering – he had no secretary – before escaping to the Palace Bar, across Westmoreland Street.

The main room in the Palace lay past a row of 'snugs', in which reporters would normally drink if they went to the Palace, and did not care to be seen by the editor. Smyllie would walk through and sit down at one of the tables – the drinks were served to customers by 'curates' – and around him would gather a remarkable collection of Dubliners, along with occasional visitors from the country or abroad. It was not a cross-section of Dublin life; there were rarely any politicians, or sportsmen. But there was usually a sprinkling of civil servants among the authors, artists, playwrights, poets and hangers-on, as well as journalists, who on most evenings filled the room.

A caricaturist from New Zealand who was working in Dublin at the time, Alan Reeve, drew a remarkable panoramic scene of the room and its regulars, all at their tables. Reeve enjoyed the same faculty as Low, the ability to make his characters instantly recognisable; the cartoon brings them back as vividly as if they were still living, which only a handful of them are. A surprisingly high proportion of the leading figures in Dublin's world of art and literature could be found there any evening, some of them every evening. And although they did not come to sit and talk with Smyllie, unquestionably it was his patronage which made the Palace the centre for the gathering.

A little earlier, in Lionel's time, it had attracted Oliver Gogarty, whose witticisms were still remembered, particularly his comments on the effect of the compulsory education system introduced by the Free State – all it was doing, he claimed, was bringing the graffiti lower down 'on piss-house walls'; and in particular, of the introduction of compulsory Irish – the money spent on it was turning Ireland 'into a race of bilinguals ignorant and gullible in both languages'. These, at least, were credited to Gogarty, though most were regarded as the work of Jimmy Montgomery – Gogarty getting the credit simply because his name was better known.

Yeats, too, had come occasionally to the Palace. Smyllie would recall him reciting a limerick he had just heard, about the bestially-inclined undergraduate of St John's, leading up to the last line 'The swans are reserved for the dons' which Yeats would repeat, as if to underline the point: 'the swans, Smyllie, are reserved for the dons.'

Yeats was dead, and Gogarty no longer living in Ireland, when I began to join the Palace throng; but it was impressive enough for somebody who had never found himself in such company before. Yeats had pulled several Irish poets into recognition in his slipstream, as it were: *The Oxford Book of Modern Verse*, which he edited in 1936, contained poems by Joseph Campbell, Padraic Colum, Gogarty, F. R. Higgins, James Joyce, Thomas McGreevy, Louis MacNeice, Frank O'Connor and James Stephens. All were still living; it created no surprise when any of them walked in to the Palace, though by 1940 Higgins was the only regular. His 'Boyne

Walk', included in the anthology edited by Cecil Day Lewis and L. A. G. Strong, was dedicated to Smyllie.

Far from feeling flattered by the inclusion of so many Irish poets, the Palace's consensus was that Yeats had fallen down on the job. Where were Austin Clarke, Donagh MacDonagh, Patrick Kavanagh, Francis MacManus, Roibeard O Farachain, and Seumas O'Sullivan – all in Reeve's Palace cartoon? An anthology of poems which had appeared in the *Irish Times* literary pages, edited in 1944 by MacDonagh – the son of one of the executed leaders of the Easter Rising in 1916, who in public life was a District Justice – was to show that the Palace view was by no means unjustified. As Smyllie observed in his Preface, however, the collection revealed that poets writing in Ireland appeared to have been left almost entirely unaffected by the impact of the war. To what extent this had affected the quality of their work, he decided, he would leave the critics to determine. For a time critics were contemptuous, but in the most recent *Oxford Book of Twentieth-Century English Verse*, edited by Philip Larkin, the Palace of those days still qualifies as a Poets' Pub. All Yeats's choices are there except McGreevy and O'Connor. L. A. G. Strong and Robert Graves are there, too – they were not in Reeves's cartoon, but would certainly have been expected in the Palace if they were visiting Dublin. Larkin also includes Clarke, McDonagh and Kavanagh – though not O'Sullivan, who in the 1930s was deemed to be the victim of Yeats' idiosyncratic dislikes.

Two authors in the cartoon were well known at the time, Lynn Doyle and Maurice Walsh; they are now all but forgotten. But one, then hardly known, has since become a cult figure; Brian O'Nolan. His *At Swim Two Birds* – written under the pseudonym Flann O'Brien – had just come out, but in spite of an enthusiastic review from Graham Greene had flopped; his 'Cruiskeen Lawn' column in the *Irish Times*, for which he called himself Myles na gCopaleen, had not yet started. And one other writer not in the cartoon, but who came to the Pearl whenever he was in Dublin, was to gain even greater fame: Samuel Beckett.

I cannot remember how we sorted ourselves out at the Palace, but tact stopped anybody on the *Irish Times*, except Alec, from joining Smyllie unless beckoned over. There must have been bores to be avoided, gurriers to beware of, as the evening wore on. But I know which table I would have joined for preference; the one where

'Pussy' O'Mahony was to be found. He had acquired his nickname, according to Lionel's recollection in *Head or Harp*, because he had been found one day trying to show a kitten which had been orphaned how to take milk by going down on his hands and knees – one knee, actually; he had a wooden leg – and lapping from a saucer.

Pussy was in the advertising department, along with a chubby, jolly-faced youth who preferred acting, and was getting parts at the Gate, but needed to earn a living: Wilfred Brambell (I was to find it hard to believe that he and the gaunt Steptoe could possibly be the same man). There was no love lost between those who were trying to obtain ads for the paper and those who, as they thought, were thwarting them by writing critical articles about the products that would otherwise have been advertised; but Pussy transcended the boundaries by being funny. He particularly enjoyed playing practical jokes on Smyllie; when Smyllie was seen setting out for a Masonic banquet 'all dressed up like a pox doctors's clerk', as Alec put it, leaving instructions that he was only to be called for in the event of some emergency, Pussy used that excuse to gain entry to the exclusively Protestant gathering to deliver a greeting and 'a blessing from His Holiness the Pope.' Practical jokers are not necessarily amusing: Pussy was. On form, he could reduce us to helpless laughter.

My first 'pup', on after dinner speaking, had been turned down; but the second delighted Smyllie. It described the villainy of a dictator who had once had artistic leanings, but had become a ruthless tyrant. Anybody reading it would assume it was about Hitler – as would the wartime censors de Valera had appointed, who would certainly reject it outright. In fact it described the career of Frederick the Great, two centuries before, but the parallels with Hitler were so close that I could hear Smyllie muttering, 'what on earth . . . ?' until the last sentence revealed it was about 'der alte Fritz'. My reward, that weekend, was to be told to follow again in Lionel's footsteps and become the *Irish Times's* Cinema Correspondent.

Ordinarily, as I had found on my first day, the complementary tickets were distributed among the reporters; each of them wrote a short notice, usually from the hand-out before going to the film (if they bothered to go at all) to save them coming in at the week-end to deliver their copy. This suited the trade, as there was no actual criticism; and if any reporter wanted to see a film in advance or, more commonly, if a cinema manager wanted publicity, a showing would be arranged during the week. But managers – except for Desmond Rushton, a Palace regular – were not inclined to help an active critic by inviting him to earlier showings. I usually had to see five, sometimes six, new films at the week-end.

On Sundays during the winter some of us would go out to Portmarnock strand, there to play mixed hockey on the hard, damp sand. One afternoon Barbara Strickland brought with her, as a looker-on, an older man – much older, he seemed to us (he must have been about thirty). Bryan Rogers, it turned out, was also awaiting call-up for the RAF; he had already logged some fifty hours flying from a makeshift airfield near Leixlip in County Dublin. Would I like to come up with him?

I would, indeed. A few days later I had my first lesson in 'straight and level' flying and gentle turns; easier, and much pleasanter, than learning to drive a car. I have no recollection, for some reason, of learning to drive; but in 1938 Michael Charlesworth, who had come up from Oldham's to Magdalen, and I had bought a bull-nosed MG, complete with a bulb horn and a belt over the bonnet, for £5. The self-starter did not work; the starting handle had a vicious kick-back when the engine fired; changing down the gears required nicely-timed 'double-declutching'; and the tyres were puncture-prone. Good service though it gave us, the contrast between driving even the MG's successor, a snazzy Sunbeam Talbot, and flying, was marked. I arranged to have some more formal lessons with Darby Kennedy, who leased the airfield.

At this point, in March, a summons reached me to report to Padgate, the RAF's receiving centre in the north of England, for a medical and an interview. There was only one hitch: asked 'to factorise X squared minus Y squared', I found I had forgotten elementary algebra, dinned into me year after year at school, as completely as if I had never had a lesson on the subject. The interviewing Board told me I had been accepted, but to have any chance of qualifying as a pilot I must brush up my maths, including trigonometry, which would be required to pass navigation tests.

Back in Dublin I went to a 'crammer' and learned, or tried to learn, trigonometry, finding it totally baffling; not that this mattered, as it was never mentioned, let alone required, during my training.

A few days later, the Phoney War came to its abrupt end with the invasion of Denmark and Norway. Bryan Rogers rang to say he had been called up; as I expected to follow him within days, Smyllie suggested I should concentrate on the cramming and not worry about office hours. Knowing the Germans as he did, he was full of foreboding; *Jam proximus ardet Ucalegon*, 'Now nearest Ucalegon burns', had found its way into his editorials with each fresh German move. But there was still no summons when, on May 10, Dubliners woke up to read that the Blitzkrieg had opened, with the thrust into the Low Countries.

Dubliners who took the *Independent* or the *Press* would not have been able to read about it in their papers. It had reached the *Irish Times* just before the late night sub, Jimmy Meagan, had left the office; he had stopped the presses, and inserted a small paragraph on the front page giving the news. As a result quite a few extra copies of the paper were sold that morning. If Jimmy expected to be congratulated, he was quickly undeceived. Smyllie, when he realised what had happened, was furious that such an earthshaking event had not been given more prominence. Jimmy, when he came into the office, was told he had been suspended – temporarily sacked.

During the winter I had come to know Francis 'Hank' Cobbe whose brother Tom owned the land on which the Island links had been constructed. He had a job as a mining engineer in Rhodesia, but had come back to join the Navy. Waiting for the call-up, he was staying in the family home, across the estuary from Malahide; we had found ourselves equals over the Island course; and we had planned what we would do when either of us received the week's notice which, we had been told, would be given to us when the call-up came. As things were, with the Allies' resistance in France crumbling, we suspected that the week's notice might be reduced; we had better put our plan into immediate action. We would devote a whole day to settling the issue which of us was the better golfer.

There were no trolleys in those days, and ordinarily we did not have caddies; for this occasion we had four, two to carry our clubs and two to carry crates of Guinness. The plan was to complete the first nine holes of the Island; move over to the adjacent course at

Corballis; then on to the Donabate course; and finally back over the Island's last nine. Corballis, unusually, was a sixteen-hole course, so the match would be over fifty-two holes, for a stake of £1. For this contest, it was laid down that the winner of a hole must drink a bottle of Guinness before driving off from the next tee.

Not merely did both of us play rather well, that morning; unluckily we tended to play our best at different holes, so the two Guinness-bearing caddies' load was quickly lightened. I had not played golf with drink taken before, apart from the occasional beer at lunch. The effect was to make both of us misjudge distances 'through the green', but this was compensated for by brilliantly uninhibited driving and putting. At the fifty-first hole I was one up; but the twenty bottles of stout I had consumed on an empty stomach proved too much, and Hank won the last to square the match. Honour was satisfied, I suggested. Hank would have none of it; we must go on to a 'sudden death' extra hole. He drove off, down the fairway of the first hole at the Island. Trying to follow, I fell over. Hank calmly claimed the match, and the stake.

The next day I woke up in a bed in the Cobbe household, with no recollection of what had happened in the meantime. 'Never so ill as at 4.30 a.m.,' I noted in my diary. Yet that morning we were on the course, and later, on the Guinness again. I knew, too, that the following week-end was to provide what Dublin journalists who played golf, and some who did not, described as the finest hooley of the year; the annual trip to the Great Northern Hotel in Bundoran, County Donegal, laid on by the Great Northern Railway for journalists and advertising reps.

We left early in the morning on what had once been the Royal Train, a breakfast of Guinness or Jameson being followed by bridge or poker while it ambled through the countryside. In the hotel bar, when we arrived, there was a large bowl-shaped silver cup; casually looking at the inscription I was given a macabre shock. It read

Bundoran Golf Club
Gordon Inglis Challenge Cup
The Bequest of Gordon Stuart Inglis

Elected member 4th April 1896
Won Club Cup 6th April 1896
Died on 9th April 1896

Gordon Inglis was the one of my father's brothers who had died young. His father had leased the fishing on the river which flows from Lough Melvin to the sea, and the house, Larreen, which went with it; it was there my father had learned to fish for what he called 'gillaroos' an indigenous Melvin species, and for brown trout. But after Gordon's death – from peritonitis – Malcolm gave up the lease – as the correspondence between him and the golf club which Joseph Roarty, the Hon. Secretary, still retains, makes clear. Malcolm also gave up his membership of the club, but presented the Challenge Cup in his son's memory. There it still stands, Mr Roarty tells me, in the bar.

I was determined to emulate Gordon, and did, winning the Publicity Cup the next day, much to Smyllie's satisfaction; he had 'bought' me in the Sweep on the event. The celebrations lasted long into the night, with 'Pussy' laying on an informal cabaret act for us. After some desultory golf the next morning, we were brought back in leisurely fashion to Dublin in the Royal Train. A letter was awaiting me in the office, with O H M S on the flap. I was to report at Padgate at the end of the week.

Among the farewell parties was a last game of golf at the Island, with Hank, Smyllie and the Polish Consul-General. There was a dance, somewhere – there were few nights in Dublin, then, when there was not a dance somewhere. I spent a night at Seamount, where Guardsman Mungo Park was back on leave; visited cousin Ida and dentist Sheridan; had dinner at the Dolphin with the medical students, and at the Royal Irish Yacht Club in Dun Laoghaire with Charlie and Wendy. The British Expeditionary Force was penned in around Dunkirk; the feeling was that it had no prospect of escape. And then? Presumably England would fight on, as Churchill had made clear; it could hardly be expected to survive a German invasion. But as I left by Aer Lingus, in a blacked-out aircraft, for Manchester, the gloom perceptibly lifted. The lead story in the *Irish Times* that morning of 3 June was about the safe evacuation of four-fifths of the B E F from Dunkirk.

On Saturdays the Irishman's Diary was by 'Nichevo', the editor's pseudonym. 'I was sorry to say *au revoir* yesterday to my friend Brian Inglis, who is flying to England this morning and will be absent from Ireland for an indefinite period,' Smyllie had written, before going on to say something about my time as a member of his editorial team, as film critic, and as a performer at the Island – 'it is a liberal education to watch him and his friend Mr "Hank" Cobbe trying to out-drive each other.' Brian had been interested in flying, Nichevo went on, but with few opportunities to enjoy it; 'I should be surprised if he has any further cause for this complaint in this regard' – as near as Smyllie could get to saying I was joining the RAF without bringing the Censors down on him. In theory, everything which appeared in the newspapers had to be sent to their office for scrutiny to ensure that nothing appeared which might be held to jeopardise Ireland's neutrality. In practice, much of their effort was concentrated upon ensuring that the *Irish Times* gave no indication that many of its past subscribers, or the children of present subscribers, were in the British forces.

'Nichevo' made a reference to my 'nervous' style which was momentarily disconcerting; from Smyllie, though, it meant that the style varied according to the task to which it was being applied, whether a leader or one of the Diary paragraphs which, at 3/6*d*, had been my sole source of income from the paper. 'In the meantime, he has other fish to fry,' Nichevo concluded (his Diary was always packed with colloquialisms of the kind; originally deliberately indulged in to distract him from leader-ese, but eventually pouring out unchecked) – 'Good luck to him!'

The seven months on the *Irish Times* had themselves represented extraordinary good luck. If Smyllie had not played golf at the Island, I would not have gained the experience which the spell as a reporter provided. If the winter weather had been less vile, I would have been called up before working with Smyllie in his office as a leader-writer, and taking on the films. As things had turned out, in spite of the fact that I had not been on the pay-roll I could regard myself as having been in the *Irish Times*' employment, and could assume that if I came through the war I would be returning to it. If gloom settled in again on the flight to England it was not the result of worry about the future; it was simply that I had already had a sight of the Padgate reception centre, and had thought it the most depressing establishment I had ever seen.

8

R.A.F.

Padgate turned out to be even gloomier than I had thought it on the earlier occasion. Its Nissen huts cast a chill even in mid-summer. Predictably, as nobody was likely to stay in them for more than a week, no attempt had been made to brighten them up. As if to ensure that the earliest experience of RAF life would be the most unpleasant, the first day was devoted to a medical examination, chiefly designed to catch anybody with V D, followed by vaccination and inoculations against typhoid, cholera and other diseases. The queues of airmen waiting their turn were frequently disrupted by men fainting at the sight of the needle, or even at the prospect of it. The second day, for most of us, was spent miserably recovering from the side-effects.

The *Irish Times* experience turned out to have done little to change my English public school conditioned reflexes. I had not realised before that what men wore when they went to bed would be an even clearer class distinction than their everyday clothes; I was uneasy to find myself the only one in the hut to put on pyjamas. When we were kitted out the next day, and our new AC2 uniforms blurred class distinctions, I found myself listening to voices in the airmen's mess and the canteen, hoping unavailingly to hear one which would identify a likely companion. It was not until the evening that the arrival of a new batch in the hut offered relief. A few beds away, a craggy-looking man, older than the rest of us (as with Bryan Rogers, five years was enough to make me think of him as much older) was swinging an imaginary golf club. It was as easy an excuse to introduce myself as I could have hoped for.

Willis Roxburgh's Scots' accent came as a relief. Scots' accents, far more than Irish, were refreshingly exempt from class distinctions. He had worked for some years for an oil company in Abadan, and looked like a Big White Carstairs. We teamed up immediately, and were lucky to find ourselves on the same draft to proceed to our Initial Training Wing. Security declined to let us know where it was; but when I looked out of the train window in the early morning light I knew from earlier visits – in spite of the absence of identification on the station's name boards, removed during the invasion scare – where we were: Cambridge.

ITWs were a concession to the tradition which the RAF had inherited from the Royal Flying Corps, which the RFC had itself inherited from the army. A few weeks square-bashing, the assumption was, would instil a sense of discipline, before we were allowed to proceed to an Elementary Flying School. At Cambridge we quickly found that a few old sweats, army-style sergeant majors, took this and their work very seriously. But most of the officers, and many of the NCOs, were a joke.

When the RAF had begun its rapid expansion, a severe shortage arose of officers and NCOs needed to run the ITWs. Brigadier-General Critchley, a noted aviator and golfer, offered to remedy the deficiency, which he did by promising quick commissions, or NCO status, to golfers, cricketers, footballers, tennis players and boxers. A further inducement was that they would be relieved from the fear of having to go to the Front (people still tended to think in First World War terms). At St John's College, where our 'squadron' was billeted, a Davis Cup player was the officer in charge, with a faded professional boxer as our drill instructor. The tennis player was preoccupied with getting married (and even more preoccupied, we noticed, when he returned after a brief honeymoon). The boxer would march us smartly out of sight of the college buildings, behind bushes, and then fall us out to lie in that summer's brilliant sun, and smoke. We had two months of numbingly boring, time-wasting marching up and down by the 'Backs' and, ludicrously, doing 'sentry-go' at night over the Bridge of Sighs – to give warning, should there be parachute landings, of an enemy force arriving off the street.

Yet there was no defeatism. After the fall of France the Group Captain in overall charge paraded us for a pep talk; his line was that we now had nobody to let us down. We accepted it gratefully, as we accepted that we would resist an invasion with pitchforks, if nothing else was available. That there were politicians still contemplating appeasement never crossed our minds.

Willis was in a different 'squadron', in King's; we saw each other occasionally in the evenings, but the lack of anything useful to do in the way of training had not prevented the imposition of the seven day working week, following the fall of France. With so little useful to do to occupy our time, our course began to behave like schoolboys, with a hint of what William Golding was to portray in *The Lord of the Flies*. After a ruction which had led to our being confined to college for a few days, a kangaroo court was held to put one member of the course on trial for not having admitted he was involved; he was sentenced to have his balls blacked with Bluebell Boot Polish. It came as a relief when, a few days before we were due to take the formal ITW examinations, we were told one morning that they had had to be brought forward. A new Flying Training Wing had opened earlier than had been expected, in the north of England.

At this point I had another of the succession of curious pieces of good luck which anybody less agnostic might, in retrospect, be tempted to attribute to a guardian angel. The only one of the papers which mattered, we had been forewarned, was Navigation. I had taken notes during the lectures, confident that – as in Haydon's form at Shrewsbury – I could mug them up at the last moment, the evening before taking the paper. There was to be no such opportunity. The navigation paper, we were informed that morning, was to be taken there and then. Along with a few of the others, I failed.

Ordinarily this would have meant being taken off pilot training; but we were told that as we had taken the exam before the course formally ended, those of us who had failed would be allowed to sit a fresh examination which the rest of the course, from King's, would soon be taking. In the meanwhile our tennis-playing officer relaxed sufficiently to lay on demonstrations with another Davis Cup star, R. A. Shayes, who was on the next course; and P. B. 'Laddie' Lucas, a Walker Cup player, who was also training to become a pilot, showed us how to play golf shots on John's immaculate lawn. The delay enabled me to repeat the mugging-up technique, and to pass the examination. Instead of having to re-muster as an air-gunner, or leave to join the army, I could go on to flying training. Better still, instead of going to the station in the north of England we were to be sent, we heard to our delight, to one of the new flying training establishments, in the Empire scheme.

'Security' meant that we did not know whether we would find ourselves in Canada or Southern Rhodesia. The fact that we were issued with tropical kit was not to be taken as settling the issue, we were warned; we were to give nothing away in our letters home. With Willis and others from King's, we celebrated our last evening with drinks at the Piccadilly Brasserie and dinner at La Coquille, catching an early train the next morning to Liverpool. There, at Princes Stage – where I had so often caught the B. & I. boat to Dublin – we boarded the *Stirling Castle*, a 22,000 ton luxury liner, to be told that Rhodesia was indeed our destination. We were to sail the following day for Cape Town.

That week the Battle of Britain reached its peak. Soon, the Blitz was to begin. Yet ours might almost have been a peacetime voyage. A destroyer escorted us for a couple of days; thereafter the *Stirling Castle* relied on speed and frequent zig-zags to prevent any U-boat from getting into position to loose off its torpedoes at us. We were treated no differently from the ordinary cabin class passengers, having the same huge meals, playing the same deck games, going to the same bars, where the drinks were at duty-free prices. Soon, we were in and out of the swimming pool during the day and dining and dancing at night with the wives of service men who were stationed in South Africa and Rhodesia, and had been allowed to leave England to join their husbands. We threw silver down for the diving boys in Freetown harbour (as there were 150 ships there, the boys no longer bothered to dive for coppers, though they could be deceived by pennies wrapped in silver paper); visited Napoleon's home on St Helena; and, in general, apart from the occasional brief spell as look-outs for U-boats, behaved as if we were on a holiday cruise.

I kept a log of the voyage to send to my mother; there was little constraint between us in correspondence except that, as a friend of hers once remarked to me, 'I cannot imagine telling her a dirty story'; I could describe getting drunk, but not getting randy. Most of it was a routine description of people, events and sights, but there were a couple of revealing asides. Willis and I were in a three-berth cabin with Robin Whelldon. We had come together at Cambridge when I found Robin had been in Balliol – the only other Oxford, or indeed Oxbridge, graduate in our group. Yet I did not like him. We had come together, I explained in the log, because of our shared prep school–public school–Varsity background. Although in theory I did not care for the system, it was a bond when we were among other types 'simply because our minds have been pushed along the same channels – drains, possibly.' On the *Stirling Castle*, though, we found ourselves with several other products of the system. Outside the cabin, Robin and I rarely spoke.

The other parenthesis in the log was the outcome of finding C. E. Montague's *Disenchantment* in the *Stirling Castle*'s exiguous library. Montague's disturbing account of his experiences in the First World War set me reflecting on the reasons why I had joined up for the Second after boasting of my pacifism. The fact was, I had to admit, that I would not have dared to stay on in Ireland; 'it would have needed tremendous strength of mind to be a "fly-boy", far more than I possess.' Sooner or later, when almost all my friends had joined one or other of the services, I would have been ostracised at places like the Island, and could hardly have faced the friends when they came back on leave.

By the winter of 1940 almost all the men in our set – except the medical students, who were waiting to qualify – and most of the girls I had known, were in the forces. The only 'fly-boy' I knew of was an Englishman who had been in Oldham's with me; and he was in a rather different category from, say, Paddy Campbell, who had failed to make his mark with Beaverbrook and had come back to Ireland. Although at first, during the Phoney War, his friends did not think the worse of him, he suffered. 'Some people gain a life-long inferiority complex from not having been to a public school or a university,' he was to write in his autobiography. 'Not having been in a war that nearly all one's contemporaries endured was a great deal worse.'

Yet I would have joined up anyway. Although for me it was still a capitalist war, and I had no expectation that if it were to be won, the peace settlement would be any better than Versailles, my time in Heidelberg had convinced me that those who had wanted to crush Nazism before it grew too powerful had been right, even if sometimes for the wrong reasons. 'Under Nazism the curtain rings right down on civilisation as we know it,' my rousing peroration ran.

'Better a shot in the back from a Messerschmitt than living under a fascist régime.' Then, as if a little embarrassed by such an expression of feeling, unusual in my letters, I concluded that having no powerful home ties I could indulge in a pleasant fatalism about survival; but should I be killed, if anybody suggested it was for king or country 'I shall return and haunt them at the earliest opportunity.'

The reference to being shot in the back from a Messerschmitt reflected my mind's eye picture of a wartime pilot. It had been established by such films as *Dawn Patrol*, in which a pilot would be seen grinning contentedly as he prepared to shoot down a German plane, only for his face to be transformed into a rictus of agony as he himself was shot in the back by Von Richtofen, or some other World War One German ace. And the flying we did at No. 25 Elementary Flying Training School, after we had landed at Cape Town and been brought up to Salisbury in Southern Rhodesia, did little to erase this image. The Tiger Moths which we flew were so manoeuvreable that as soon as we were sent solo, it was tempting to put them through the aerobatics which we had been taught – not, our instructors always emphasised, because they were to be trusted in dog fights, but simply because they would help us to obtain complete mastery over our aircraft.

For the first few days all of us had one preoccupation: when would we go solo? Here, the experience I had gained from the Leixlip airfield proved invaluable. The RAF selection board had told me not to waste my time paying for lessons when soon I would be receiving more professional instruction for nothing. But the Flight-Sergeant responsible for most of my instruction had a massive chip on his shoulder; he had been turned down for a commission, and took it out of those of us who had a public school background. He failed a former bank manager, the course leader (Willis took over from him), and he might have failed me if those early flights had not given me a confidence which his sarcasm, sometimes degenerating into angry abuse, could not entirely dispel. He was a show-off, liking to demonstrate his mastery over the Tiger Moth. Not long after he was to come in to land just too low, clip a fence and kill himself; but he showed me what could be done in the way of aerobatics. As soon as I went solo I tried to emulate him, and Errol Flynn, looping the loop and tracking Huns around 'fair-weather cumulus' clouds.

Further north, Rhodesian and South African forces were preparing to dislodge the Italians from Abyssinia; but Salisbury
might have been a peacetime city. We had plenty of time off;
Willis and I borrowed clubs from the local professional and played
golf whenever we could. Seeing an attractive girl wave her
boyfriend off at the railway station Willis presented himself as a
substitute; soon, we had the benefit of the house, 'The Mess',
which she shared with two delightful friends, Marize and Jake,
and we went with them to dinners and dances at establishments
whose names I was to forget until encountering them again in
Doris Lessing's novels.

Politics became a serious issue only once during that spell in
Salisbury. The day after we arrived a rumour was put out over the
wireless that Ireland had been invaded; not by Hitler but by Britain.
Two of us were Anglo–Irish, on the course; Willy Humphrey and I
got together to decide what we should do if it turned out to be
correct. There was no doubt in either of our minds that we could not
simply continue with our flying training as if it made no difference.
An invasion would have been resisted, and even if the resistance
quickly collapsed, as it was bound to do, Britain and Ireland would
have been in a state of war. In that event, we knew which side we
would be on: Ireland's.

We realised, though – or at least we hoped – that the decision to
invade would only have been taken for the same reason as the British
mine-laying off the Norwegian coast, which had given Hitler his
excuse for the invasion of Norway: a pre-emptive strike, based on
information that a German invasion of Ireland was planned, to try to
forestall it. We were not inclined to think in terms of a campaign of
sabotage on Ireland's behalf, or any move which might help the Nazi
cause. If Ireland had been invaded, we decided, we would simply ask
for an interview with the Group Captain, explain the position to him,
and accept whatever treatment he might decide upon: internment,
we thought, being the most likely outcome.

The world over, Irish men and women would have been faced with
the same decision – and not only those of us who were in the forces.
'My only serious moments of misgiving were when Churchill was
threatening to seize the Irish ports in order to use them as anti-
submarine bases,' Lionel was to recall in *Head or Harp*. By this time
he had established himself in the BBC, and was determined not to

return to work in Ireland; but 'if the British Government really had done that, I do not know what I should have done – gone back to Dublin, I hope.'

I have often wondered since what would have happened if the decision *had* been taken to invade Ireland. In the summer of 1940 General Montgomery had been asked to prepare for an attack which would enable the port of Cobh, near Cork, to be restored for use as a British naval base; and a more general scheme, code-named the 'W' Plan, had been prepared which would have been adopted if the Germans had been about to invade. If de Valera could have been persuaded that the invasion was genuine and imminent, it is just possible he would have accepted British forces, descending from Ulster, as allies. More probably the British government, impatient, would not have waited on him, and Hitler might then have presented himself as Ireland's liberator.

What seems certain is that a British occupation of Ireland which required actual hostilities, even if only for two or three days, would have left literally hundreds of thousands of Irishmen in the British forces or in civilian jobs as potential enemies, many of them dangerous. If Humphrey and I felt the way we did, there would have been very many who would have felt even more strongly that they had been let down. I still have an uneasy feeling that this may not have entered into Churchill's calculations at the time.

At the end of October those of us who had completed the fifty-hour course were promoted to become flight sergeants and divided into two groups, one staying on at another base near Salisbury to continue on single-engine aircraft; the other to move south to Bulawayo, there to learn to fly twin-engined Oxfords. We were inclined to assume (though this was not made explicit) that the intention was to part the likely fighter pilots of the future from the more staid and stolid bomber types. Errol Flynn fantasies had to be banished when my name appeared on the Bulawayo roster.

Still, there were compensations. The next stage for the single-engine trainees would be on the American Harvards, which had a poor reputation: Oxfords were slow, but safer. And my friends from the *Stirling Castle* cruise were all on the Oxford list, including Willis. He had bought a car, and we drove down to Bulawayo, along with his girl, to book in to the Palace Hotel for a last night of liberty before the course began.

At this point our good luck temporarily deserted us. I woke up the following morning with a sore throat; and at the reception desk there was an ominous instruction to the two of us to report to the Chief Ground Instructor immediately. We had committed three serious offences, he informed us; staying at the Palace, which was for officers only; bringing a girl with us; and bringing the RAF into disrepute by having our three names, as staying in the hotel, displayed in the Bulawayo newspaper he had read that morning. Willis was told he could not expect to lead the course any longer. I do not know what my punishment would have been; but the CGI, seeing I was not looking well, told me to report to the station sick quarters, where I was put to bed with a diagnosis of acute tonsillitis.

It turned out that there were too few Oxfords to cope with the size of the course which had arrived; the CGI took me off it, to await the start of the next one. Worse, although for a while I was still with the old course in the Sergeants' Mess, a few days later Willis and other friends were told that they were to join the Officers' Mess, the idea being to observe whether they were officer material, while the remainder of the course had to continue in the knowledge that they were not regarded as likely to qualify for commissions.

For the RAF, the whole army legacy of 'commissioned' and 'non-commissioned' was being rendered farcical by the speeding up of the training process. In peacetime there had been a fairly clear distinction between the two; promotion from non-commissioned to commissioned, though not uncommon, was an unhurried affair, which could take years. Now, the gap between becoming a sergeant automatically at the end of elementary flying training and receiving our 'wings' had narrowed to three weeks, and soon after we would be commissioned – if considered suitable. The CGI and the Station Commander would have some information to work on from earlier confidential reports, which doubtless was why Willis's gaffe had not been held against him; but the selection of those who were regarded as officer material was arbitrary and, as I could see from my knowledge of my former course-mates, in some cases unfair. I also found out why; while waiting for the next course to begin I was employed in the Flight Office in some capacity which included filing the instructor's reports on their pupils – useful enough about their ability as pilots but erratic in the estimates of them as individuals.

The new course arrived; the flying training for a time went smoothly; within a week I had joined Willis and the others, nearing the end of their training, in the Officers' Mess. I was returning from my first solo cross-country flight, which had entailed finding and landing on a remote, bumpy airstrip in the 'bush', congratulating myself on how well things were going, when I remembered I had not put on my safety harness, with its shoulder straps – uncomfortable, so we usually threw them off during solo flights, but a wise precaution for landings. Coming in to the airfield at Bulawayo, I put it on. As the Oxford touched down, it slewed to the right. From the feel and the sound of it, I knew what had happened from past experience on the roads with the MG: the tyre on that side must have burst. To straighten up an Oxford slewing right while on the ground, the normal procedure was to apply the brake on the left wheel of the undercarriage. With the right tyre punctured, this was disastrous, as both wheels were part locked. The Oxford promptly turned over on its back, sheering off its nose, leaving me dangling from the straps.

We had been warned, should we find ourselves in that predicament, not to release the straps: many a neck had been broken that way. But we had also been warned that we might have to extricate ourselves as best we could, if the Oxford caught fire. It did not catch fire, and the station ambulance was there in seconds to pull me out; soon, I was in the sick bay, with no more than superficial cuts and bruises on one leg. The RAF followed the same principle as riding instructors; a trainee pilot must go up again at the earliest possible moment after an accident, for a Chief Flying Instructor's test. My first circuit and landing was so abysmal that he almost grounded me there and then; the second was immaculate, as were the next three; and without a break, I was off solo again.

It was 23 December. Willis and I took the road back to Salisbury for Christmas in 'The Mess'. It was the first Christmas I had spent away from home; yet home it seemed. Willis by this time had his wings, and was completing his advanced training course, still at Bulawayo. I was due to begin mine, if I passed the written 'Wings' examination in the new year of 1941. There were papers in airmanship, morse and armaments, but the crucial tests, we knew, would be in practical and theoretical navigation. To fail, even narrowly, meant being put back a course; to fail badly would mean being grounded.

'Wings Exam', I noted in my diary. 'Navigation awful. Certain fail. Airmanship o.k.' Almost half the course, we heard a week later, had failed – including 'Trilby' Freakes, a laid-back South African who had been at Magdalen with me, and had played rugger for Oxford and England. To my astonishment, I had passed.

Again, luck had intervened. The theoretical paper was indeed awful; I had completed the relatively easier of two parts and was wrestling, baffled, with the other when an officer came into the room and conferred with the invigilator. We need not do that part, we were told; a mistake had occurred in the setting, and it would not be marked.

This was small consolation, because – as I wrote to tell my parents, 'I made an awful mess of the Plot' – the filling in of the course taken by a hypothetical aircraft from the information provided – 'owing to taking the wrong air speed at the beginning, which put me out all the way through'. When we were given our papers back, though, to compare them with the correct version, it turned out that later mistakes in my Plot had mysteriously corrected the initial error, so that my aircraft ended up at the right place at the right time. Although I had failed even the easier part of the Theoretical, the marks for the Practical just made up for it. I could 'put up my wings.'

At this point we were asked to decide what type of operations we thought ourselves best suited for. To go on to fighter aircraft was hardly an option, after Oxfords; the choice lay between army co-operation, heavy bombers, and medium bombers. Army co-op was despised in the RAF. Heavy bombers would mean long night raids over Germany to attack the marshalling yards at Hamm, and other sinister destinations. Medium bombers, Blenheims, were associated in our minds with the remarkable success of General O'Connor's thrust, in December, into Libya, comprehensively destroying the far larger Italian force with which Mussolini had planned to drive the British out of Egypt. Unhesitatingly I put down 'medium bombers' as my choice.

It was the custom of each course to give a party to its instructors, before leaving; and the squadron leader in charge, when lubricated, was prepared to confide in some of us that we would shortly be in the

Officers' Mess in our own right. He also had some startling news. The entire course, with only a handful of exceptions, would be posted to George in South Africa, to the School of General Reconnaissance.

It was particularly unwelcome for me because it meant, by implication, that we would be destined for Coastal Command. I had nothing against 'Coastal'; the problem was simply that it required a higher standard of navigation than the other RAF Commands. Ordinarily only trainee pilots who had shown particular ability in their navigation tests were selected for further navigational training of the type provided at George. A course of these select few, we were told, had been on its way from England, but the ship had been torpedoed. Whether we liked it or not, we must take its place.

On reflection – and on making inquiries from one of the earlier course who was at George, but had come back to spend a few day's leave with his girl in Bulawayo – the prospect began to look brighter. The atmosphere there, he had found, was relaxed. There was a good golf course and, nearby, a celebrated holiday resort, 'the Wilderness', at Knysna, with a beach for surfing and an attractive hotel. Obviously there was no possibility of passing the navigation exam at the end, but that would matter little. They would not, at that late stage, ground me. And in the meantime, there was no incentive to return to Britain while the Blitz was still at its height.

Those of us who had been given our commissions were formally made members of the Mess at a Dining In night, followed by a sing-song with a South African clergyman at the piano until the songs, or the words which were put to them, took their inexorable turn. It was still summer in Rhodesia and I invested in a tropical uniform; in photographs I look like one of the notorious 'Gabardene swine' – army staff officers in the Middle East. A week's leave in Johannesburg followed. On the strength of an introduction from one of our hosts in Bulawayo a vast car arrived to collect three of us and bring us to the Shacklock's country house; my diary recorded 'beauties draped round bathing pool', and for the rest of our stay we spent as much of the time as we could draped round them, and with sundowners, by the pool dinners and dances, at clubs and night clubs, enjoying hospitality of a kind we had never had before and could not reasonably expect ever to enjoy again.

So far from my mind was the war that it had ceased to feature in the diary, returning only after we reached George to find we had a week before the course began, with nothing to do except play golf and bridge, and enjoy surfing for the first time. 27 March has the entry 'News of Jugoslav rebellion comes through'. It was to be the last bit of apparently good news from Europe for a long time; three days later, Rommel's counter-offensive began to drive Wavell's forces out of Libya. But on April Fools' Day we put the war out of our minds again, all of us taking off on exercises designed to show how to navigate over the ocean.

The RAF could hardly have chosen anywhere less suitable than George for a navigation school. It lies 250 miles east of Cape Town, and between them stretches the Little Karroo, a chain of mountains visible from great distances out to sea. We flew in Ansons – so ancient that one of our duties, when the pilots had taken off, was to crank up the undercarriage by turns – by hand. Their range was so limited that we were never out of sight of land; however incompetent our navigation, we could always correct mistakes by eye. We learned how to estimate wind speed and direction from 'white horses' or, on calm days, by tossing out smoke canisters; and from the observations, to give the pilot courses to steer which would eventually bring us back to the air field. But that was about all.

Every other day there was golf – 'Trilby' Freakes arrived for the next course, to join us on the links – followed by sundowners, and bridge or surfing, dinner and dancing, at the Wilderness. We were not required to do any flying, except as navigator-trainees; and the ground instruction, in subjects such as meteorology and ship recognition, was quite absorbing. When, in June, we had to sit the examination which would give us a passport into Coastal Command, we could almost feel we had been on extended leave for three months.

The papers turned out to be easy except, inevitably, navigation. But at this stage our instructors were in no mood to fail anybody; far from being more difficult, it was actually simpler than its predecessors. In any case, it was possible to make up for poor marks on it by doing well in ship and aircraft recognition, and meteorology. All of us passed; and into my Pilot's Flying Log Book went an Air Ministry inscription – the initials typically incorrect:

This is to certify that
Pilot Officer E. S. Inglis, Royal Air Force has successfully
qualified as an Air Navigator Second Class

Never, I suspect, has anybody less deserving received that Certificate.

Within a week, we were on another Castle liner on our way north. Apart from the twenty-four of us, the crew and a handful of passengers, the ship was empty; with the winter approaching in the southern hemisphere, the weather was villainous; and when we were in the tropics, U-boat watches – four hours out of every sixteen – began. One night we saw rockets, presumably a distress signal; but the captain had orders to ignore them, as they might simply be a U-boat's lure. Bridge was the only distraction, apart from a book a day from the ship's library, with Pickwick as a standby, my selection varying from Aldous Huxley's *Ends and Means* to *Rebecca*.

The first aircraft seen turned out to be one of ours, a Hudson from a station in Northern Ireland. As we neared Liverpool we held an adjudication to decide the winner of a contest begun out of boredom on the voyage; for the best newly-grown moustache. Mine finished down the field. In the cabin mirror it resembled Wodehouse's description of Roderick Spode's; it looked like the faint discoloured smear left by a squashed black beetle on the side of a kitchen sink.

We arrived in mid-July to find that Germany had invaded Russia, and her armies were rolling irresistibly forward on three fronts. But at least the Blitz was over. Our instructions were to proceed at once to Bournemouth, where there was a Receiving Centre; we had time only for dinner in London, before catching the train on south. At the Centre, however, the indications were that they had not been expecting us. They did not know what to do with us except, as if through routine, to give us a night blindness test. No, we could not go on leave. Some of us had had no embarkation leave, we protested; were we to have no disembarkation leave, either? After some prodding, they eventually got through to Coastal Command and we were told we could have one week.

No restrictions had been placed on Irish members of the forces returning to Ireland for their leaves. Dublin, with no black-out and few shortages, was the obvious place to be. Apart from the absence of friends who had joined the forces in the meantime, it had hardly changed. The medical students were still there, soon to take their First MBs; among them Jerry Slattery, later to become GP to half the literati in NW1 and NW3. He was a formidable member of the Trinity rugby team, astute enough to offer drinks to the sports reporters who covered the matches; the next morning we could expect to read something to the effect that the Trinity pack was undistinguished 'except for that clever forward, Jeremiah Slattery'.

The medics could usually be persuaded to abandon their studies to come to the Hibernian Buttery; so, too, could Judy Post, whose mother had decided to stay in Ireland, rather than return to the United States, when war broke out. There was golf at the Island, and late night sessions at the *Irish Times* club. This, I assumed, might well be my last fling in Dublin for a long time. The real war would now catch up with those of us who had escaped it in South Africa. We would be returning to Bournemouth to find what squadrons we had been assigned to, and where we would be stationed.

It was to be 53 Squadron for half a dozen of us, to fly Hudsons from St Eval in Cornwall. The twin-engined Hudsons, imported from the United States, had a poor reputation; they were inadequately protected for the jobs they were being called upon to do – reconnaissance of the enemy-held coastline, to shoot up any shipping which was found. They were clumsy to fly, and tricky to land. Still, St Eval sounded quite agreeable, and the defences of the northern coast of France less menacing than those of the Low Countries and Germany. At the station, however, they looked at us with astonishment, before grinning at each other and tapping their heads: 'Coastal, again!'. 53 Squadron had indeed been at St Eval, but it had left a month before. After some telephoning, we were told there had been a mistake; we were to proceed to Bircham Newton, in Norfolk.

At Bircham Newton the first officer I saw in the bar was Robert Tyrrell, who had been one of the Dublin crowd I had met from time to time at parties and dances. As soon as he heard I was joining the squadron it was 'Right. You can be my second pilot.'

Robert had a famous grandfather, Robert Yelverton Tyrrell, regarded as the foremost classical scholar of his time. The grandson's talents lay in other directions. The story used to circulate in Trinity how he had managed to survive the entrance exam. The college had a curious system of vivas; they were marked out of nine, three being the pass requirement. Robert had come up before the formidable Sir Robert Tate; and his score at the end of the viva was nil.

'What did you say your name was?'

'Robert Yelverton Tyrrell.'

'Robert Yelverton Tyrrell,' Sir Robert had repeated, incredulously. 'I tell you what: I will give you one mark for Robert, one for Yelverton, and one for Tyrrell.'

I knew Robert, as he knew me, as a party-goer. Neither of us, I feel sure, was the other's idea of an accomplished, safe pilot of a Hudson. I went up with him the next day on an exercise described as 'Air Experience' – not one that either of us would have wished to repeat, as the Hudson turned out to be every bit as tricky to land as I had heard. When we came back to the Mess, however, we were greeted with the same grins as at St Eval: 'Coastal, again!' Too many of us had been posted to 53 Squadron; only a few of the new arrivals could stay. The rest of us would be told where to go in a day or two.

In my case it turned out to be Iceland, to 204 (Flying Boat) Squadron. The idea of joining Coastal Command at all had seemed far-fetched, but Flying Boats . . . I recalled that when the Squadron Leader at Bulawayo, tipping us off that we were to go to George, had suggested 'Boats?' when I asked what the course might lead to I had assumed he must be joking, as he surely was.

Flying boats were the naval equivalent of Army Co-op aircraft, but it would have been unwise to draw that parallel in the company of their crews. They considered themselves to be an elite. They even felt rather more at ease, I was sometimes to find, with the navy than with land-based squadrons. This pride was partly derived from the fact that they could fly wherever they were called upon to fly, knowing they would be able to come down, provided there was sea, a lake or a broad enough river, without the need for a prepared airstrip; and they could begin to operate from that base without the need of a ground crew, provided that they could get aviation fuel. Each Boat had its two 'fitters' – flight engineers – and a 'rigger' capable of keeping it in working order between major overhauls.

Because of this adaptability, the crews had to be of a high standard. The pilots, in particular, were expected to be able to double for any member of the crew, up to a point, in the event of sickness or accident. Navigators necessarily had to be prepared to plot their courses in and out of Reykjavik, one week, and Rangoon the next; in emergencies the pilots must be able to pick up where a navigator left off, carrying on as if nothing had happened. They must also be capable of receiving and decoding radio signals, and much else besides.

This much we had learned at George. Waiting in the Orderly Room at Bircham Newton for the formalities to be dealt with, and to get my travel warrant to Iceland, I had mixed feelings. Relief at escaping from Hudsons predominated; had I known that, soon afterwards, the squadron was to be sent to Singapore, it would have been still more heartfelt. But, flying boats? There could hardly be anybody less suited, less adequately trained. And Iceland, with the winter approaching, would surely be grim.

As I was waiting, one of the AC2 clerks – 'erks', as they were known – came up a little diffidently to say that if I had been posted to Iceland, I could not be joining 204, and if I was joining 204 I should not be going to Iceland. His brother was in 204, and for some days he had been in Pembroke Dock, in South Wales. A couple of weeks earlier the United States had relieved Britain of the need to protect Iceland from any German incursion, and the squadron had returned. More grins, when this was confirmed by telephone calls; more headtapping: 'Coastal, again!'

Pembroke Dock, it turned out, was 204's maintenance base, where the 'boats' – Short Sunderlands – were serviced: we would not be staying there long, but no decision had been reached about the next posting. I liked the atmosphere of the Mess; in particular I was relieved at the discovery that my flight commander, Flight Lieutenant Alan Wood, had been a contemporary at Oxford, where he had been in the University Air Squadron. He looked indecently young to have achieved such promotion, but he might be more sympathetic than the other two flight commanders, old hands, who aroused something of the uneasiness that Marsden had, in Rhodesia. Better still, he played bridge. Kibitzing on the first evening, I could see that at least one of the four must have been roped in out of desperation.

I was still not securely in the squadron, even when a few nights later I joined the bridge players. Two of us had come down from Bircham Newton; it turned out that the squadron needed only one.

But towards the end of August, when it was learned that the squadron was to move to West Africa, I was the one who had to report for the battery of injections, to be told that I would be going out with the 'odds and sods' by sea, while the crew to which I would be assigned flew out via Gibraltar. Even then, owing to some further cock-up, some of us were sent by mistake by rail up to Glasgow for a couple of nights. Willis had been there only the week before; I had dinner with his parents. He was stationed at Aldergrove in Northern Ireland, they told me; he would surely be piloting one of the aircraft despatched to protect us as we sailed from the Clyde. But we did not sail from the Clyde. Liverpool, it transpired, was where we ought to be. And again, the ship we boarded was tied up at Prince's Stage.

The SS *Northumberland*, though, was no *Stirling Castle*. One of the B & I boats would have been far preferable. 'Looks bloody', I noted in the diary; and it was, with three of us in a cupboard of a cabin. Still, they were good company. Rose, a massive red-head, had been an all-in wrestler; for some reason which mystified him he had been made an Intelligence officer. Bell – 'Clapper', as Bells found themselves called – had got married the day before. His best man, reading out the telegrams, had put a damper on the festivity by announcing that he must report to Liverpool forthwith.

As an old, slow troopship, the *Northumberland* sailed in a large, slow convoy, with the aircraft carrier *Furious*, the battleship *Repulse*, and sundry smaller warships for our protection. It was a week before we parted from them, to turn south, making a landfall at Freetown before trundling up the coast to Bathurst, at the mouth of the Gambia River. The HQ turned out to be an old but comfortable liner, the *Dumana*. It was still served by its former crew, and was still run, at least in the officer's accommodation, as if it were in normal service. In the bar, tots of whisky or gin cost 2½*d*; in the restaurant, waiters brought round our meals. Bathurst, I had been assured, vied with Freetown for the title of arsehole of the Empire. Standing in the evening sun on the boatdeck, looking out over the estuary, we found it hard to accept that the port of Bathurst was called Half Die, because when it was first colonised, half did.

Two days after my arrival I was sent on my first operational flight, a ten-hour anti-U-boat patrol; followed the next day by another with the crew of Sunderland 'C', which I was now to join. The previous captain's name had been Bunt; inevitably it was known as 'C for

Bunt'. His successor, Flying Officer Dart, looked like a schoolboy – he was to celebrate his 'twenty-first' a few months later. There was nothing to do except keep watch, and from time to time regulate 'George', the automatic pilot. It was going to be dull work, I decided. But at least it was safe . . .

Two days later, we were briefed to carry out a reconnaissance of Dakar. Dakar was in Vichy French hands; a year before, a British and Free French naval force which had been sent out to liberate it for de Gaulle had been compelled ignominiously to retreat. An eye needed to be kept on it, as the battleship *Richelieu* lay in the harbour; there were fears she might slip away, some night.

Dart did not spell out how he proposed to conduct the reconnaissance – not, at least, to me. Flying first at sea level, and then at tree-top level, he swung in over Senegal a few miles north of Dakar, returning from a little way inland to fly over Dakar harbour, so close to the *Richelieu* that our tail gunner later boasted we had severed some washing lines on its deck. We then flew on out to sea, encountering another Sunderland, captained by Flying Officer Douglas, returning from patrol. We joined in with him, in loose formation.

A minute later, four Vichy fighters appeared; seconds later they were on to us, with their machine guns – luckily they had no cannon. The advice given to Sunderland pilots, if attacked, was to stay as close as possible to the sea, to restrict the fighter pilots' range of approach; occasionally 'skidding', to give the fighter pilots the illusion of a turn when the Sunderland was in fact not turning, the idea being that the fighter pilots would be misled into turning, too, only to find that they could not correct course again in time – their guns being fixed on the wings, so that the fighter's nose had to be pointed a little in front of the Sunderland, to hit it.

'Duggie' took this course. 'Daisy' did not. I do not know how Dart had come by his nick-name; perhaps somebody had remembered that Steerforth had given it to David Copperfield, as it certainly did not imply femininity. Daisy was only one example of the weakness of the RAF's system for deciding what individuals would be best suited for; he was a born fighter pilot. This was his opportunity. In most pilots' hands, the Sunderland was a staid, almost lumbering, carriage horse of a flying boat, as befitted its pre-war past in its Imperial Airways civilian role. In Daisy's, it was put through bucking bronco contortions of a kind from which, if I had had time to worry about the strains to which it was subjected, I would have expected it to disintegrate.

Daisy had two main tricks. The second pilot, Flight Sergeant Gough took his post with his head in the observation 'bubble' dome in the pilots' cabin; whenever he reported an imminent attack, Daisy would pull back the controls so that we rocketed up, leaving the fighter pilots firing into the sea. If attacked when we were up, he would turn and dive, 'skidding' and 'slipping' to add further confusion, down to sea level again. It seemed as if the fighter pilots regarded us as a challenge, or perhaps realised we were the culprits they had been despatched to deal with; they concentrated on us. And for a time there was confusion – not surprisingly; they cannot have had any experience of making such attacks singly, let alone together, when there was the risk of shooting each other down. Eventually one of the four disappeared, apparently damaged. Two hovered around above us, perhaps instructed over the intercom to leave it to their leader.

Daisy's manoeuvres, though, also created difficulties for our defenders: a machine-gunner on the nose, another on each side of the Sunderland, just under and behind the wings, and the tail gunner in his turret. The gravitational forces made it difficult for them to aim their guns. The second pilot, standing in the dome, had a bar to cling on to; sitting in his seat, beside Daisy, I could hold myself down; but the unfortunate nagivator, just behind us, was flung from side to side, up and down, his charts, compasses and pencils with him, until the cabin looked as if it had been ransacked.

Eventually our attacker began to try what proved to be the most effective approach, from above and a little behind us, on my side; beginning by firing down at the sea. I could see the bullets churning up the water as they approached; a spatter of them could then be heard hitting us. When Daisy hoisted the Sunderland, the attacker rose too; and eventually he got it right, riddling us with bullets. The second pilot, who had one through his wrist, collapsed out of the 'dome' falling onto the navigator; two other members of the crew were slightly wounded; one of the port engine's throttle controls was severed; and a fire was started in the rear of the aircraft by an incendiary, so that in seconds the cabin began to fill with smoke.

We did not know it at the time, but as the Vichy pilot lifted his fighter over us he exposed it to one of the gunners on the other Sunderland, who claimed he shot it down. The others broke off the attack, and we were able to set course for Bathurst without further interruption. The blood spurting from the second pilot's wrist had drenched the cabin, but he had managed to put his thumb on the artery, and hold it until we got a tourniquet onto his arm. There were no further problems until we landed, when it became necessary to haul 'C' up the slip, or the water gushing in from the bullet holes would have left her sinking.

When we went ashore a couple of days later, to look at 'C' she presented an extraordinary sight; terms such as colander, or sieve, leapt to mind. The most awesome news, though, was that one of the depth charges had a machine-gun bullet in it. We felt we had been fabulously lucky to survive what, as we were now told, had been a misunderstanding. When, at his briefing, Daisy had been told to do a reconnaissance of Dakar, there had been no intention of asking him to enter Vichy French air space, which was not precisely measured but usually reckoned to extend about ten miles out from the coastline. He had not been warned against breaching this unwritten rule, because nobody had thought he would be so foolish. The assumption had been that he would fly past Dakar to take photographs, which would be quite sufficient to provide the required information about the *Richelieu*.

As for flying over the battleship at 'nought feet', it was crazy. Would Daisy have to be court-martialled for exposing himself, his crew and his Sunderland to grave risk, unnecessarily? Wing-Commander Coote decided that the best way to avert that embarrassing outcome was to gloss over the misunderstanding and concentrate in his report upon the heroic action which followed. A few weeks later, we heard that Daisy had been awarded the Distinguished Flying Cross.

There was to be a curious postcript, a year later. When Senegal came over to the Free French, some of the pilots who had been stationed there were sent to Invergordon to train on Sunderlands. Alan Wood, who by that time was an instructor there, asked them if they remembered the occasion. They remembered it very well; they boasted that they had shot the Sunderland down. Alan could not resist taking them out to where 'C' lay at its moorings, pocked with patches but still in service.

A couple of days after the Dakar affair, a party was held to celebrate 204's arrival in the Gambia, the guests including some Hudson pilots from the nearby airstrip at Jeshwang, and some officers from the destroyer *Vimy*. One of the pilots turned out to be my cousin Ian Henry, whom I had never met, as his family lived in Durban. The M.O. of *Vimy* was Henry Fitzgibbon, one of the Dublin medical students I had known. And another of *Vimy*'s officers was one of the Cowley twins I had known at the Dragon School. After a return visit to *Vimy*, Alan managed to get hold of a car to take us to Jeshwang, on my cousin's invitation. We found the officers sitting in the open-air mess bar, gloomily drinking; Ian's Hudson, they told us, had just sent out a distress signal and was presumed to have ditched some 150 miles away. I asked the next day to go with Duggie's crew to rescue them from their inflatable dinghy (a Hudson had found them in the meantime); but by the time we arrived *Vimy* had picked them up, and Henry Fitzgibbon was treating them with medicinal brandy.

Within the space of a fortnight I had encountered more action than was to be my lot for the whole of the rest of the war. As I wrote to my mother, she need not worry about any repetition. Daisy remained incorrigibly slapdash; later, we were to be fired on by a Spanish anti-aircraft battery near Tangier because he was hugging the coastline on a flight back to the Gambia from Gibraltar; and, on another occasion, by a Vichy destroyer which resented our failure to keep our distance. But both times, they might simply have been warning us. Otherwise I was not to see or hear shots fired in anger again.

Apart from the brief search for Ian, I did not fly again until, a couple of weeks after the Dakar episode, 'C' was considered sufficiently seaworthy to be taken down the slip and flown to Pembroke Dock for a major overhaul. There was no need for me to go with her: Wing Commander Coote was to take the opportunity to fly back for some leave, so there would be four of us pilots on board. Tradition did me proud: I was a member of 'C's' crew, even if I had only flown in her a couple of times. I had said my farewells in Dublin and Malahide in July in the expectation that my next leave, if I survived to take it, might be a year or more distant. I was back, three months later, having been on operations, and in action.

Not that, so far as friends and relations were concerned, it mattered how long I had been away, or what I had been up to.

Dubliners had a remarkable capacity for telescoping time, as Lionel was to note in *Head or Harp*. If after twenty-five years he decided to return to Ireland, and met the nutcracker-faced Cathal O'Shannon – one of the Palace regulars – Cathal would say 'Where have you been?' but in a tone 'as if I had been delayed overlong in the pub lavatory between drinks.' Cathal, or any of the others, would then talk as if there had been no gap; in fact some would not notice there had been any absence at all.

The week's leave was hardly distinguishable from the one before, except that in Malahide I had to face visiting Kay Russell, whose son Beano had joined the RAF, caught meningitis while training in Canada, and died there. When the telegram had come to the Post Office, Miss Holton – still there, running it, with her infectious cackling laugh – had kept it until she could call around to find a friend of Kay's to break the news to her.

I flew back to the Gambia in November, settling down for a year of largely uneventful operational flying. Twelve-hour patrols looking for U-boats – we saw only one; it had dived long before we dropped our depth charges on the wake it had left – was as boring a wartime job as could be imagined. But there were compensations. Sunderlands were the military version of the Empire flying boats, and the modifications had not removed all the benefits; we had a jakes, and even a galley, in which the rigger prepared hot meals to be eaten in the wardroom, where it was possible to stretch out for the occasional siesta. 'Dull trip', my diary kept on recording; but at least the only danger we had to contend with was the weather, as in the summer fierce tropical storms would blow up, making landing hazardous.

Our tranquillity was seriously threatened only once. The battlecruisers *Scharnhorst* and *Gneisenau*, it was feared, were about to leave Brest as sea-raiders. We were despatched to Gibraltar to watch for them in case they came south (instead, they sailed boldly back to Germany through the Channel). Landing in the bay, we struck some hard object; the Sunderland was holed, and had to be brought up the slip; so instead we spent an agreeable few days in the Rock Hotel in the company of an Intelligence officer who had installed himself there. He was a fellow Anglo–Irishman,

I found: John Perry, 'Binkie' Beaumont's partner in H.M. Tennent's, the leading theatrical impresarios of the time.

I had seen *Spring Meeting*, which John had written with 'M. J. Farrell' – to be better known, nearly half-a-century later, as Mollie Keane when her novels, old and new, began to enjoy their well-deserved popularity. In fact I had seen it twice: in the West End, with Nicholas Phipps as the juvenile lead, and in Dublin, where the actor who played the part – I told John, when I was introduced to him in the Rock Hotel bar – had been no good. 'I was the actor,' John said; but he was inclined good humouredly to agree with the assessment. He was excellent company, and proved a useful ally, arranging for some of the shortages which had begun to plague us in the Gambia to be removed.

Gibraltar was the ideal stepping-stone, at this time. The shops appeared to lack for nothing, and it was possible to bring back as Christmas presents products rationed in Ireland, such as tea, and unobtainable in England, such as silk stockings (which the unmarried members of the crew were sure would enable them to win the favours they hoped for on the 'one before, one after' basis). Alan Wood, who had come with us, and I whiled away the time, climbing to the top of the Rock and playing bridge with John and a group captain who happened to be staying in the hotel, and drinking in the bar with passers-through – including Terence Rattigan.

I had met him briefly at Pembroke Dock; he was waiting for the Sunderland on which he was an air gunner to bring its crew out to Sierra Leone, where his squadron was stationed. I was soon to meet him again, at Bathurst. A message was picked up one day from a Sunderland flying down the coast, about on a level with Senegal, saying that one of its four engines had failed, and another had started to give trouble. Sunderlands could fly on two of their four engines, but only if they carried no load except the crew. When it had staggered in to the estuary and landed safely, we heard that the crew had thrown everything movable, including all their personal belongings except what they stood up in, into the Atlantic.

One of them turned out to be Rattigan. I had seen his *French without Tears* in the West End's two-year run; I had also seen his *After the Ball*, which surprised him, and had thought highly of it, which pleased him, because it had been a flop, and soon closed. Hating to admit to failures, he did not include it in his collected plays.

Rattigan, I wrote from Bathurst,

> is a quiet fellow, or appeared to be, here. I don't think he
> would be in civil life. We got arguing after dinner one
> night and were at it till midnight, mostly on plays and
> books; he is well read. He said that some people he'd met
> during training seemed to sheer off when they heard he
> wrote plays whether from fear of being used *à la*
> Maugham, or embarrassment at meeting a celebrity, or
> just mistrust of writers, he wouldn't know!

In his autobiography Rattigan was to describe how he had lost
everything he had brought with him except one possession he could
not bear to throw overboard: the script of *Flare Path*, which was to
re-establish his reputation.

The end of 'Daisy's' operational tour meant another return to
Pembroke Dock, and another leave in Ireland – this time considerably longer. It was apparent that the 'Emergency', as the state of
neutrality had come to be described, was beginning to make life
difficult in many ways. Tea had been rationed – a severe depriva-
tion, as the Irish were very heavy tea drinkers. Soap was hard to
come by; petrol was simply not available for private cars. Determined to get back to Connemara for a few days, I took a decrepit
train – running on turf: Todd Andrews' *Bord na Mona* was proving
its worth – to Galway and a bus on to Peacocke's Hotel in Maam
Cross, for four halcyon days of trout fishing. But back in Dublin, if
I wanted to get to parties or dances I sometimes had no choice
except to bicycle.

Smyllie, I found, was showing signs of wear and tear. The *Irish
Times* was down to a single folded sheet – four pages; and he had
been involved in a protracted battle with the Censors. A couple of
notable victories had been gained, including one which had
featured in newspapers all over the English-speaking world. Commenting on one of Churchill's speeches, in which he had named
nine military commanders who had won fame in the Middle East,
an Irishman's Diary paragraph noted that only one of them had

been British. Three, it went on – Generals Wilson, Dill and Brooke – were Japanese (North Island); four – Generals O'Connor and O'Moore Creagh; Admirals Somerville and Cunningham – were Japanese (South Island). Nobody was later able to discover how this spoof got past the Censors; but they had retaliated by becoming even more tough than before.

Smyllie's other success was achieved with more subtlety. John Robinson had left the paper to join the Navy, and was known to be serving as an A.B. on the *Prince of Wales* when it was sunk off Singapore. A few days later the *Irish Times* carried his photograph, along with a front page story about John having been in 'a boating accident'; his many friends would be 'pleased to learn that he is alive and well'; as he was a good swimmer it was possible he 'owed his life to this accomplishment'. It looked a little ludicrous among the world war news, as it was meant to: the story of the way the Censors had been fooled quickly circulated through Dublin clubs and pubs. But again, the Censors' noose tightened.

In one respect, at least, the Censorship was having an unfortunate effect. It encouraged rumours in Britain that it was disguising the extent of German activities in Ireland, where Nazi agents were supposed to be active, and where U-boats were believed to be refuelling. There was not enough fuel for the Irish, let alone for U-boats; and the record of German agents in Ireland was feeble. The small embassy staff was well-known to Smyllie; I once joined him in the Pearl Bar, unaware that he was talking with Karl Petersen, the Embassy press officer – Smyllie was embarrassed, fearing I might be reported to the British authorities for consorting with the enemy.

By this time it was the Pearl Bar – 'the Cultured Pearl', as somebody had derisively named it – where Smyllie was to be found, after a dispute had led to an unmendable rift with the Palace Bar. He had carried most of the Palace regulars with him, but the atmosphere was wrong; the saloon bar was the wrong shape, divided by a thick pillar into two. Gradually, many of the former regulars went elsewhere. The court was never to be the same again.

Back in London, I went with Michael Jefferson to Charles Phillips' wedding, and on to Ward's Irish House in Piccadilly, where by chance there were some members of another 204 crew with girl friends. At some point we moved up Regent Street to the

Café Royal, where I was particularly attracted to one of the party who seemed unattached, and who offered me a bed for the night. Michael told me not to be silly; she was obviously a pro. Why not? I thought. I had been beginning to feel embarrassed at being almost as old as Bernard Shaw had been before he lost his virginity; here was the opportunity to lose it.

A taxi took us to a house in Sussex Gardens, the property, I was later to find, of the Church Commissioners. At this point she stated her terms; five shillings, or thirty shillings for the whole night. My diary records 'not bad', but my chief recollection is of waking up the next morning with a headache and a throat – in the simile popular at the time – like a Chinese rickshaw-coolie's jock-strap. In the morning light she still looked attractive, watching me dressing; and when the time came, thinking it would be impolite to hand her the money, I put the two bank notes on the chimney piece. 'Bring them here!', she barked at me, furiously; calming down when I did. She had been caught that way by the RAF before.

It was a relief to have had the initiation. In Ireland the smooching had continued to be uncomplicatedly innocent – the stage Byron described when Don Juan and Haydee enjoy 'such kisses as belong to early days, where heart, and soul, and sense, in concert move'. So little suspicion did our love-making arouse that on one of the leaves during the war, when I stayed a couple of nights with the parents of one of the girls I had known, they put me to sleep in her former bed, in spite of the fact that this meant sharing a room with her disturbingly attractive seventeen-year-old sister. In the RAF petting of the adolescent kind was jeered at. The relief at the change, however, was to be punctured when I got back to the Gambia, where the squadron doctor had to prescribe for NSU and an infestation of 'Sandy McNabs', as RAF rhyming slang called them.

I had been promoted, I found, to take over as captain of a crew, and given Sunderland 'M'. Traditionally flying boat crews became almost mawkishly attached to their Boats; and I was sorry to leave 'C for Bunt'. But 'M' had a certain kudos; it was the very first Sunderland to come off the production line.

We saw no U-boat during the next six months of operational

flying; but they were not entirely without incident. When in July the S S *Honolulu* was sunk 400 miles to the south-west of the Gambia, we managed to find the lifeboats. It was too stormy to land beside them, so we flew to a liner which happened to be nearby, to direct it to them. Three months later the S S *Oronsay* was sunk even further to the south west; we flew to Sierra Leone, and took off from Freetown harbour on a search. This time the weather was calm, when we found nine lifeboats crammed with people understandably delighted to see us. It was sorely tempting to land, but there was a heavy swell. Landing – and still more, taking off – in a swell was hazardous; all the more so, in calm conditions, as it took longer to become airborne. Besides, a corvette looking for the survivors was not far off. It was able to pick them up that night.

The crew were as disappointed at the decision not to land as I was. Before I had become captain, they had won the reputation of being the best in the squadron; the experience of the rigger and the fitters – flight engineers – stretched back into peacetime, when they had regarded themselves primarily as tradesmen, rather than aircrew. When a directive came round insisting that all aircrew must have the rank of sergeant, at least, they actually wanted to refuse to join the jumped-up air gunners in the sergeants' mess, who had been in the RAF for only a few months.

The absurdity of the division between officers and NCOs also came home to me again, at this time. Aircrew who were manifestly incompetent but had public school voices were in the officers' mess; accents often decided who would be sergeants. Yet I was still affected by the same conditioning. Alan had become the squadron's second in command. He and I shared many tastes, including playing classical music on an ancient gramophone on the top deck of the *Dumana*, in the evening sun. 'Did I tell you he was at Bryanston, the "Hum" favoured "advanced" public school?', I asked my mother. I was still finding it hard to shed the public school habits of mind, little though I liked them, to 'make friends of any other types, since they don't "speak the same language"'. So I had continued to find myself gravitating towards public school products, even when they were still recognisably in the mould which I hoped I had broken out of; I was lucky to have found 'Willis and Alan, whose education was reasonably enlightened'.

Enlightenment was slow in my case: later in the letter there was a disparaging reference to the local 'wogs'. The only Gambians we encountered were the 'boys' who were the camp cleaners, whom we treated much as Shrewsbury monitors had treated douls – not actually beating them but sometimes wishing we could. But towards the end of our tour of operations Alan introduced me to Wilson Plant and K. C. Jacobs, colonial civil servants, who were to do something to promote a change of attitude. 'W.P.' could have been a force in the Labour Party, if he had not been a civil servant; 'Jake' was diffident and self-effacing, but his home with its library and its stock of cool beer was a delight. There, I met Gambians in the civil service, intelligent and articulate, providing the first inkling that they would be ready to take over the running of the country when the time came.

Squadron life, though, was deteriorating. A shore camp had been made ready; that *Dumana* had left – so encrusted with barnacles that she had to wait for the tide to begin to ebb in order to get out of the estuary; soon afterwards we were told she had been sunk by a U-boat. The camp was primitive. Supplies of food and drink, too, dwindled; the Mess catering officer had to fall back on ingenious variations to disguise the basic bully beef, and beer was rationed to a bottle and a half a week. A new C.O., Wing Commander Cecil-Wright, wielded a new broom, causing consternation among the flying boat crews, who had considered themselves largely exempt from squadron chores. Alan, his operational tour completed, left for home.

I fell back on omniverous reading. Chivvied by Cecil-Wright to do something to offset the adverse report he had given me, I started up a Mess library, collecting from the stock other officers had with them. Most of them were Penguins or Pelicans, the quality surprisingly high; I read works which I was highly unlikely to have embarked upon in other circumstances, *Don Quixote*, and even the *Critique of Pure Reason*. Cecil-Wright, mollified, told me I had been promoted to Flight Lieutenant, and despatched me with 'M' and its crew back to Pembroke Dock for its next overhaul, along with instructions to me to report to Coastal Command HQ at Northolt to warn them just how difficult life was becoming in the Gambia (even razor blades would have run out, if John Perry had not been able to supply us with a consignment from Gibraltar).

Returning to Pembroke Dock after leave in Ireland, I found a message from Coastal: a thousand operational flying hours, they thought, was enough. Somebody else would have to bring 'M' back to the Gambia. I was to proceed to 131 Operational Training Unit at Killadeas, on Lough Erne in Ulster.

9

Catalinas

For a Sunderland pilot, 'Cats' were a sad come-down. They had no wardroom, no galley, not even a jakes. Still, with trains running between Enniskillen and Dublin, Killadeas on Lough Erne was preferable to the Sunderland training base at Invergordon. Luck was with me, still.

I was to be an instructor for over a year, but the routine varied so little that the months have fused into a jumble of vague impressions. Day after day, and periodically night after night, we would taxi our Catalinas from the moorings at Killadeas down to the main lake, each of us with two pupil pilots, and watch them do take-offs and landings, practice bombing, and other standard exercises. We were lucky in our C.O., Wing Commander Lywood, at first encounter unapproachable but mellowing when his confidence was won.

When I opened up the wartime letters which my mother had kept, it was to find that almost the only ones from Killadeas were those in which I described visits to Dublin. These were frequent, as 'forty-eight-hour passes' could be granted every month; by choosing the days next to the weekly day off, this could be extended to seventy-two hours; and by leaving Enniskillen around tea-time it was possible to get to Dublin in time for dinner at Jammets or the Dolphin, 'chiselling' an extra night. Sometimes as many as ten of us went down, bringing with us contraband in the form of soap, tea, and mustard – Colman was refusing to export it to Ireland as a protest against her neutrality; and bringing back meat and whiskey. Or we would cross the border to Bundoran, to stay in the Great Northern Hotel.

Hearing that the annual Press and Advertising week-end was coming up in May, I cycled over to the nearest station and caught the train to meet Smyllie, Alan Montgomery, Lynn Doyle and others; joined in the golf and the dinner; made a short speech of thankfulness for being there; and stayed up until it was time – 4.40 a.m. – to take advantage of a lift back, in a snowstorm. A few hours later, those revellers who were still sleeping off the effects were woken by a low flying plane, which they assumed was mine doing a 'beat-up'. It turned out to be an American Flying Fortress, gone astray on the flight across the Atlantic, which had to make a forced landing on the Bundoran beach. 'Judge the amazement of our respected editor,' Pussy O'Mahony wrote to tell me,

> when he woke up some three hours later, and, like Sister Anne, looked out of the gable window. Below him, lounging outside the Hotel, were a group of Yankees, talking in a southern, nasal drawl, smoking Camel cigarettes and attired in moccasins, zip-fastened trousers, wool helmets and all sorts of odd kit. He thought first that he was in a foreign country and secondly that there had been an invasion. Finally he decided that he was (as, in fact, he *was*) in the rats.
>
> With his well-known aplomb, however, the Editor dismissed the incident as one which should be viewed later in the day, and sent for a ball of malt, which brought him round.

In April Alan Lywood told me that Coastal Command planned to post me to Sullom Voe, in the Shetland Islands, but that he had another idea. A few days later I was astonished to hear that my next move would be to Gibraltar, to 202 Squadron, as Flight Commander – which would mean promotion to Squadron Leader. This was baffling, and remains baffling. On Lough Erne I had distinguished myself by allowing one of my pupils to land in a sheltered part of the lake, on a stormy day, unaware that it contained a hidden rock, which had ripped a gash in the Catalina's hull. On another occasion the rigger who was responsible for letting go the mooring rope when the engines started had let it go before they started; we had drifted back into another Catalina – the rigger's fault, but the captain was supposed to take the blame for the failings of his crew. Counting the Oxford which I had written off, that would surely qualify me for one of the most expensive pilots in the history of the war. And as I was to find when I met some of the former pupils in 202, I was more highly regarded as convivial company in the Mess, and the inventor of ingenious excuses to get to Dublin, than as an instructor. Still, mine not to reason why . . .

It turned out to be a very different Gibraltar, when I arrived in May. Clearly there would soon be a Second Front, and, almost as certainly, a Third, in the Mediterranean – a landing in the South of France. 'Fagin' Finch, my co-flight commander, turned out to be an Irishman, as was the Adjutant, Paddy Meakin; the three of us were to become close friends. For a start, Fagan suggested, I should have a crew and do some operations, leaving him to deal with all the squadron problems; and this was to launch me into three months of more intensive flying even than on the Gambian tour, as the opening of the Second and Third Fronts required a constant watch for U-boats operating in the Mediterranean, or returning from the south Atlantic to harass the shipping in the Channel off Normandy.

It had been realised by this time that the U-boats had the benefit of a new 'schnorkel' system which enabled them to remain submerged for long periods. The chance of detecting them was very small; the main purpose of the patrols was simply to keep them submerged, reducing their range. It was boring work, all the more tedious because the Catalina's endurance was considerably greater than the Sunderland's. Only one operational flight remains vivid in memory, partly because it was the longest, partly because of the circumstances in which it was undertaken.

Coastal Command had come through to say that an aircraft on a trans-Atlantic flight had ditched some four hundred miles off Cape Finisterre; as no suitable air sea rescue aircraft happened to be available from Britain, could 202 take a look to see if there were any survivors? It struck us as odd that Coastal could not mount the operation from Plymouth, which was considerably closer; but nothing Coastal did any longer greatly surprised us.

With an additional fuel tank fitted into the Catalina, we took off at midnight, flew through the night around the southern tip of Spain and north along the Portuguese coast to take a reliable bearing as soon as it was light enough, before turning westwards into the Atlantic. There was no sign of wreckage, no oil slick, when we reached the point we had been given; but this was encouraging, as if the pilot had managed to land the aircraft in one piece it might have sunk, after the crew got out, leaving no trace. There was a prescribed search procedure for such occasions, designed to cover the maximum of sea without missing an object as small as an inflated dinghy; the quiet, workmanlike Australian navigator, Flying Officer Cavill, plotted it; and we began the search, changing course every few minutes on his instructions.

The sea was rough, and after a few hours, white-caps began to prompt hallucinations of dinghies. The second pilot, Flying Officer Buckmaster – an Old Etonian; a rare species in Coastal Command – and I took turns to 'zzzzz' for a while, as best we could in the discomfort of the main hull, occupied as it was by the spare fuel tank. Just as I was beginning to fear we would have to return to report failure, a member of the crew shook me awake and there, below us, was a dinghy – two? I forget – and we counted seven survivors, waving like mad.

A Catalina might have landed safely even in that rough sea; its hull was much better at taking a battering than a Sunderland's. But we could not have taken off again safely, with the additional load; so we contented ourselves with chucking out the air-sea rescue stuff we had brought with us; climbed high enough to ensure that we had an accurate 'fix' on their position with the help of the radio beacons; reported it to base; and then flew back the way we had come, landing shortly after 11 p.m.

But for two things, it could have been described as a routine flight. One was that nobody at Gibraltar could recall any operational flight lasting so long – over twenty-three hours (somebody years later suggested it should qualify for the *Guinness Book of Records*). The other was Coastal Command's reason for calling on us to make it. They did not, in fact, need to tell us the reason; when we got back we knew. We had looked for, and found, that ditched crew on June 6; D-Day. Every available aircraft in Britain must have been concentrated upon the support of the massive fleet crossing the Channel. Yet Coastal Command had still worried about the fate of the ditched crew (we heard later that a ship had picked them up) and found time, in those anxious hours, to arrange for our search. I still find that moving.

Early in September, 202 Squadron moved back to home waters – Castle Archdale, a few miles down Lough Erne from Killadeas. Coastal Command, realising that the introduction of the 'schnorkel' was allowing U-boats to avoid surfacing in daylight, had decided that the best chance of sinking them was to catch them unawares at night with the help of radar and a 'Leigh Light', mounted under one of the Catalina's wings, which could be switched on at the last stage of the approach.

Learning how to make the approaches in darkness was tricky. I had to give up operational flying, to concentrate on training the crews. It was a slow business, as the training flights could only be made in reasonably good weather (though not too good; clear moonlit nights made it too easy); and the weather that winter was foul. My diary recorded the occasional Mess party, for which there was always some excuse or other, at Killadeas as well as Castle Archdale; and a few games of rugby against Portora school. But the only times it came to life concerned the 'forty-eight-hour passes' to Dublin, and a leave spent partly in London where I was able to see a couple of that remarkable 'New Vic' season's offerings, Olivier's *Richard III* and Olivier and Richardson in *Arms and the Man*.

Towards the end of January Lough Erne was iced up – not a frequent occurrence – and for a couple of weeks the only serious activity was keeping the Catalinas' hulls from being scrunched. By that time it was becoming obvious that the Leigh Light idea was not working successfully in practice. Occasionally a radar contact would be made, but no schnorkels were illuminated. With the collapse of the German offensive in the Ardennes, the Russian advance through Poland and the success of Slim's 14th Army in Burma, the pressure was off; our thoughts were turning to what we could do when Germany finally collapsed. Even after VE Day, we were still for a while called upon for a few anti-U-boat patrols; I did my final one on 27 May. But five days later, we heard that the squadron was to be disbanded; and in mid-June I was told to proceed to Benbecula, a Coastal Command station in the Western Isles of Scotland, as Squadron Leader (Admin.).

So it was to be a desk job . . . I had not put in quite enough hours to complete my second tour of operations, but Coastal Command had decided it would not be worth sending me with the others to re-train on land planes, Liberators, for the hours that remained. The notion of being an admin type, spending the day hearing evidence about airmen brought up on charges of various kinds, was appalling. Fortunately – the luck held out to the end – Alan Wood was involved with the Empire Central Flying Training School at Hullavington in Wiltshire, which had a post for a trained journalist, to try to report what was happening there in colloquial English, when required; he assured ECFS that I was their man; and although it meant temporarily dropping a rank, to flight lieutenant, the opportunity was too good to miss.

Hullavington at the time contained some of the most remarkable individuals in the RAF: two, in particular. Wing Commander Kermode – 'the Prof', a nephew of 'Hum' Lynam – as the leading authority in Britain, and probably in the world, on the theory of flight; a shy man, but his prowess as a lecturer was such that many of us who would never have thought of attending lectures for pleasure went to his. And in the Navigation section there was Squadron Leader Francis Chichester, who almost single-handed – we had been taught at George – had developed the techniques which we had to learn to navigate while over the sea. In *The Lonely Sea and the Sky* he was to describe how he did it. This was after his remarkable victory in the first solo yacht race across the Atlantic; but even before he became internationally famous, he was awe-inspiring for us. Yet all the time, those of us who were not going to stay in the RAF were watching the progress of demobilisation, conducted on the points system based on age and length of service.

As the day approached, the temptation was to do little more than put in token visits to our offices, to leave messages when we might be expected back. In my last few days, however, I spent some time working on a project which had been brewed up in the course of one of the parties which were becoming increasingly frequent, to say farewell to those about-to-be-demobbed. It had ended with the familiar songs, and somebody had suggested there ought to be some record of their words. I had volunteered to compile it, with assistance from the regulars in the mess bar, I produced a typed song-sheet of all that we could remember.

I did not keep a copy, but recollection of the words of some of the songs suggests that somebody, coming across it, consigned it to the flames. They were shocking in their banality, relentlessly dealing in fornication and defaecation, and rarely displaying any trace of inventiveness, let alone of wit. Seen on the page, too, they looked more nauseating than when they were chorused; even such amiable old favourites as 'The Ball of Kirriemuir'.

In a way, though, that last task at Hullavington was appropriate. There was something about life in officers' Messes which protracted adolescence. In some ways they were closer to school than to university, with their uniforms and ranks and conventions. Women played a very subordinate part. There were none in 204 squadron while it was in the Gambia; none in 202 in Gibraltar. Except when actually flying, too, pilots had few responsibilities. The Battle of Britain had left us at the top of the popularity charts, in the public mind; in pubs and in restaurants, it was not uncommon to find a round of drinks presented, or a bill paid, by a stranger as a 'thank you' offering. Some of us left for civilian life almost as immature as when we had joined.

Coastal Command, admittedly – flying boat squadrons in particular – were hardly representative. To have flown fighters would have meant having a very different war; and the thought of being a pilot in a wartime bomber squadron still provokes a shudder. Casualties in flying boat crews were comparatively rare. In other commands, many friends I had made had been killed: among them Bryan Rogers, who had given me the first lesson, and 'Daisy' Dart – who had eventually achieved his ambition to fly less cumbersome aircraft. He had joined a Mosquito squadron, and killed himself 'beating up' his home to celebrate his liberation.

Again: looking back, it is only too easy to speculate about the existence of guardian angels, or good fairies, or lucky stars. At the time, I was ready to put it all down to luck. And the luck held. Smyllie was still editor of the *Irish Times*, and I could feel confident that he would find room for me in some job there, even though I had no formal right to one.

10

Features: Specials

My demob number came up on New Year's Day, 1946. The last night in the RAF turned out to be even gloomier than Padgate; thirty of us spent it in an un-heated Nissen hut – 'out', my diary recorded, 'as we went in'. The next morning we collected our civilian clothes, shoes, socks, a shirt, a suit and a choice of cap or trilby hat, before leaving in a lorry for the railway station. We were not, strictly speaking, released. In the event of another threat of war we could be recalled. But few of us would put on uniform again – though RAF greatcoats, stripped of their shoulder straps and brass buttons, would continue to identify many of us for years to come. Willis Roxburgh and Alan Wood had been demobbed ahead of me; both were in London, and we celebrated having come through the war. Ours were to be enduring friendships.

Also in London, just back from India, were my parents. Correspondence had made me feel closer to my mother than I had ever been; or, as I was soon to find, would ever be. She still hoped for a closer relationship; I shrank from it. My father was still easier to be with. He had made the Poona research station a show piece internationally; and he had managed to demonstrate the practical value of the models there by explaining how a threat to a vital Bengal–Nagpur railway line – the one used to supply the Burma campaign – from an erratically meandering river could be averted just in time to bring the river under control before the monsoon. Like his father before him, he was knighted, and his reputation would enable him to choose between the offers of consultancies which began to flow in, to keep him occupied.

146

My mother had also been awarded an honour: the Kaiser-I-Hind medal. It was for her services as, among other things, a prison visitor. The jailbirds were an unusual collection; among them, men and women who were soon to be the rulers of India. They included Mrs Sarojini Naidu, who had established a reputation as a poet, a feminist – one of her most successful campaigns was against purdah – and a nationalist; she had been the first woman to take the chair at the meetings of Gandhi's National Congress, and had accompanied him to the London Round Table Conference of 1931. One of my mother's wartime letters described how pleased she was to have been rung up by Mrs Naidu asking to come round to say goodbye: she had just been let out of jail.

> Along she came and amused Claude who had never met her before. She had been let out 'cos 'her heart is weak', but I hope it is because her humour and commonsense may keep Congress from being silly. She made Claude laugh describing Reggie Martin from Portrush, the C.O. of the jail she had been in before: 'he had such Beautiful Blue Eyes and he Would keep looking at the ground . . . I used to do All in my power to shock him into looking up . . .' She is definitely an actress and a fine one in the Ellen Terry class, full of unconquerable spirits and fun despite none too good health.

Mrs Naidu was off to meet 'the "old boy", as she calls Gandhi' in another jail; my mother begged her to 'throw in her weight for peaceful and sane behaviour'. Reading the letter – one of a series from which she made carbon copies, to circulate round the family and friends in Ireland – makes me regret that inability to reach out to her, when she returned, but also to recall one of the reasons for it: her belief that if people only behaved reasonably, and did not resort to threats or violence, all problems could be solved. She could not face the possibility that in India in the 1940s, as in Ireland in thirty years before, 'reasonable' politicians would inevitably be swept aside if the tide of nationalism came up against unreasoning resistance.

'Take away our hearts o' stone, and give us hearts o' flesh! Take away this murdherin' hate, an' give us Thine own eternal love!' Mrs Boyle's last cry, in *Juno and the Paycock*, was my mother's favourite

147

quotation; it rang in her ears as she had heard it spoken by the first
and greatest 'Juno', Sara Allgood, in the Abbey Theatre. My mother
was to use it in another of her circulating letters, written after the
death of the man whose company she had enjoyed in all the years in
Poona: Armine Wodehouse, brother of P.G. As the elder and
academically-accomplished brother, Armine was given advantages,
such as going to a university, denied to the younger; yet he had ended
up in a poorly-paid teaching job in Poona. My mother was attracted
to him by the discovery that he was 'Senex', the contributor of
entertaining light verses to *The Times of India*; some were to be
collected and published in 1933 as 'Verses from Senexpur'.

P. G. Wodehouse's biographers have tended to suggest that his
relations with his brother, which might have been soured by the
different treatment they received from their parents, were good. My
mother could not forgive the well-off P.G. for not helping with the
impoverished Armine's son's education; and in her letter she
described how a friend of hers and of Armine's, entertaining him and
P.G. in England, had been 'horrified to see the look of concentrated
hate cast on him by P.G.', which suggested lingering jealousy. 'The
hates in family life are tragic', she commented, 'indeed "murdherin'
hate" seems the curse of the world . . . could children be made to
realise that hate destroys every worth-while thing in the world?' For
all Bernard Shaw's influence on her, she thought in simple terms of
love – or, rather, sanity – and hate. Her 'if-only-people-would-be-
kind' attitude became an irritant.

Still, there was no need to worry about the uneasy relationship.
My father had decided to stay in London, as there was the prospect
that a research station on the lines of the one in Poona would be
established in England. He expected to be asked to act in some
advisory capacity (a year later, when the Hydraulics Research Board
was set up, he was in fact appointed the first Director of Research). I
would be in Dublin if, as I assumed, the *Irish Times* would take me
back. It did, at six guineas a week – the then minimum wage which
the NUJ had managed to extract from the newspaper proprietors. I
was to go back to the reporters' room, under Alan Montgomery, who
had become chief reporter, but no longer *as* a reporter. My job was to
be 'Features, Specials'.

Ideas for 'Features' were discussed each morning. My first
working day consisted of a tour of the dance halls (they were just

becoming a familiar aspect of Dublin life; though the ballroom dancing which I witnessed was soon to fade away.) 'Specials' proved to be more satisfying. Airliners were beginning to cross the Atlantic in ever-increasing numbers. Flying boats were on their way out, as uneconomic; there was controversy over whether to concentrate upon upgrading Rineanna airport, by the Shannon estuary, or Collinstown, near Dublin; and further controversy over how the airports should be developed – whether, say, the terminal buildings should be alongside the runways or in the middle of them, as at Heathrow. Smyllie appointed me to look after the subject, suggesting that I get together with Seamus Kelly, in the public relations office of Aer Lingus, as he would surely be helpful.

Coming into the office one morning when I was on leave I had seen a man in Irish army uniform, who I was later told was Seamus, climbing the stairs ahead of me. To my surprise, he turned into the office on the right at the head of the stairs, where Smyllie now worked while the *Irish Times* premises were being rebuilt. I did not see him come out, but heard later that he had appeared dazed. If he wanted a job, Smyllie had told him, he could start on one even before he was demobbed: he could be the *Irish Times* theatre critic. The previous incumbent, the Abbey playwright Brinsley Macnamara, had just resigned in a huff because the paper had published a letter from Michael MacLiammoir and Hilton Edwards criticising him for something he had written about them. Smyllie, fearing that he would be inundated with applications for the job from people who would be deeply offended if he chose anybody else, had decided to pre-empt them by appointing the successor before they would have time to offer their services.

Demobbed, Seamus had found the job with Aer Lingus. I took an immediate dislike to him when we met. He had a face like a discontented tomahawk, thin-lipped and, when *he* took a dislike – as he, also immediately, took to me – uncompromisingly hostile. Ordinarily, too, the relationship between a journalist trying to find what is going on, and a PRO seeking to feed him only such information as will show the company in a good light, would have been calculated to nourish such mutual hostility. We thawed when we found we had a common enemy, bureaucracy.

The minister in charge of aviation, Oscar Traynor, kept interfering; as Aer Lingus was nationalised it was poorly placed to resist. Seamus, though, could keep me informed; and much to Smyllie's delight, it was not long before the *Irish Times* was being denounced by Traynor in the Dail for publishing information which Our Air Correspondent could only have obtained illicitly. Seamus and I were to form a lasting alliance, cemented by his love of the theatre – he was to continue as the *Irish Times* critic for over thirty years.

I saw little of Smyllie in this 'Features, Specials' period, but enough to realise the change in him. He was no longer the Falstaffian figure Lionel Fleming and Paddy Campbell were to portray; he had lost weight, and self-confidence. He came in to the office in the afternoon, but crossed the road to the Pearl as soon as he could. And he did not come back for the late night sessions, which he left to Alec Newman and Bruce Williamson, his latest recruit.

During the war, Smyllie had received many threats from the IRA, whose members had actually thrown a bomb into the *Irish Times* Cork office. Visiting him on my leaves, I had been scrutinised by the detective whose duty it was to sit outside the editor's door whenever Smyllie was inside. But Smyllie had received no protection on his journeys home, by bicycle. As it happened, the IRA was in such a shambles at the time that he was not likely to be a target; but he could not have known this.

He also had had the Censors to contend with. Tony Gray, another of Smyllie's 'direct entry' recruits, worked for a time in his office and recalls that when the Censor who was on duty felt bloody-minded he could make things difficult both for Smyllie and for the management; if he delayed decisions the early editions might miss the trains which took them across the country. Eventually, Gray suspects, Smyllie came to a deal with the Censors, promising not to play any more tricks on them if they would play none on him. But he had kept one in reserve. On the last night of the wartime censorship, due to end when the war in Europe ended, he arranged that the photographs of Allied leaders scattered innocently through the paper in its early editions – as the Censors permitted – should be brought onto the front page to form a V – for Victory. For readers, it was an effective Parthian shot; but it was small consolation for Smyllie after what he had been through.

Before the war ended, Smyllie had begun to suffer from another nagging threat to his peace of mind. A Dublin businessman, Frank Lowe, had joined the board. Appalled at the chaos he found in every branch of the newspaper, he had staged a boardroom coup which made him effectively Smyllie's boss. Although he did his best not to interfere with the journalistic content, his attempts to shake up the management from time to time shook up Smyllie; in particular, his commissioning of Harold Brown to compile a report on what could be done to improve efficiency all round. Brown, still the Motoring Correspondent, advocated greater collaboration between journalists and management – something which Smyllie had always resisted.

To avoid having to attend the conferences which Brown's report recommended, he settled for Lowe's suggestion that Brown should be given the job of organising the collaboration, with an office and a title, News Editor. It seemed obvious to Alec Newman that this could only be the first of a series of moves Lowe must have planned to follow up his boardroom coup with the replacement of Smyllie, and in all probability of himself. To be on the safe side, Alec decided to throw in his lot with Harold Brown. There was not much they could do, except plot, so long as Smyllie remained. But at least, Alec thought, he could secure his own succession when Smyllie was sacked.

Smyllie, however, was too firmly entrenched. He had won the respect, during the Emergency, both of de Valera (in spite of the teasing of the Censors) and of Sir John Maffey, the British representative in Ireland, who used to consult Smyllie to gauge what the reactions would be among old Ascendancy – still influential in industry, though no longer a political force – to moves by Churchill designed to coerce the Irish into abandoning neutrality. *Irish Times* readers, too, were grateful for the stand Smyllie had made, when the end of the Emergency brought the realisation of his difficulties with the Censors. And Smyllie had two trump cards in his hand: Myles na gCopaleen's Cruiskeen Lawn, and Patrick Campbell's Irishman's Diary.

Myles – Brian O'Nolan in private life and in his capacity as a civil servant – was 'a small man whose appearance somehow combined elements of the priest, the baby-faced Chicago gangster, the petty bourgeois malt drinker and the Dublin literary gent', as Anthony Cronin has described him in *Dead as Doornails*, a fond but far from foolish portrait of the post-war literary scene in Dublin, with particular emphasis on the locations – the pubs. In the 1970s Myles was posthumously to become a cult figure in Britain, partly because of the republication of *At Swim-Two-Birds* but largely on the strength of the reprinted collection of some of his Cruiskeen Lawn columns; their merits can consequently still be savoured without the need to visit the British Library's newspaper repository at Colindale. They were unlike anything that had appeared before, or has appeared since, in the press.

It had often been suggested to Smyllie that he should have something in the Irish language in the paper. He had jibbed at the idea, not so much from hostility to the language as from irritation at the way it was being forced down schoolchildren's throats; but he had eventually consented on the understanding that the articles must stand up in their own right. In other words, if they had been submitted initially in English they would have been accepted only if they were good enough.

Myles was a leading Gaelic scholar, combining the ability to write fluently in the language with an acerbic contempt for the pedants who, in his opinion, were undermining its chances of becoming again widely spoken. Although *At Swim-Two-Birds* had flopped, it had come to be greatly admired by the Dublin avant-garde, among them Alec Newman, who liked to keep abreast of cultural developments. When a letter to the editor came in from Myles, under one of his numerous assumed names, starting up a controversy, Alec encouraged him to enter into the fray under other assumed names.

According to Tony Gray, who was privy to the plotting, it was weeks before Smyllie realised what Alec and Myles had been doing. Alec by this time had taken charge of the correspondence. Smyllie, initially worried, eventually decided that if Myles was offered space in the paper and paid for it, he might cease to send in near-libellous letters. By this time, Tony feels sure, Smyllie would have become familiar with Myles' background, his mastery of the Irish language, and his ability to write amusing prose; Myles was invited to contribute a column in Irish. But when the first Cruiskeen Lawn arrived, Smyllie nervously asked Tony, who had learned Irish at school, to translate, before sending it out to the compositors.

Cruiskeen Lawn was a success from the start with those *Irish Times* readers who could understand it – and even those who had only a smattering of the language were encouraged to turn to it if they knew that a 'cruiskeen lawn' was a jug of porter. Manifestly it was not going to be too serious. Before long Smyllie was basking in the plaudits it brought in, and listening to the pleas of those who did not understand Irish to allow translations, too. Soon, Myles was writing alternately in Irish and English, bringing in subscribers who ordinarily would have felt embarrassed to be seen reading, let alone buying, the *Irish Times*.

Although Myles had been a regular at the Palace, he was not to be seen at the Pearl, or in the office. I encountered him chiefly on occasions when British or American feature writers and foreign correspondents came to Dublin to write about the post-war scene; if they had not heard of Myles before, they would be intrigued by the column and ask to meet him. Usually they would assure him that their editors would be delighted to take articles from him – I can recall a representative of *Time* magazine actually telling him the fee, in precious dollars, that he could expect to get. But one of the reasons for his growing embitterment was that rarely, if ever, were his pieces actually commissioned. Editors thought them too Oirish, or eccentric, or over their readers' heads.

A play which he wrote, too, had failed when it was put on at the Abbey Theatre in 1943; and apparently he was having trouble with the book which was eventually to emerge as *The Dalkey Archive* – Cronin thinks he left it uncompleted, at the time. My chief recollection of Myles is of him sitting, or standing, a little aloof from the group in the hotel bar or pub where a visiting journalist was the host – though frequently not in the sense of paying for the drinks; Myles in a black hat (as the cartoon of the Palace regulars showed, hats, and poets' black hats in particular, were still worn in pubs) and dark overcoat, looking as if he were worried that he would be expected, perhaps even asked, to say something witty for the visitor's benefit.

Patrick Campbell had returned to Ireland, as I had, on the day Chamberlain declared war. He knew Smyllie would not take him back, and decided to see if he could write – a book, short stories, anything – in a cabin cruiser on the Shannon. His typewriter was never even taken out of its cover; his only positive achievement was to grow a fine, flowing reddish-white beard. Standing marooned on a mudbank just below water level, he frightened the wits out of passers-by, as he appeared to be walking on the water.

A few days after the evacuation of Dunkirk, de Valera had warned on Radio Eireann that as the German drive through northern France left Ireland exposed to the risk of sudden invasion, he was calling upon every able-bodied man to volunteer for the forces, or for the Irish equivalent of the British Home Guard. Ashore for supplies, drinking in a pub in Carrick-on-Shannon, Paddy heard him, and decided this was his chance to justify his return to Ireland; he would join the Dublin Port Control Service – a branch of what was facetiously called the Irish Navy, but described itself more modestly as the Irish Marine Service. 'For the first time since 3 September', he was to recall in *My Life and Easy Times*, 'my conscience was clear.'

The next four years were not to be in the 'easy times' category, though they provided him with the material for some hilarious recollections. Eventually he reached the rank of Chief Petty Officer, but he had no chance of obtaining a commission, as he could not hope to pass an examination which would require a fairly high standard of mathematics, including trigonometry. He spent interminable boring hours bucketing about in Dublin Bay waiting to board any ship which arrived, to check it for 'unauthorised persons' – who, if they *were* unauthorised, would certainly have hidden themselves carefully enough to avoid any risk of being discovered. When the Allies landed in Normandy, he felt that he had done his bit, and applied to Smyllie through an intermediary – the Sports Editor, Paul MacWeeney – to return to the *Irish Times*. The request was turned down; but when Paddy turned up in his uniform and pleaded his own cause, Smyllie relented. 'You'd better come and do something about the Diary. It's a shower of lapidary crap.'

I had met Paddy for the first time – in his uniform – in the course of one of the leaves from Lough Erne, at a Dublin party, and had fallen at once for his gift of exploiting his stammer to lend point to his accounts of the assorted catastrophes which dogged his career in the Dublin Port Control, and which were later to delight the readers of *Lilliput* and the *Spectator*. By the time I rejoined the *Irish Times* he had established the Diary as the most popular feature in the paper – at least with the Anglo–Irish readers, who tended to be a little wary of Myles. But it was no labour of love; he hated being 'Quidnunc'.

When he took it on he had been expected to incorporate paragraphs sent in by contributors; he was determined, though, to make the Diary all his own work. To this his immediate boss, Alan

Montgomery, raised no objection so long as it contained plenty of personalities. Every morning, five days a week, Paddy did the rounds of Dublin's leading hotels – on a bicycle, until petrol became available again – to try to inveigle receptionists into letting him know if anybody suitable for an interview was due. At the Shelbourne, he was to recall in a recording thirty years later, the formula never varied:

'Miss Carter, are there any famous people staying here?'
'Mr Campbell, there are only famous people staying here. Which one would you want to talk to?'

But quite often there would be nobody famous, or the famous declined to be interviewed. Paddy would have to come in to the *Irish Times* to find if something was happening which he could attend, to scrape up a paragraph or two. Off he would go on the bicycle, his elevated centre of gravity (he stood about six feet four) conspiring with Dublin's intricate tramlines to cause some monumental purlers, so that he would return bruised and shaken to type his piece for the following morning.

By the time I rejoined the office he had made his mark sufficiently to abandon the conventional formula of unrelated paragraphs and plenty of personalities, in favour of his preferred method: 'What I wanted to find was a situation with a beginning and a middle and an end – almost a short story – with myself right in the middle of it.' When it clicked, it could be as funny as he was when he was relating it in advance, to test it out. But when no suitable situation presented itself, he would come in desperation to the reporters' room – which ordinarily he avoided, preferring to work in a room above, cold but solitary, with only a table and a chair – begging us for something, anything, out of which he could squeeze a paragraph. 'I used to have your actual nightmares,' he recalled. 'I would see the *Irish Times* coming out, and I'd open it, and on the Diary page there would be a huge blank space. In capital letters, I would see HE COULD NOT THINK OF ANYTHING TO PUT.

We saw little of Paddy on his Diary stint except on days when he was really desperate; and they became fewer when he teamed up with Frank Launder, in Ireland to make *Captain Boycott*, with Stewart Granger and Kathleen Ryan. He was welcomed by the film crew, as always, as a resident jester, keeping the unit happy when they were not actually filming, and in turn getting material for the Diary. In his absences, I would be called upon to be Pro-Quidnunc; useful experience, as things were soon to turn out. The time was approaching when, following the policy Smyllie had adopted of broadening the experience of these recruits he had taken in off the street, I would have to do a stint as one of the sub-editors, cleaning up and if necessary re-jigging and re-writing the copy coming in from reporters, feature writers and agencies. Before the move could take place, Paddy came to the rescue by leaving for London.

The editor of the *Sunday Dispatch* had come to Dublin to look for somebody who might help to sell more copies of the Irish edition of the paper, which sometimes had to be considerably different from the English version. When English readers were getting *Forever Amber*, in serial form, it was deemed wise to treat the Irish to an adulatory life of the Pope. Paddy was selected to write a weekly column for eight guineas, more than he was getting for writing the Irishman's Diary five days a week. Soon afterwards Frank Launder and the producers of *Captain Boycott* paid him £25 for some 'additional dialogue' which was never used ('There's an "and" of yours in there somewhere,' Launder told him). Once again, London began to beckon, particularly as Paddy's marriage was breaking up.

Invited to stay with Launder in London, he took the opportunity to visit the *Dispatch* office to hand in his column. It was used in all editions; he was paid thirty-two guineas. When the column appeared again in all editions the following week, he decided not to return to Dublin. In his account in *My Life and Easy Times* he was to imply that he wrote immediately to inform Smyllie; in fact days passed before it began to dawn on us that he was proposing to stay in London. And by that time I was established as 'Pro-Quidnunc'.

11

Quidnunc

For a time Alec Newman and Harold Brown managed to persuade
Smyllie that the Diary should revert to the former system of separate
paragraphs, contributed by anybody who cared to earn 7/6*d*. I would
continue as editor, filling in whenever there were insufficient
contributions. The contributions turned out not merely to be
insufficient, but almost non-existent; the remuneration was inadequate, and the management declined to allow it to be raised.
Then it was decided that I should share the job with Tony Olden,
another of Smyllie's discoveries. Tony had proved to be a perceptive
film critic, and would have been an asset to the Diary; but he had had
TB, and suffered from protracted spells of illness. Gradually it came
to be accepted that I was Quidnunc. The contrast with Paddy's
entertaining column must have been painful to readers; but largely, I
suspect, thanks to Smyllie's backing, I stayed on throughout 1947.

Only one Diary event has stayed firmly in memory: the last voyage
of the *Muirchu*. The *Muirchu* had originally been the *Helga*, the
gunboat which the British had used to help crush the Easter Rising in
1916. From the port of Dublin it had shelled the General Post Office,
where Pearse, Connolly and other rebel leaders had their HQ. When
Bernard Shaw was taken to France to see the devastation in towns
such as Arras after two and a half years of artillery bombardment, his
reply was that the *Helga* had done more damage in a week – though it
would not be quite true to say that not one stone was left on another,
'for the marksmanship was so bad that the Post Office itself was left
standing amidst a waste of rubbish heaps'. Was it coincidence, or
somebody's black humour, that led to the *Helga* being presented to

the new Free State government to be the first, and for two decades the only, ship in the Irish navy?

It had been used chiefly to try to protect the fishing limits from penetration by French trawlers; and as most of them were faster, the *Muirchu* had become the butt of *Dublin Opinion* and of Dublin's leading comedian, Jimmy O'Dea. Towards the end of the war, the government had managed to persuade the British to release some corvettes; the *Muirchu*, redundant, could be sold for scrap to Davie Frame, owner of the Hammond Lane Foundry in Dublin. Frame was a neighbour of Smyllie; Smyllie, hearing from him about the deal, suggested that I should go down to Cobh, where the *Muirchu* had been in dry dock, and sail with her round the coast on her last voyage.

I joined the scratch crew – cobbled together for the purpose: the mate was a young English naval officer who happened to be in Cork, unsuccessfully wooing a girl there, and had run out of money to get home – after the *Muirchu* had been re-floated in the dock. There were thirteen of us, but with the help of a crate of Jameson's we cruised hilariously down the estuary, seen off by the newly-commissioned corvettes with the help of all the sounds they could raise from hooters, bells and voices. A little further on we ourselves similarly greeted the merchantship *Irish Plane*, which had managed to survive the war under the tricolour – not always respected by German U-boats or aircraft – but had run aground on its way up to Cobh.

Night fell as we reached the open sea. When I woke up the following morning, it was as if the hangover had taken a new and unwelcome form: it felt as if my aching head was hanging below my heels. This was, in fact, the case: the *Muirchu* was at an alarming angle, down by the bows. Staggering out on deck I found the captain (who must have been older than his ship), the mate, and the representative of the Foundry nervously conferring, wondering what to do next.

Gradually, during the short summer night, the bows must have been dipping downward, and the stern lifting; but with the *Muirchu* trundling along at little more than walking pace, nobody had noticed until the dawn broke. What had happened, it later transpired, was that chocks used to hold her in dry dock had been removed, or had collapsed, too soon, before she had floated; and her fall had sprung some rivets. If we continued on our course, the front bulkhead might collapse under the weight of water pouring in.

Somebody had an idea: suppose we put the *Muirchu* into reverse? The propeller would then lift the bows; the water would pour out again; and we could go on our way stern first. At first it looked as if this was the solution; the propeller blades had just enough purchase to lift the bows. A few seconds later there was a yell through the intercom from the engineers below; the water which had accumulated in the bows was not flowing out to sea, but bursting through the bulkhead. The engines stopped, and all hands assembled on the bridge.

We were in sight of land – the Waterford coast. But we were also almost within hailing distance of some fishing trawlers. One of them, the captain decided, should be called to our assistance. How? I recalled that hoisting flags upside down is a recognised distress signal; but the *Muirchu* had been stripped of almost everything movable, and a search produced only one tattered flag which attracted no attention from the nearest trawler. We fell back on the other standard distress signal, familiar to passengers on sea crossings: a quick succession of toots on the ship's siren. But there was hardly any steam left; the only sound when the captain pulled the cord was a sigh we could barely hear ourselves.

The captain decided that as we appeared to be sinking, we should abandon ship. There was a lifeboat and a dinghy; ten of us would be lowered in the lifeboat, and he and the two others would launch the dinghy as best they could. Although there was no wind, a heavy swell was running; the *Muirchu*, beam on, was bucketing up and down. None of the three left on board had ever lowered a lifeboat before; we were not so much lowered as dropped, plummeting down and hitting the water with a thump. I was at the sharp end. Innocently, I assumed that the casting-off would be done from the deck above. The sailor at the other end knew better, and cast off. As the *Muirchu* rolled in the swell, the sharp end was lifted out of the water by its davit until the lifeboat was almost vertical; we were left clinging to our seats as if to the rungs of a ladder. The man who had cast off was face down, almost in the sea. When we rolled back, I had just enough sense to unhook us, and avert a repeat performance.

One of the oars proved to be rotten, and broke while we were trying to fend the boat off from the *Muirchu*'s hull; but the other three took us across to the trawler, its crew lining the rail, watching us sardonically.

We were not lifted aboard until they had had some fun at our expense, asking each other why they should do anything for the *Muirchu*, which had chased them if they strayed within the fishing limits; but they relented, and said they would take us back – not to Ireland; to Milford Haven. The last we saw of the *Muirchu* she was like a duck feeding, at an angle which suggested she would sink at any moment. Neither we nor anybody else, apparently, saw her end.

The first report reaching the *Irish Times* had it that the *Muirchu* had gone down with all hands; Smyllie had gone to the Pearl to recover from the shock. When the news we had been rescued came through, he stayed there to celebrate. Much to Alec's indignation, the story I telephoned through from Wales appeared under my name the next morning: the first such by-line in the paper's history.

In ordinary circumstances, to be Quidnunc of the *Irish Times* would have been a headily satisfying job to be given to somebody with so little journalistic experience. Unlike run-of-the-mill reporters, a columnist attracted invitations. I found myself in the Embassy party circuit, notoriously boring for those diplomats who have to attend the functions, but intriguing – for a while – for outsiders. Among the people I encountered at one of the parties, at the Spanish Embassy were Tommy Gilmartin, a Dublin anaesthetist, and his beautiful wife Peggy, whom I had met on one of my visits to Bundoran. On their way back to Dublin they had stayed for a few days with friends in County Monaghan, near the border, and come over to the Officers' Mess at Killadeas, bringing with them Erskine Childers. He was with them again at the Spanish Embassy, with his daughter Ruth. We got talking; I invited her out; she invited me back to her home in Highfield Road, in south Dublin; and soon I found myself in a new society.

Up to this point my social round had been with pre-war company. Living in a bachelor establishment, shared with Patrick Jameson and John Stokes, I played golf and bridge with them and other old friends. But the girls we had known had married, and were dispersed. Ruth, I thought, was just what I needed to take the place of Rachel, and the others.

I soon found, though, that Ruth had her own social circle – or her father's and mother's. They included people from the theatre. Edwards and MacLiammoir ('Arsenic and Old Lace', as Jimmy

Montgomery had dubbed them) came by, from time to time, as did artists, some distinguished, others unknown, and a variety of eccentrics.

I do not recall meeting any politicians, though Erskine was one himself, in the Dail. His father had made his name with *The Riddle of the Sands*, which might still come out top in a poll to decide which is the best book in its adventure/espionage category. Staying with his cousin Bob Barton near Glendalough on his holidays, Erskine Childers the first had been infected with Irishness, rather as Cyril Connolly was soon to be; eventually he was drawn into the Home Rule cause, progressing to the republicanism of de Valera. After the Treaty of 1921 he had stayed with the rebels seeking to overturn the Cosgrave government; he was captured, sentenced to death and shot. His son, a schoolboy at the time, had been welcomed into de Valera's Fianna Fail as soon as he grew up; a seat had been found for him in County Wicklow; and he was now a Parliamentary Secretary, clearly in the running for a ministerial post when the older generation, who had fought alongside his father, died off.

Erskine the second, though, was a long way removed from my picture of a Fianna Fail T.D. He had been to an English public school, Gresham's; and by Irish standards, as a young man, he had led what he would have regarded as a cosmopolitan life, and others might have called raffish. He had infectious enthusiasms, for the theatre, for pictures, for sculptures, for people. The first time I came to lunch at Highfield Road it was to meet a young civil servant whose conversation he enjoyed: Conor Cruise O'Brien.

Conor was in the Department of External Affairs, as it was then called. He was engaged on a thesis for a Ph.D. at Trinity College – it was to be published as *Parnell and his Party* in 1957. He was occasionally to be found in O'Dwyer's pub on the corner of Stephen's Green with as un-diplomatic a bunch of colleagues as one could hope for, among them the poet Val Iremonger. Val was to gain the distinction of twice being banished from the Department, once for writing a letter to the *Irish Times*, in his own name, deploring the American government's decision to sentence Ezra Pound to incarceration in a mental hospital for aiding and abetting Mussolini during the war; the second time for standing up in the Abbey Theatre during an interval, along with Professor Roger McHugh, and denouncing the management for the policies which, they claimed, were destroying the theatre's reputation. On both occasions this led to Val being sent to the civil service equivalent of Siberia, the Ministry for Local Government; but as his superiors privately agreed with him about the iniquity, in both cases, he was soon brought back.

Ruth Childers, I was gratified to find, held her own in the sparkling talk with Conor at the lunch table. She was taking a degree in Trinity at the time, but seemed to me to be much more attractively self-assured than her contemporaries. It was satisfying to be able to show her off to my friends, even though she was not at ease with them as with the visitors to Highfield Road. It did not occur to me that she might find my predominantly male circle boring. I had no inkling that anything was amiss until an evening when Ruth had been invited to a dance at Luttrelstown Castle, where one of the Guinness sisterhood had come back with her teenage daughters to live in Ireland; and I drove Ruth there. On the way in to the castle, we passed the bar which had been set up for the evening. Seeing some of my friends there, I told Ruth to go on to the ballroom, where I would join her in a few moments. They turned out to be more than a few. When I eventually reached the ballroom, there was no Ruth.

This troubled me not at all; I went back to the bar. But she was not in the ballroom when I returned. Minutes, and then hours, passed without a sign of her. Eventually I went in search of her in the grounds, finding her at last with one of the Guinness family I did not know, and immediately loathed. They came in eventually, and I brought Ruth back – along with Paddy Campbell, who was over on holiday from London, and needed a lift; so we said nothing at the time about the evening. But I was not invited in, when she got back home; and Ruth soon made it clear that she was tired of being treated as an appendage, to be called for when I wanted her around, but left for my other friends when I encountered them. I was not that much catch as a lover, she indicated, either.

It was a repetition of the affair with Jean at Oxford, I thought. If Ruth calmed down, we could resume our relationship on the same terms as before; but when she made it clear she had no intention of resuming the relationship, unlike with Jean I found myself growing desperate. Our social paths by this time criss-crossed. It was not difficult in Dublin to guess what she would be doing, and where. I would attend, say, the opening of an art exhibition, and catch a glimpse of her there, only to find she would slip away when she saw me. I wrote her long letters, pleading for a fresh start, mixing flattery with criticism of her behaviour. Occasionally she would agree to a meeting, but with obvious reluctance. I was not jealous, I reassured myself when it became clear there was no other man in her life; merely impatient to make her see reason. Soon, I could think of little else. Each time something came up to remind me of her, it would bring a sigh. I had never sighed before – or, rather, I had only heaved sighs, as an intimation of annoyance. This was different; the sighs heaved me.

At this point a measure of relief came from the entry into serious political contention of a new party, Clann na Poblachta, led by Sean MacBride – son of Major MacBride, one of the leaders of the Easter Rising, the 'drunken vainglorious lout' of Yeats's '1916', and Maud Gonne. Its professed aim was to revive the true spirit of Sinn Fein, lost by de Valera's Fianna Fail party during its fifteen years in office; but it collected a kalcidescope of discontented supporters from all over the political spectrum. That October, when campaigning began in three by-elections, the main interest centred on how well, or badly 'the Clann' would do – an interest the Irishman's Diary reflected, as I did the rounds of the election meetings and the pub gossip following them. The Clann won two of the seats; I went to the celebratory party, there to be thanked by Sean MacBride, who had won his Dublin seat by a massive margin, for the publicity the Diary had given.

This prompted an idea. The Clann's success was the measure of the flatness of the political scene; as I was being scathing about that, in and out of print, I should try to do something about it from the inside. The encounter with some of MacBride's republican henchmen at the party celebration, however, had put me off the Clann. When I discussed the subject with one of the *Irish Times* reporters, Michael McInerney, a disillusioned Communist, he suggested that some of us should ease our way into the Irish Labour Party by offering to help in the production of its weekly, the *Irish People*, edited by Peggy Rushton. I knew her slightly; her genial husband Desmond, as well as being a Palace regular, had extorted admiration for his skill at sliding puffs for the films which the cinema he managed was about to show into the *Irish Times*. Peggy arranged a meeting with William Norton, the complacent, fat (he was known as 'Puffing Billy') leader of the Labour Party, 'young Jim' Larkin – son of the celebrated trade union orator-leader – and Roddy Connolly, son of the Labour leader executed in 1916. We would revamp the *Irish People*, we promised, and turn it into an effective propaganda-conveyor in the General Election which de Valera, stung by the by-election defeats, had decided to hold in the new year of 1948.

Ruth's refusal to have anything more to do with me, however, had prompted more than the decision to forget sorrow in political activity. The Diary was at last going well; I had developed a more personal formula which was making it easier to write and – I gathered from Alan Montgomery, not given ordinarily to paying compliments – less boring to read. But, what then? The threat still hung over me of a spell as a sub editor, when Smyllie decided it was time for a change.

I had read somewhere about the forthcoming termination of the British Government's Forces Grant scheme, established to help individuals whose careers had been interrupted by their war service, to make up the ground they had lost. There was just time to post off an application for a grant to resume my academic career, by taking a Ph.D. at Trinity. The reply was curtly discouraging. I had worked on the *Irish Times* at the beginning of the war, and returned to the *Irish Times* at the end of it. How could my academic career have been interrupted?

In the course of the round of Legation parties I had often met Reggie Ross Williamson, a friendly soul who was the Press Officer in the British High Commissioner's Office, where he had succeeded John Betjeman (he had a book of John's poems, inscribed by him with a reference to Joan Hunter-Dunn 'whom we both loved'). When we next met, I told him what had happened. I had gone the wrong way about it, he said. I should have claimed that my *journalistic* career had been interrupted. Warming to it, he drafted an impressive-sounding letter explaining that while I had been heroically at the controls of my Sunderland, young whipper-snappers had joined the *Irish Times* and moved into secure positions ahead of me. A Ph.D. from Trinity would offer a chance to redress the balance. I did not keep the reply, but its tone, I remember, suggested that somebody had been amused by the switch, and had relented. Provided that the Ministry received satisfactory progress reports, I would receive a year's grant payable in three instalments, £60, £60 and – mysteriously – £55 19s 1d.

It remained to persuade T. W. Moody, Professor of Modern History at Trinity, to take me on. This proved difficult. I had only achieved a second at Oxford; I was a journalist; what was I up to? But the proposition which Reggie and I had presented to the Ministry – research into the history of the press in Ireland – interested him. There was only one historian, he knew, in the same field, and he had been labouring there for decades without ever showing any sign of publishing his findings. Theo agreed to be my supervisor for a year, at the end of which I would aspire to a B.Litt. Only if the material I presented then was sufficiently acceptable would he allow me to re-fashion it, after another year, for a Ph.D.

As one of the regulations in connection with the grant was that full-time employment must cease, I told Smyllie that I would be leaving the staff after the general election. He was less annoyed than I had feared; at least it was not to take up another newspaper job. He realised, too, that there was something in the case Reggie had made to the Ministry. Jack White, who had joined the *Irish Times* during the war, was being tipped as the next editor, and being groomed for it, we believed, by a spell in the London office. Bruce Williamson, who had been at Shrewsbury after I had left, was now the paper's literary editor and film critic. In hierarchical terms, I had fallen behind. In any case, I could continue writing for the paper – 'pups', in particular, Smyllie assured me, would be welcome.

The reporters' room resources were stretched during the campaign; the Diary's role was to provide additional colour pieces, in particular to follow MacBride on what his supporters hoped would be a triumphal tour. MacBride had 'a gaunt, cadaverous appearance', as Noel Browne was to recall in his autobiography. 'His rare smile was a momentary muscular response, as used by a well-mannered diplomat; it did not infuse a sense of warmth, nor was it ever completely reassuring.' In the course of this election campaign, it constantly reminded me of Peel's smile, described by Dan O'Connell as like the silver plate on a coffin. MacBride, too, was a wretchedly poor speaker, with an unattractive accent he had retained from his upbringing in France. Although crowds came to hear him, he could not stir much enthusiasm. The Clann was clearly not going to sweep the country.

It was, though, attracting votes away from the other parties in Dublin. In the hours spared from the Diary I canvassed in Dublin South-East for Eleanor Butler, the Labour candidate. As a respected member of one of the oldest Catholic families in Ireland, she was able to attract speakers to her meetings who would not ordinarily have thought of supporting Labour; at one, where she had asked me to speak, the others on the platform were the authors Robert Collis and Terence de Vere White; the Earl of Wicklow, who was soon to make Eleanor his Countess; and Louie Bennett who, though she had devoted her life to setting up and running the Women Workers' Union in Ireland, came of old Ascendancy stock. It was a strange team for the occasion; but all of us, including Eleanor, knew that she had no chance of attracting the workers' vote in the constituency. Those who were prepared to abandon their loyalty to Fianna Fail and Fine Gael were likely to give their First Preference votes to Noel Browne, the youngest and most impressive of the Clann's candidates in the election.

As a schoolboy, Noel had been adopted by the Chance family; I had occasionally met him at dances in the Phoney War period when he was a medical student. Later he had contracted TB and, appalled by the conditions he had found as a patient, had decided to dedicate his career to remedying them. He hoped that the Clann would provide the political clout he would need; the Clann was happy to exploit the reputation he had already made by his campaigning.

Canvassing, I found that the well-to-do element in the constituency had also been impressed by this unusual candidate. He swept in on the first count, to take one of the three seats and join the nine other Clann T.D. – six of them from Dublin constituencies; the results from outside the capital had been disappointing for the Clann. Still, the opposition parties mustered just enough seats between them to enable them, after some energetic wheeling and dealing, to vote de Valera out of office and form a government, with John A. Costello as Taoiseach and Norton as his second-in-command. The *Irish People*, Norton decided, had served his purpose. It should make way for what, it was planned, would be a bigger and better Labour newspaper.

The pause was welcome. It would give me more time to indulge in that most addictive of obsessions: historical research in an area which had remained unexplored, or at least had not been exposed in published form. I would try to justify G. N. Clark's verdict after my History Finals viva; I would become a historian.

12

Researcher

The shake-up in my life was taken a further stage when Alan Lywood, whom I had seen from time to time since the Killadeas period, told me of a firm who wanted to sell caravans in Ireland: would I like to have one, live in it, and attract custom? I mentioned my uncertainty whether to accept in a letter to my mother, which elicited a typical exasperated comment from my father. He had been appointed head of the Wallingford Research station, but was fuming over the delays in getting it ready. My letter, he wrote, 'only confirms what has long been my opinion that people only consult you either in the hope that you will agree with them, so that they can quote you against somebody who holds other ideas, or in the hope that you will agree with them that something they know is rather foolish, isn't perhaps so foolish after all.'

I had given various reasons why moving into a caravan might be a good idea; 'another experience of mine,' he went on, 'is that if one has a sound proposal, only one reason is required. Giving several reasons nearly always shows a weakness being bolstered.' Clearly he thought the idea foolish, but 'after all, you are 33.' I would accept the caravan offer, I decided. I managed to persuade the owner of a building site in South Dublin to let me live on it; and though I failed to sell even one caravan, it compelled me to learn to cook.

The forces grant was soon spent, but leaders, 'pups' and the occasional book review helped to keep me solvent. I also became Pro-Quidnunc, again, when Tony Gray, who had taken it on, was on holiday; and later, when he moved to a new venture, the *Times*

Pictorial, stood in for his successor, Seamus Kelly. Better still, when Seamus was away I inherited his duties as theatre critic.

Not that the Dublin theatre was in a healthy condition. At the Gate, MacLiammoir was becoming a parody of himself, continuing to play juvenile leads when into his fifties; and although the Longford company, which shared the theatre, had some fine actors – notably John Welsh, who was later to have several meaty parts in the West End and on television, and Blake Gifford, a wonderfully decadent Burgoyne in *The Devil's Disciple* – the standard of productions was erratic.

The most melancholy aspect of the Dublin theatre, though, was the Abbey. Ernest Blythe's determination to keep the Irish language as his priority kept out actors who would otherwise have maintained some of its former standards, difficult though this would have been in view of Hollywood's attractions. Sarah Allgood, Maire O'Neill, Barry Fitzgerald, Dudley Digges, and J. M. Kerrigan had been lured away, between the wars. The only actor of stature who remained was F. J. McCormick: Seumas Shields in the *Shadow of a Gunman*, Joxer in *Juno and the Paycock*, and Fitzgerald's successor as Fluther in *The Plough and the Stars*.

McCormick was a revelation. One of the characteristics of the Abbey casts under their first producers, Frank and Willie Fay, was stillness. 'As a rule they stand stock-still. The speaker of the moment is the only one who is allowed a little gesture,' A. B. Walkey noted in *The Times* on their first London visit: 'When they do move it is without premeditation, even with a little natural clumsiness, as of people who are not conscious of being stared at in public.' He could have been describing McCormick. He held us with 'the authority of absolute repose' – a snatch of one of Christopher Hassall's poems which recollection of McCormick, particularly in *The Shadow of a Gunman*, brings to mind.

Unluckily the only film part he accepted was as a stage Irishman in *The Third Man*; funny though he was, the part gave hardly a hint of his greatness on the stage. For Denis Johnston, a shrewd critic who wrote and directed plays both at the Gate and the Abbey, McCormick was the greatest actor he had ever seen. He was also the most self-effacing. Recalling him is a constant recipe for irritation in London theatres, with the constant movement dictated by directors for movement's sake, to prevent a scene looking static.

Two years followed of burrowing among the old newspapers in the National Library. Such absorption could be fatal to the chance of ever presenting a completed work – as it was in the case of Francis O'Kelley, who had amassed an impressive collection of card-indexed material about old Irish newspapers without being able to commit himself to preparing a book from it. But I had to satisfy Moody that it was worth my spending the second year on the subject, to move on from B.Litt. to Ph.D.; and then to provide a full length thesis which would satisfy not only him but an examiner from some British university. The temptation to pursue trails leading away from the main theme had to be resisted.

One of them, though, proved irresistible. The indignation aroused ten years earlier by the realisation of the responsibility of British governments for the Famine of 1845 was now revived, by the discovery of the ways in which they had systematically controlled the Irish newspapers in the period I was dealing with, from 1770 to the 1840s. This was partly by corruption – payments to proprietors and editors: partly by repression – putting journalists on rigged trials for seditious libel, as criticisms of the government were assumed to be by the judges who tried the cases, as well as by the government lawyers who brought them. And as the chief sufferers were journalists in the period leading up to the rebellion of 1798, there was the excuse to study its origins and development, and the careers of the participants, in particular those who had grown up into the Protestant Ascendancy.

Lord Edward Fitzgerald, Wolfe Tone and Robert Emmet had been little more than names to me. I had not even known that Lord Edward had served in the British army during the American War of Independence, or that Wolfe Tone had tried to get a job from William Pitt in the embryo British colonial service. Lord Edward's conversion to Irish nationalism, and eventually to acceptance of the need for a rising, appeared entirely understandable in the light of the information that research disclosed about the corruption not only of the press, but also of the judiciary. Promotion to the Bench and to the higher levels of the Irish peerage could be obtained by finding for the prosecution and passing sentences in cases which the Castle – the English-controlled executive in Ireland – wanted a guilty verdict. The harsh lesson of the 1790s was that reforms could not have been achieved by constitutional means.

Tone's motives were more equivocal. His republicanism arose initially out of frustration at his inability to impress the authorities in London. Still, it was impossible not to warm to him, reading the journal that he kept in Paris when he was trying to persuade the French to send an expedition to Ireland:

> Feb. 29th 1796. I have now six days before me, and nothing to do: huzza! Dine every day at Beauvilliers for about half-a-crown, including a bottle of choice Burgundy which I finish regularly . . . A bottle of Burgundy is too much, and I resolve every morning regularly to drink but the half; and every evening regularly I break my resolution . . .

Tone was still a national hero in Ireland, as were Lord Edward, Emmet, Thomas Davis and Charles Stewart Parnell, all from the Protestant Ascendancy. No Catholic, not even Dan O'Connell, was held in so much esteem as they were. Ought it not to be possible, then, for a defector from the Ascendancy to become accepted as a nationalist in the mid-twentieth century?

The meetings of the Dublin South-East branch of the Irish Labour Party were discouraging. Most of the active members during the campaign had been Ascendancy defectors, too. Still, the Party was now in office, with a share of power; might it not be possible to stir things up, at larger party meetings? And to attract recruits through the medium of the new journal, which was in the planning stage? We would need a banner to fight under. Fortunately one was ready to hand: James Connolly's legacy, to be found in his *Labour in Irish History*, and his other works. Connolly had the requisite nationalist qualifications, as one of the Easter Week martyrs: Marxist interpretation of events, too, presented a clear picture of the way in which nationalism had been corrupted by capitalism in the past; and by extension, showed how it was still being corrupted.

I had come across Arthur Koestler's *Darkness at Noon* in Gibraltar, and read it long into the night, realising that it provided an explanation for the otherwise baffling treason trials of the 1930s, the pact with Hitler, and the invasion of Finland. Russia had ceased to be communist in Marx's sense; it had become a Stalinist dictatorship. Surely, though, that fate could have been averted? It was impossible to think of Connolly as an embryo Stalin. He was not even, as Larkin had been, a demagogue. Connolly's oratory, Cathal O'Shannon – a former Palace regular who was still to be found in the Pearl – recalled, 'aroused enthusiasm of the more lasting kind, a quiet, enduring enthusiasm which forced the hearer to act on Connolly's side rather than cheer.' Surely Connolly's brand of socialism, with its human face, could be our oriflamme?

It very soon became clear that the leaders of the Labour Party, when they attended our meetings, regarded even the mention of Connolly's name with deep suspicion. Socialism, too, was a dirty word. The Party's main support lay among farm labourers, in those constituencies where the farms were large enough to employ labour, and they tended still to accept unquestioningly the authority of the Church. To the Church, Marx was anathema. Norton and the others were determined not to allow their supporters to be alarmed by mavericks in the city. The successor to the *Irish People*, when it appeared, was scrupulously anodyne. Very soon, it disappeared.

Still, absorption with the thesis and with Labour Party affairs had done much to take my mind off Ruth, and the fact she had gone to study on the Continent made her absence easier to bear. At least she was not at home, with some other lover. And at this point serendipity led me to Proust. I had read some of *Remembrance of Things Past* at Oxford, but had been advised by Michael Jefferson not to start at the beginning, which at the time was sensible (he was gently to remind me, when I had written to him saying that he must read *Darkness at Noon*, that he had recommended it to me a couple of years before). This time I started on 'Swann in Love', and it hit like a blow in the solar plexus. Here was Swann, behaving in just the same childish ways I had behaved with Ruth, when he found himself out of favour with Odette, trying out the same ruses to restore himself to favour, blaming her if they failed . . . So it was not love, after all; it was the loss of possession which had been responsible for the torment, the sighs. I would write to Ruth, and show I understood her feelings, and her reaction.

To the surprise of both of us, it worked. We went to the Dordogne, hired bicycles, took the sun, swam, and visited what have since become show places, such as the caves with their wall paintings at Lascaux. It was August, yet we met hardly any other tourists; the currency allowance of £30-worth of francs had been a deterrent. It lasted us for over three weeks. Some of the hotels charged only the equivalent of two shillings a night; meals were similarly inexpensive, and always included the local wine. It was delightful. Yet at the end of it, we both knew it was the peaceful end of the affair.

From the caravan I moved up into a cottage above Ticknock on the mountainside – the hills to the south of Dublin are always given the courtesy title of mountains – overlooking Dublin, there to complete and polish the thesis. Fortunately for me, it went to Asa Briggs as external examiner. Though he made some criticisms he passed it without demanding any changes.

To become a Doctor of Philosophy was unlikely to meet the specifications laid down by the donors of the Forces Grant on the basis of Ross Williamson's recommendation, that it would restore my position in the journalistic world, set back by the years in the forces. In the *Irish Times* it was chiefly a source of amusement; would I begin to style myself 'Dr'? And if so, wouldn't I be in request to treat people for their pimples and their piles? But by a stroke of good fortune the editors of *Irish Historical Studies* had negotiated a contract with Faber and Faber to publish a series, 'Studies in Irish History'; the thesis was chosen as one of them. It was to attract little notice, apart from a friendly review from Conor Cruise O'Brien; but it later prompted Faber to ask me to contribute to another series they were running of the histories of a number of countries. A published Ph.D. thesis hardly counts as a real book – Castaneda's *Teachings of Don Juan* being a remarkable exception – but *The Story of Ireland* turned out to be a launching pad.

13

The Leader

When the delivery of the thesis meant that I was free again to resume journalism as a full-time occupation, Conor suggested I should take a temporary job with the Irish News Agency. It had been set up by Sean MacBride to try to ensure that the Irish case – chiefly, the case for a reunited Ireland – received more attention abroad. It was formally to begin its operations in the summer of 1950, Conor – who was supervising it – told me, by covering the proceedings at the first full meeting of the Council of Europe. One of Fleet Street's most travelled and seasoned foreign correspondents would be in charge; I would be his assistant.

O'Dowd Gallagher was a legendary Fleet Street figure. He had been in Madrid when it was being shelled by the Franco forces; on a warship which was torpedoed by the Japanese in the Pacific; in Jerusalem covering the activities of Irgun Zwei Leumi (his reports marking him out for assassination; the bullets had missed). He also could claim to be the original of Corker in Waugh's *Scoop*. When he realised my limitations, even before we reached Strasbourg, he took to calling me 'Mr Boot'.

Admirable and entertaining mentor though O'Dowd was, he was as much as out of his element in the hack work of a news agency as I was. He was looking for scoops and scandals, where none existed which would have been worth reporting. He felt badly let down, too, by MacBride, who had complained the evening after his arrival in Strasbourg that since we had not been there to interview him, he had had to accept an invitation to be interviewed by a representative of one of the American news agencies. O'Dowd had been pre-occupied with setting up the INA communications system, which ought not to have been his job; he was understandably angry when a telephone call from Dublin admonished him. We both felt that MacBride might at least have complained to us, first. For me the episode bred a mistrust – soon to be increased by his slippery political manoeuvrings – which survived all his climb to international fame, and to a Nobel Prize.

The meeting had attracted many of the leading European politicians, some then in office, some in opposition: Churchill and Bevin from England, Schuman and Bidault from France, Spaak from Belgium, von Brentano from Germany. Both MacBride – who happened to be, by rota, Chairman of the Council of Ministers –and de Valera thought that this was to be their great opportunity to put Ireland's case where it would have to be heard. Both of them botched the opportunity.

MacBride chose to speak in French, which not only irritated everybody who was not French but also irritated the French; they found both his use of the language and his accent excruciating. De Valera's plea for the reunification of Ireland met with a stony reception, less for any lack of sympathy than because the over-whelming desire of most of those present – apart from Bevin, who looked ill (as it turned out, he had not long to live) and clearly was bored by the proceedings – was to set up the machinery to bring about European unity. The main controversy was on whether it should be achieved 'federally' or 'functionally' – still in dispute, thirty years later. The feeling was that the Irish issue, however important to the Irish, was irrelevant. Our report of the debate in which de Valera spoke, incidentally toppling the microphone with a spirited left hook, and the reactions, appeared on the front page of the *Irish Times* the next morning. But it was the only Irish News Agency story to be given any prominence. Irish newspaper editors had disliked the idea of the INA, and in general boycotted its copy.

Unintentionally, O'Dowd did me a good turn. Climbing up into my press seat, I found an American girl sitting in his, which he had offered her. She was a postgraduate student working in London University; and she was to become the ideal antidote to lingering nostalgia for Ruth. When O'Dowd returned to, as he had thought, his capture, he found we had flown.

*

That autumn, somebody showed me an article in a fortnightly magazine published in Dublin, the *Leader*, which referred to me in passing as a 'left-wing socialist'. Although it was true that I was on the left of the Irish Labour Party, which stood well to the right of Labour in Britain, the attribution surprised me. The article was unsigned, but Val Iremonger, I knew, wrote for the *Leader* occasionally; and he suggested a meeting with the writer, Desmond Williams, Professor of Modern History at University College.

At one time the *Reader's Digest* used to run a series of pieces about the most unforgettable characters the writers had ever met. For me, it would be Desmond. At first encounter he was unprepossessing: overweight, with a limp from childhood osteomyelitis, a squint and a sprinkling of cigarette ash over his jacket from chain smoking – he would light his next cigarette from the droop of the one he had not yet finished. But in conversation he quickly came across as sympathetic, as well as highly intelligent.

It struck me he was remarkably young to have been elevated to a university Chair – he was still in his twenties when we met; but a study of his career as a student showed how it had come about. At UCD students took 'subject combinations' for their Finals; Desmond had obtained a first in four of them. He had gone on to win more firsts, reading for the Bar; then, in 1944, he had decided to return to history as a postgraduate student at Peterhouse, Cambridge, where Herbert Butterfield – a Fellow of the College and Professor of Modern History at the University – was to describe him as the ablest and most promising student he personally had encountered. Together with Michael Oakeshott, Desmond had founded the *Cambridge Journal*. He would have been given a Fellowship at Peterhouse had he not been involved with Colin Welch in an elaborate practical joke played upon a member of the College staff who was hated, but who had sufficient influence to block the appointment. Instead, he had come back to the UCD Chair.

Brilliant students often make poor teachers; Desmond was the exception. Both as a lecturer and at the tutorials and seminars which he introduced, he was to captivate generations of students. Every meeting with him, I was soon to find, turned into a kind of seminar; he was expert at probing for weaknesses in an argument on all subjects, particularly politics. In his youth he had been a fervent admirer of Hitler; secondment from Peterhouse to the Allied Commission, set up at the end of the war to edit the German Foreign Ministry's documents, had changed his views about Nazism but not about socialism. He was an adept, though, at concealing his own opinions, preferring a Socratic approach, so that the particular maverick brand of Toryism which later became identified with the 'Peterhouse Mafia' and their associates in journalism – Colin Welch, George Gale, Peregrine Worsthorne – and which Desmond and Michael Oakeshott had done so much to instil, rarely surfaced on the Saturday evenings which he and I spent at the Unicorn restaurant with his friend Patrick Lynch, a civil servant in the Department of the Taoiseach, later to be Professor of Economics and Chairman of Aer Lingus.

To the best of my recollection Desmond never failed to turn up for these dinners, which was astonishing. He was notoriously incapable of keeping appointments, as everybody who knew him could testify; frequently because he had made two at the same time – or even more. Tim Pat Coogan, editor of the *Irish Press*, has recalled arriving to have dinner with him at the Stephen's Green Club, to hear him on the telephone explaining to somebody that he could not turn up to dinner with them as he found he had another engagement. Flattered, Tim Pat greeted him as he came out of the telephone booth, only to see from Desmond's crestfallen face that the other engagement was not, in fact, with him.

There was no question of Desmond going to the most important or useful function, socially or academically. He once refused to answer repeated calls to the club where he was dining from the wife to whom he was briefly married – only to find afterwards that they were to tell him that, without telling her, he had invited the head of UCD and his wife to dinner, and they had arrived. Not surprisingly, the marriage did not last. Nevertheless Desmond continued to exercise a remarkable attraction for women. At any party, whether in London or in Dublin, he would always have two or three of them, usually the most attractive ones, around his chair. After one party which I gave for him later in London, two young actresses rang me to say how fascinating they had found him, and how they were looking forward to meeting him the next day in the Ritz bar – his favourite London hang-out. Desmond had asked them separately, it turned out, but both for the same time. I could not resist appearing to see his face when he arrived.

As I should have guessed, he did not arrive. I was left to give the two of them lunch.

Paddy Lynch was the perfect foil. He shared many of my left-wing opinions, though as a civil servant he had to take care not to profess them publicly. He had the ability to work in harmony with both governments, de Valera's and Costello's, and behind the scenes, as well as occasionally in front of them, he was to become one of the most influential figures in Ireland in the transitional period in the 1960s, when the retirement of de Valera made it possible to introduce the policies which were to transform the Republic – as it had become, under Costello.

In 1951, Costello's inter-party government fell, brought down by the dissensions over the Mother and Child Bill. Noel Browne, as Health Minister, had introduced it to provide free maternity services, without a means test. The medical profession prepared to oppose it as strenuously as their fellow doctors in Britain had opposed Bevan's measure; but they were not called upon to fight. The Catholic hierarchy sent a letter to Costello telling him the Bill was contrary to Catholic moral teaching; Costello withdrew his support; and when MacBride, too, ratted, Browne resigned.

14

Dail Eireann and T.C.D.

I had been working on, and moving into, a derelict cottage, a former
gate lodge with no bathroom and no jakes, even, in Dundrum, to the
south of Dublin; earning just enough to live on by spending
afternoons in the National Library in pursuit of the early history of
Guinness, which Paddy Lynch was preparing, and evenings in the
Irish Times, writing leaders. The resignation of Noel Browne
transformed the political scene. Smyllie, shocked at the discovery
that Costello had given way to the Catholic hierarchy, and disgusted
at MacBride's readiness to ditch Browne in order to cling to office,
wrote a powerful leader, *Contra Mundum*, and asked me to write a
Dail diary while the crisis lasted. It did not last long. The inter-party
government tried to restore itself to favour by bringing in a gentle
budget, but then went to the country.

Labour's role in the Mother and Child affair had also been craven;
I had no urge to canvass for the party. In any case, Smyllie sent me
round the country to do election specials. One tour was to be around
the West, bringing in Connemara; and for this I offered a lift to the
correspondents of *The Times* and the *Manchester Guardian*, who
happened to be in the Pearl talking to Smyllie the night before.

A. P. Ryan of *The Times* was an academic by inclination, I judged;
he had written a sober history of the Curragh mutiny in 1914, and
reporting was not his bent. He remained reserved throughout the
trip; we never quite knew what he was thinking. Gerard Fay of the
Manchester Guardian was in his element. The son of Frank Fay, the
Abbey's first producer – director, as the species are now called – had
grown up in England, but he retained an Irish manner, and his

features were of a shape and colour that cannot be described except by saying that they singled him out as Irish in any gathering.

On the way down to Connemara from Dublin I had come to observe certain rituals: a pause at the top of the rise where the Twelve Pins first come into view; another at the bridge in Galway, to look at the salmon below waiting to move up into Lough Corrib, when the weir permits. To this, as I grew older, had been added a visit to Lenihan's Bar, reputed to have the best wine, port and sherry in Ireland. When we went in, we were greeted by Lord Glenavy; to my astonishment, a man transformed.

Paddy Campbell in his autobiography described his father's expression as morose. I had occasionally seen him in Dublin, and in his home, and had never seen any but a lugubrious look on his face. In Lenihan's he was alight with fun and mischief. The reason was immediately obvious: an attractive woman at his side. Paddy, I was later to find, was also fascinated by her. She lived somewhere near Galway and on one occasion, when he had been knocked out of the West of Ireland Golf Championship at Rosses Point, he had sought to console himself by driving down to see her. Not wanting to arouse the household he had thrown pebbles up at her bedroom window. When it opened, it was his father's head that popped out.

Hilariously funny though Paddy could be when the mood was on him, in Lenihan's he could not have competed successfully with his father. Years later I was to conjure up a fantasy in which I would present a TV programme with Paddy and Dave Allen as the guests; I would tell the audience, 'The two funniest men I have ever met . . .' before turning to them and saying 'were your two fathers' – Dave's being Pussy O'Mahony. There could not have been a better start to our election tour; even Ryan softened, and Gerard was entranced. As things turned out, the entertaining time we had together was to prove invaluable for me. When I was next in London I began to join the group from the London office of the *Manchester Guardian* which assembled at lunchtime and in the evening at the Clachan off Fleet Street; among them Iain Hamilton, a Scot with a keen interest in all matters Irish. Three years later, when a job vacancy occurred at the *Spectator*, it was to be Gerard who suggested me, and Iain who took me on.

*

The outcome of the election was the annihilation of Clann na Poblachta. MacBride just retained his seat, along with one obscure member of his party; three others who were returned had left the Clann to become Independents. Although the Clann survived for a time, it was never to recover; I thought it safe to label MacBride as the Grey Subsidence of Irish politics – as politically he was, and remained, though he was to bounce back into international eminence in his old age. Fianna Fail increased its representation, but not by enough to provide de Valera with an overall majority; he would have to depend on the support of some Independents to survive. Smyllie, who had liked the Dail Diary during the Mother and Child affair, decided to revive it in the form Paddy Campbell had adopted fifteen years before, and asked me to take it on.

The seating in the debating chamber of the Dail is in the form of a semi-circle, facing the Speaker, with the government ministers and deputies on his left, the Opposition on his right. The press gallery is immediately above the Speaker. Convention dictated that as a sketch writer, rather than a Dail reporter, I should sit on the extreme right of the row of seats in the gallery; and on the first day of the new session, that autumn, a newcomer joined me, introducing himself as Jim McGuinness from the *Irish Press*. Before long we were adjourning to the Dail bar whenever debates began to become tedious, which was often, and helping each other out if something happened worth reporting when one of us was not there.

Jim had been in England in 1939 as a member of the IRA, preparing the explosives which were to be put in letter boxes in the course of that brief and botched campaign to rouse the English to recognise the justice of the republican cause. That the campaign was singularly repulsive, as well as disastrously misguided, was a view widely shared in Ireland as well as in England; my mind's eye picture of a typical IRA man of that period was a fanatical hoodlum devoid of any moral scruple. Yet here was Jim, eminently sensible. It was impossible to visualise him as an accessory to such an ugly form of indiscriminate murder.

He had become a fanatical republican as a Catholic boy growing up in Protestant-dominated Ulster in the between-the-wars period; and because he had looked too young and innocent to be suspected, he was thought to be all the more useful to the IRA when the letter-box campaign was launched. But he was quickly caught and, as he was just old enough to have received a life sentence, lucky to escape it; one of the jurors had taken pity on him and blocked the verdict of guilty.

Deported back to Ireland, Jim had managed to get a labouring job on Bord na Mona, in the period when the need to win turf from the massive peat bogs of central Ireland by machinery was most urgent. There, he had attracted the attention of Todd Andrews, who had managed to obtain what almost amounted to a free hand to run the company, and who faced fearsome labour problems, stirred up by the politically ambitious Sean Dunne, founder of the Federation of Rural Workers and, I was to find – by the 1950s Dunne had gained a seat in the Dail – one of the more unsavoury deputies. Todd needed people at all levels in the company whom he felt he could trust; Jim had been one of them. His recommendation had helped Jim, when the Emergency was over, to find a job on de Valera's newspaper; he had made an immediate impression there by his reporting from London; and the editor, Bill Sweetman, had decided to give him the chance to become more familiar with the leading political figures in Dublin by seeing and listening to them in the debates and drinking with them in the bar.

This was not, as it happened, my first intimation that menacing die-hard republicans might turn out to be reasonable, likeable people. In the weeks when I was working as a reporter at the beginning of the war, I had come to regard sub-editors as the natural enemies not just of reporters, but of good reporting. Only one of those in the *Irish Times* subs' room had ever had a good word to say about my copy: Larry de Lacy, who had gone out of his way to tell me he liked the story of the dire effects of the milk strike on the animals in the Dublin Zoo. I had exempted him, as did the other reporters, from our detestation of subs as a species. So I was astonished, returning on one of the RAF's leaves, to hear that he had been a leading figure in the IRA at the time, and the brother-in-law of Stephen Hayes, the republican Chief of Staff.

Larry's IRA connection had been exposed when he had featured, though at one remove, in one of the strangest episodes in its history. In 1941 the respectable residents of Rathmines had been astonished to see a barefoot man staggering down the main street loaded in chains, with a rope round his neck. Clearly in a state of near collapse, he had managed to stagger as far as the local police station, where he explained that he had been held a prisoner for weeks, and periodically beaten up, before he had contrived to escape. He gave his name, Stephen Hayes, and his occupation, 'Chief of Staff of the IRA'.

It had become obvious within the IRA that there were informers at, or near, the highest level. All its plans were going awry, and its members were being picked up by detectives every time they attempted to stage some act of sabotage in Ulster. Suspicion had fallen on Hayes and de Lacy; the IRA's Adjutant General and some colleagues had decided to arrest them, and they had been hoping to beat a confession out of them. Hayes's escape led to the arrest of the Adjutant General and to Larry's release, to become the respected editor of the *Drogheda Argus* (where for a time one of his employees was Dave Allen).

Jim McGuinness introduced me to his former boss, Todd Andrews. Todd had been just too young to have been 'out' with the rebels in 1916; he had joined the IRA soon afterwards and fought on under de Valera in the civil war that followed the 1921 Treaty. His success in building up Bord na Mona into a major industrial enterprise had won general respect, and even popularity, in a country starved of coal during the Emergency; but his next job, running the state transport corporation Coras Iompir Eireann, had left him with the kind of reputation that Richard Beeching was soon to acquire in Britain, as a ruthless butcher of the railway system. With the development of road transport, Todd had realised there was no alternative except bankruptcy; but his decision to close down the small suburban line running out from Harcourt Street in Dublin through the stockbroker belt of Foxrock and Carrickmines and on south to Bray, though it seemed justified at the time – stockbrokers had their cars – was to turn sour when suburban development restored the potential traffic the line had lacked.

Of all the older republican generation, I found Todd the most impressive and the most engaging. He was one of the best-read individuals I have ever encountered, in the literature of America, Europe and Britain as well as of Ireland; and he managed to keep abreast of current affairs the world over. J. K. Galbraith, whom he admired (and who was one of few acquaintances who could give him a centimeter or two in height: Todd stood over six foot three), once ruefully observed to Paddy Lynch, who had introduced them, 'Todd makes me feel like a provincial.' Not that he flaunted his erudition; after I had left to work in London I would find on my visits to Dublin that he had a more complete knowledge and shrewder appreciation of the British political scene than I could claim.

Yet Todd had remained a republican, to the extent of continuing to maintain that Ireland must be reunited. He would even have approved the use of force in that cause, if he had thought there was the remotest prospect of its succeeding. As things were, he despised most of his contemporaries in politics, de Valera always excepted. Yet listening to him, in his home in Dundrum or his cottage in Connemara, it was impossible to think of him as having anything to do with physical violence of any kind – or even verbal violence, caustic though he could be about those he mistrusted, such as Sean MacBride. My admiration for him was to grow with each meeting, as the years went by.

There was one other former IRA man I came to know in this period: Brendan Behan. In *Borstal Boy* he was to describe how he, like Jim McGuinness, had been picked up by the police while he was engaged in manufacturing the explosives which would be put in letter-boxes; but as he was sixteen, he could not be sent to jail. His recollection of the arrest rings true. 'How would you like to see a woman cut in two by a plate glass window?' one of his captors asked. Brendan would have liked to answer him with 'Bloody Sunday, when the Black and Tans attacked a football crowd in our street; the massacre at Cork; Balbriggan; Amritsar; the RAF raids on Indian villages. I had them all off, and was expecting something like this.' But when the sergeant broke in, in reasonable tones, Brendan decided to keep his mouth shut.

Brendan became a house painter, very ready to exchange badinage with anybody in the street below, though it was rash to do so except when safely out of range of a flick of the brush. I met him through Ruth Childers's brother Rory, a medical student at the time, who was to achieve an early reputation by diagnosing Brendan's diabetes from the smell of his breath in Davy Byrne's. He was persuaded to go into the Baggot Street Hospital, where he stayed for a while before suddenly discharging himself on the ground that he knew of a better treatment; he would go to the Gaeltacht, the Irish-speaking district of Connemara, and take the cure there: draught Guinness. To the chagrin of his doctors, it worked.

Brendan wrote surprisingly delicate poems in Irish – surprising because he had already acquired a reputation as a boozer, though not, as yet, as a drunk. He was uncommonly good company on the occasions we met, though they were few, as his pub circuit was different from mine; the circuit lovingly yet disturbingly evoked in John Ryan's *Remembering How We Stood* and in Anthony Cronin's *Dead as Doornails*. Ryan ran *Envoy*, a literary monthly which provided a lifeline for many impecunious Dublin writers: I do not recall that we ever met, but he published the one and only short story I have ever written.

Cronin – years later to be cultural adviser to Charlie Haughey; at that time, an impoverished member of the literati – was one of the handful of members of the Dublin South-East Branch of the Irish Labour Party who attended branch meetings. Afterwards we would adjourn to the local pub; but I knew nothing of the life he was leading in, and literally below, McDaid's, a step away from Grafton Street. The rooms which lay beneath the pub, originally a kitchen, pantry, wine cellar and such, had become the haven for those who its patrons who found themselves able to pay for stout, but not for digs: 'the Catacombs', whose existence was revealed to the readers of *The Ginger Man*, and which subsequently came to enjoy the reputation of having been a den of vice – a charge Cronin dismisses: most of what went on there was 'ordinary social boozing'.

Behan and Cronin took to each other from their first meeting, and remained close until the drink began to destroy Behan; Cronin's portrait of him is sympathetic and, from my recollection of both stages, entirely life-like. The early Behan was an original, endlessly funny while throwing out serious ideas; genially Rabelaisian. *Borstal Boy*, though, is the only written work which catches the flavour. The plays which later brought him fame in London (and the income which corroded him) were Behan at one remove, filtered through the needs of a script for the actors to learn.

I saw more of the other main character in Cronin's gallery, the poet Patrick Kavanagh, because he was on the fringes of Dublin journalism in his capacity as a contributor to the *Irish Press* and film critic of the *Standard*, Dublin's Catholic weekly. He was already accepted – in Ireland, though not yet in England – *as* a poet, quite distinct from the numerous tribe of aspiring poets whose contributions might be accepted by newspapers and magazines but would never be seen between hard covers. He still rates three pages in Larkin's *Oxford Book of Twentieth-Century English Verse* – though no entry in *Chamber's Biographical Dictionary*, where Behan gets a couple of inches, which would have infuriated Kavanagh.

The Great Hunger had established Kavanagh's reputation. As a farm labourer, a peasant bard, he had been welcomed in the Palace Bar, where for a while he enjoyed being shown off to visitors, and showing off himself as the inspired bog-trotter. Cronin recalls finding him, at their first meeting, 'a deeply serious man with an intellect which was humorous and agile, as well as being profoundly and apparently incorruptible'. 'Apparently' hits the mark. Kavanagh believed himself to be sea-green; but he longed for appreciation, and indeed adultation, and would readily barter some measure of incorruptibility to obtain it. He was indeed intellectually humorous and agile; but he liked to apply both qualities to bolster his own ego. I recall one small example: a party in connection with a visit to Dublin by Laurence Olivier. Kavanagh had formally applied to interview him on the Tuesday, only to be put off at the last moment to the Thursday, when it would be too late for that week's column. 'Do you know what I told him?' Kavanagh told us, with a mischievous grin: 'I *never* interview people on Thursdays!'

Gradually Kavanagh's black humour began to turn, in the early 1950s, to paranoia. Eventually he took an action for libel against *The Leader*, following the publication of a snide but accurate profile of him which it had printed. He was sure it had been written either by Desmond Williams or by Val Iremonger, or perhaps both; with the help, doubtless, of Behan. Cronin, who realises now that the action was a disastrous mistake – I doubt he did at the time – attributes it to Kavanagh's appetite for martyrdom, but admits Kavanagh dreamed of taking *The Leader* for heavy damages, which would solve his financial problems. Unluckily for this ambition, he came up against Costello, by this time Leader of the Opposition in the Dail and consequently released to resume his career at the Bar. Kavanagh hoped to appear to the jury as a wronged, impoverished writer; Costello contrived to reveal him as a boozer who preferred other people to pay for his drinks.

The decisive moment came when Costello casually asked Kavanagh whether he was a friend of Behan's – Behan, by this time, having become notorious for his drinking. Kavanagh let out a diatribe against Behan, not hesitating to give vent to his loathing. The next day, Costello was able to produce a copy of Kavanagh's *Tarry Flynn* with, inside it, 'To my friend Brendan Behan on the day he painted my flat.' The jury found for *The Leader*: they probably would have, anyway, but the evidence of Kavanagh's lying, as it must have appeared to them, settled the issue. On a point of law, the Supreme Court ordered a retrial, but neither *The Leader* nor Kavanagh could afford to continue the case. *The Leader*, which had been in existence for half a century, had to cease publication; Kavanagh shortly afterwards was diagnosed as suffering from cancer. He lived on in receipt of a small stipend as a lecturer in University College, but chronic alcoholism soon gripped him.

For a year, the job of writing the Dail sketch was satisfying enough; on occasion, entertaining. There was only one Deputy who could be described as an orator, James Dillon. At his best, and he quite often was at his best, he had a notable Churchillian line of rhetoric and a style of delivery unmatched, I was to find when I attended debates at Westminster, by any English politician. Dillon had been the only Deputy to advocate Ireland's entry into the war on the side of the Allies, which had abstracted him from his party, Fine Gael; otherwise he, rather than Costello, would certainly have led it, as eventually he did.

Otherwise the level of debate was disappointing. Of those who had broken away from the Clann, Noel Browne was infrequently heard; but Captain Peadar Cowan would occasionally appear as a one-man opposition, from his own standpoint of extreme republicanism – he was engaged in drilling a private army to invade the North. Although it was not taken seriously, he contrived to look suitably sinister, relaxing, in my recollection, only once. Irritated by one of the government ministers, Cowan intervened at the end of an altercation between the government and opposition benches – he sat between them – to ask if it was in order to call a Deputy a sewer rat. The Chairman said he had not heard the words, but certainly they would not be in order. Cowan gravely thanked him: 'the sewer rats will be grateful for that ruling.'

At the same time, during the mornings, I was doing some work for Moody in Trinity, taking seminars; and on evenings when the Dail was not sitting, taking a small class of trade unionists – a spin-off from my Labour Party efforts – in elementary economics, which meant keeping one day ahead of them. Hearing of this Professor Joseph Johnson wrote to ask if I would lecture first year Trinity students in Economic Organisation, which would take me into the Senior Common Room.

Looking back, I can see it would not have been difficult to have embarked on an academic career, as Trinity was soon to enter a period of rapid expansion. The History Faculty, too, was congenial, with Moody, R. B. McDowell – the prototype of a university professor even in his student days, with precautionary overcoat, scarf and hat, it seemed, even in mid-summer – and the future Provost, F. S. L. Lyons. (Initials, at that time, were almost obligatory in academic circles. In the common room, I once heard a junior lecturer in history say of a man who broke the convention, using his Christian name over an article, 'Why, anybody would think he was a journalist!') But the old Trinity hierarchy in those days was stuffy, hardly changed from the days of Tyrrell and Mahaffy but lacking their character. The common room turned out to be depressing, largely because those who would have made it more congenial tended to stay away. I saw more of Con Leventhal, the friend of James Joyce and Sam Beckett, in the Pearl than I did in college. I liked having the Trinity connection, but had no thought of making it more permanent.

Of all the Trinity lecturers at the time the one I most admired was the Reader in French, Owen Sheehy-Skeffington, son of the pacifist who had been murdered by a crazed British officer in 1916. A socialist, Owen had been thrown out of the Irish Labour Party for preaching Socialism, which naturally endeared him to me; and I began to see more of him when a friend of his, the Dublin solicitor Christo Gore-Grimes, founded the Irish Association of Civil Liberty, roping me in to become the Hon. Secretary. It had Moody, Lord Killanin and Sean O'Faolain among its vice-Presidents; Killanin was working in London, but Christo, Owen and Sean were around for entertaining informal gatherings, as well as formal committee meetings.

Christo had the reputation of being a hard man, as a solicitor; he proved an agreeably easy man on a jaunt we took by car across the Continent to see Italy for the first time. With Owen I collaborated in campaigns in the correspondence columns of the *Irish Times* –

Smyllie raised no objection to members of his staff contributing letters – on civil liberty issues; Owen had the ability to rouse people whose attitudes and views he mistrusted to frenzy by wonderfully delicate rapier strokes of his pen. Sean, for me, became a kind of guru, though he would have disclaimed any such role. His *Bird Alone* had been banned by the Irish Censorship Board in the 1930s, and he might easily have taken himself off into lucrative exile – American universities competed to get him. But he had stayed to found and edit *The Bell*, a literary magazine to which many of the leading Irish writers of the time contributed, from unknowns such as the young Behan to the internationally famous Frank O'Connor. I still had the urge to write, to become an author rather than simply a journalist; Sean encouraged the ambition, listening, criticising and advising with saintly patience.

I could not help realising, though, that in this company I was aligning myself with individuals who were considered to be hostile to the cause of an Irish Ireland, critical as we all were of the Church and the politicians over the Mother and Child Bill, the Censorship, and the anti-Partition campaign. And whereas the others could be regarded as Irish mavericks, my background put me in a different category: I was a West Briton.

In its original usage, the term had corresponded to 'North Briton' among the Scots. 'If given a real, not just a nominal, role in the Empire,' Dan O'Connell had once claimed, 'we are ready to become a kind of West Briton, if made so in benefits and in justice; but if not, we are Irishmen again.' By the 1950s, however, it was not a term which any of us would have used about ourselves, in the sense that some Unionist Scots still called themselves, or at least regarded themselves, as North Britons. It was used only contemptuously, as on hoardings at the time which carried posters

I AM A WEST BRITON
I READ THE BRITISH PRESS

There was nothing to stop me continuing to play the part expected of a West Briton, but it was not what I had hoped to do. It galled me when I committed gaffes of the 'Westm'l'nd Street' type. The Dail commentaries had led to my being given a slot by Radio Eireann to do a Dail sketch, and this in turn had led on to my taking over as chairman of an 'Any Questions' programme: in it I pronounced the name of a village in County Limerick, Athea, as if it rhymed with 'faithier' instead of 'Cathay'. Only now, too, did I realise that I had been continuing to say 'Roman Catholics', though they had for years dropped the 'Roman'. For all I knew, I might be giving offence in other ways without being aware of it. To outward appearances I was a successful journalist, with Trinity providing a useful second string; but I was becoming uneasy, dissatisfied, when an invitation arrived to visit Stuart McClean, Managing Director of Associated News-papers, Lord Rothermere's chain.

McClean had decided to buy Kemsley's *Daily Graphic*, a tabloid, to try to make it a serious rival to the successful *Daily Mirror*. During the war the *Graphic* had survived only because any newspaper with an established ration of newsprint could sell almost all copies; but it was always the last to be found on news stands, bought only in desperation. McClean knew he could pick it up cheaply, and thought he could see how to pick sales up, too, by making it different. Fleet Street, he had decided, was too inbred. What was needed was an infusion of talent from the provinces; and he despatched a memorandum for circulation throughout the Rothermere empire, asking for suitable candidates to be proposed.

He had no newspaper in Ireland, but working on the management side of one in Scotland there was Bobby Childers, Ruth's uncle, who had heard Ruth extolling my abilities. He had put my name forward. In the course of the interview, when I came to meet McClean, he thrust open a file of the *Irish Times*, to check that I was not trying to con him. It happened to open at a Saturday. In it, that morning, I had a leader, a book review and a feature. Without even consulting his editor-designate, McClean told me I could join the renamed *Daily Sketch* as its leader writer, for more than Smyllie was being paid as editor of the *Irish Times*, and with guaranteed expenses higher than the salaries junior reporters of the *Irish Times* were getting at their NUJ rate. But I would have to come at once, before the end of May.

This, I told him regretfully, was not possible. I had to finish my course of lectures at Trinity. That took him aback; he had gone to Trinity himself, it turned out, though he had not taken a degree. The recollection seemed to mellow him: I could stay until mid-June, by which time the Trinity term would have ended, but I must not disclose what I would be doing until he had a chance to tell his new editor, who was on holiday. This suited me: I would have been embarrassed to tell Smyllie it was the *Daily Sketch* I was about to join.

There followed the predictable farewell parties. Any sorrow that I felt about leaving was more than compensated for by the prospect of a regular pay packet, assured expenses and – perhaps the strongest lure, for a freelance journalist – a month's paid holiday annually. I could reassure myself that the new *Sketch* would be very different from the *Graphic*; it would provide valuable experience, and perhaps a toehold in Fleet Street. And if it did not work out, I could return . . .

Just as I was about to leave, I received a characteristic straight-faced letter from Smyllie:

> Dear Dr Inglis:
>
> Since you abandoned your career in the Royal Air Force and contrived by some means unknown to me to acquire a doctorate in Trinity, I have noticed that your value to the Irish Times has been diminishing steadily.
>
> Furthermore, you have gathered around yourself a large number of shady characters, who hardly are in keeping with the type of company that is expected to be kept by members of this staff.
>
> I have decided, therefore, to ask you to accept in lieu of notice, a week's salary, which I have instructed the cashier to place at your disposal . . .
>
> Yours fflly
>
> R. M. Smyllie

The 'shady characters' referred to were Christo and Owen, who, he pretended to complain, were endangering the *Irish Times* with their controversial views – which he had been delighted to encourage. Curious about the 'week's salary', I asked the cashier about it when I went to say goodbye. Smyllie had told him to remind me that as of my own choice I had opted to remain a freelance, I had no salary. Smyllie and I had an affectionate farewell session in the Pearl; I was not to see him again.

15

Fleet Street; and the Freelance Life

> You are joining the editorial staff of the Daily Sketch as a
> leader writer, special feature writer and understudy for
> Candidus. Your salary will be at the rate of £30 per week
> and in addition we will pay you £7.10s per week to cover
> all your day to day expenses in or around the London
> area . . .

In his letter setting out the terms of my appointment, McClean
made it clear that I would be there on approval – 'I hope that in
coming to this decision you are aware of the personal risk involved.'
One obvious risk was that the editor, Herbert Clapp, was on holiday
and would not be told who was to be his new leaderwriter, special
feature writer and understudy for Candidus until he returned. (Nor
was he to know who the new Candidus would be; but, as it happened,
none of the possibles accepted the offer to take on the *Sketch*'s
column, which was left unfilled.) I was relieved to get a friendly letter
from Clapp, welcoming me; and to find at the first daily conference
which I attended that he was a mild, unobtrusive figure, quite unlike
my mental picture of a Fleet Street editor. He appeared slightly
shocked when one of the conference team suggested that the ideal
front page of the paper would include an old man and a pair of tits.

I was relieved, too, that the atmosphere was friendly. I was looked
on not as a dangerous outsider, but as a country cousin who might
need to be helped to learn rough Fleet Street ways. Another of the
team shoved a note into my hand, as we left, warning me not to kick
anybody in the face on my way up the ladder; I might encounter him

again on the way down. At the far side of the table where I was to work, there was Jim Pettigrew; he had not returned to the *Irish Times* after his wartime service in the Fleet Air Arm, and was now more relaxed, and much more Oirish, than I remembered. And the woman's editor was Edna McKenna, from Malahide . . .

I had hardly settled in, though, than a Palace revolution ousted Clapp, replacing him with with Herbert Gunn ('Glad to hear you have got rid of your Clap,' a message came from Conor Cruise O'Brien; 'Sorry you have contracted Gon'). Gunn, who looked like a slightly decayed Roman Emperor, was from the Beaverbrook stable. His recollections of the old man were compounded of admiration and exasperation; there was still, he claimed, a mark on an office wall which would commemorate his departure when he had thrown an inkwell – ink was still occasionally to be found on Fleet Street desks – at Beaverbrook's portrait. He had despised the Rothermere papers; now, he transferred his loyalty to the *Sketch*, convinced that he could make it not just a good paper, but a great one.

Each day's *Sketch* – each day's successive editions, even – Gunn examined as a gardener looks each morning at the flowers he plans to exhibit in some show, hoping to carry off all the prizes. It did not cross his mind that the campaigns he waged under the slogan 'THE SKETCH SAYS . . .' were mildly ridiculous, not so much in the causes they espoused, which were usually sensible, as in his conviction that they would be influential. People in pubs all over the country, he really believed, would be drawing each others' attention to them; civil servants would be pointing them out to their minister. The *Sketch* said (among other series I wrote) that the government must give the railways more money, and the Navy, less (it was trying to keep up appearances; even pretending that the last of the battleships, the *Vanguard*, was battleworthy, when it was barely seaworthy). But the way the arguments were put in single-sentence paragraphs, some in italics, some in bold print, some underlined as if such variations were the only way to hold the readers' attention, trivialised them.

Only one of the *Sketch*'s sporadic campaigns made any impact, and it was not of the kind Gunn hoped for. A young soldier had been found guilty of cowardice in the face of the enemy during the Korean war. 'To every son's mother', the *Sketch* said, 'suppose it was *your* boy'. This, we were told, had caught the eye of the Chief Justice,

Lord Goddard, then beginning on a campaign of his own to bring Fleet Street to heel. The *Sketch* received a writ for contempt, on the ground that the editorial had been published before sentence had been promulgated. As it happened, the newspapers had earlier been allowed to comment in such circumstances, on the ground that it was only juries who might be swayed by what they read in the press; but Goddard brushed this argument aside. He even tried to have Lord Rothermere, rather than Gunn, in the dock, but allowed himself to be persuaded that this would be too massive a breach with the tradition of editorial responsibility. Gunn was made to feel he was lucky not to be jailed; as it was, the *Sketch* got away with a fine.

It was disconcerting, for a while, to be producing what Smyllie called lapidary crap – ephemeral pontifications, presented as if carved on stone. But at least Gunn was genuinely concerned – as O'Dowd Gallagher confirmed. He had retired to a haven in the Channel Islands, but had heard from some friend in Dublin of my move. 'The Sketch!' he wrote: 'Jesus, Mr Boot, I am perplexed!' Gunn at one time had been his boss, in the *Express*. 'He is a newspaperman's editor. He knows all the answers. He is a good guy, too. Has a strong sense of justice and looks after his staff if they look after him,' O'Dowd recalled. 'Very sound cove and good company, though might strike the casual observer as being somewhat austere of countenance. You'd be that way if you'd been as long in Fleet Street.'

It turned out to be a just assessment; Gunn proved to be a congenial boss. There was some good company, too, particularly Simon Wardell, son of Beaverbrook's managing director. 'There were only two good William Hickey's out of the twenty-three,' Arthur Christiansen was to recall of the *Express* column founded by Tom Driberg: Tom and Simon. He lived at the Cavendish, still run by Rosa Lewis in the fashion that Waugh had encountered in the 1930s, and described in *Vile Bodies*. She still rooked guests who looked as if they could afford it, allowing Simon to stay – or so he claimed – and to take advantage of the frequent champagne parties, without payment, whenever he could not afford to pay, which seemed to be much of the time; not surprisingly, as he spent many evenings in night clubs. He had a notable variety of illnesses as excuses for not coming in to the office; almost always, hangovers were the actual reason, but Gunn liked his copy so much when it appeared that he accepted his absences philosophically.

I had two merits in Gunn's eyes; one being that years of writing leaders and 'pups' on the *Irish Times*, different though they were in style, had taught me how to churn out the required material at speed. Competing, Bruce Williamson and I had cut the time for 500-word 'pups' down to twenty minutes. Gunn's experience with leader writers had led him to assume they would labour over their deathless prose, while he waited impatiently. The other was that he liked to have somebody he could tap on the shoulder when he set out for the pub at lunchtime; somebody who would not bother him with office politics. We got on well. But I had assured Desmond Williams before I left Dublin that I was going to the *Sketch* for the experience; that I would only stay for a year. Before it was up I wrote formally to Gunn explaining that when he had a replacement, I would be on my way.

He found it difficult to understand why I should defect, though not for the same reason as Smyllie. Smyllie felt that as he had seen us through our journalistic apprenticeships, we should not skive off for higher salaries until we had repaid the *Irish Times* for what it had done for us. Gunn could not understand why anybody who had a job on the *Sketch* should want to leave, when it was so obviously the up-and-coming newspaper. I can still see him shaking his head sadly when he heard that Ken Tynan, who was briefly the *Sketch*'s theatre critic, had accepted David Astor's offer to move to the *Observer*. It just did not occur to Gunn that the couple of hundred words into which Ken had to compress his reviews would be exchanged for a thousand, or more, and that this alone would explain the decision. Still less would Gunn have thought of the *Observer* as more prestigious.

I mollified Gunn by telling him how much I had enjoyed working with him, and how much I had learned; and also by assuring him I was not moving to the *Observer*, or anywhere else. I had in fact been invited by the great Arthur Christiansen to join the *Daily Express* as leader writer; but the prospect of being a mouthpiece for Beaverbrook's opinions repelled me. Could I join as a feature writer? Christiansen pondered, then mercifully refused. There were a dozen or more feature writers on the *Express*, some established Fleet Street names, yet often they would go for weeks without seeing even one of their stories in the paper. He would not condemn me, he said, to that depressing existence. It was not long before I was to thank him, when we met on a television programme, more fervently than I have ordinarily thanked people for offering me work.

For a time, though, a tinge of regret remained. 'To have worked in Fleet Street without working for Lord Beaverbrook is like having been in the forces without seeing action,' I commented later in a review of Christiansen's *Headlines All My Life*. 'One would not have liked it, and one might not have survived it; but without it, the sense of inadequacy lingers which used to plague Scott Fitzgerald, because his draft never went to Europe.'

The reason I had decided to leave, I told Gunn, was 'to write some deathless prose' (the term must have been common facetious currency at the time, in the office) in the form of a novel. It was not just an excuse. A couple of years earlier I had booked in for a stay in a *pension* near Menton, intending to write it there, only to find myself at the next table to a bunch from Fleet Street who were not fooled by the pad and pencil I laid beside me to stake a claim to be a writer, rather than a newspaperman (newspapermen despised pads). They brought me in to some celebration in the bar, where one of the girls provided an impromptu cabaret turn with 'Violate me in violet time'. What with the beach by day and the bar by night, the novel proceeded only fitfully.

One episode during that holiday, though, stuck in my mind. An English family living in a nearby villa used to come to the beach: the father, a Cockney who had made a fortune during the war supplying some need to the American forces; the mother, quiet and reserved; the daughter, a seventeen-year-old picture of classical innocence, a nymph, in the sea a mermaid. I used to go to the beach early and one morning, to my surprise, the girl's mother joined me and poured out her worry.

The money her husband had made, she told me, had decided them to move out of London into the country, where her daughter – Ondine, as we at the *pension* had decided she should be called – had been to a good local school, and then to a finishing school some distance away from home, to which she went each day by bus. One morning a large, blowsy woman appeared at the front door and told Ondine's mother that if she did not remove her daughter, there would be hell to pay. Remove? From where? From the local baths, the woman told her. Ondine had not been going to the finishing school; she had been stopping off at the baths, where she had seduced the woman's husband, the swimming instructor. Appalled at the revelation, Ondine's parents had whisked her away to the South of France.

At the time I thought the story would fit neatly enough into the projected novel, which, I had decided, would be based on a villa on the Riviera (as it was then usually called) to which the 'I', the narrator, would be invited as an old friend of the owner. When I actually got on with the novel, the following summer, the mix did not work; perhaps because the actual Ondine was more real to me than my cast of invented characters, making them look contrived. But during the winter I was on the *Sketch*, actuality pushed the novel in a new direction which prompted me to finish it.

Alan Wood was working in London; his wife Joan, an actress, took me to see a friend of hers, Rosemary Harris, in a play. Rosemary, Joan told me, had been a nurse who had done some spear-carrying – or whatever the women's equivalent is – in her spare time; gradually she had become hooked, working her way into rep, where Joan had met her, and eventually saving up enough to go to RADA. There, the judges of the Bancroft Gold Medal – they included Sybil Thorndike, John Mills and John Gielgud – had unhesitatingly awarded it to her for her performance in *The Heiress*; and one of the perks of that victory was a contract from H. M. Tennent, with the prospect of a West End role. As a result, she was playing the lead in *The Seven Year Itch*.

We took Rosemary out after the performance. In Dublin, critics and performers mixed freely, sometimes all too freely; a hotel bar just opposite the Gate, in particular, attracted our custom because its proprietor seemed to be able to ignore the licensing laws with impunity, the assumption being that he devoted some of the profits to helping the Fianna Fail party. I had no romantic notions about the stage, knowing that off it, actors were ordinary people; but it was precisely Rosemary's ordinariness that was attractive. She had grown up in Sussex in a village which was clearly an English version of Malahide (though uncomplicated by any religious divisions) in a family which had simple habits and tastes. Garlic was for them, as it had been for me, what French porters chewed, with revolting consequences; when she brought her young nephew round for lunch he was astonished to be offered spaghetti of the kind he had to wind around his fork, unlike the bits which he was used to from a tin.

Rosemary made her own clothes and displayed none of the mannerisms which successful actresses accumulate, except perhaps her reluctance to be separated from her affectionate but unpredictable dachshund Pinky. She was also a shrewd, though charitable, judge of people's performances, off-stage as well as on. She had a flat in Soho; I had had the luck to rent half of the actor Basil Radford's flat, after his death, across Regent Street in Old Burlington Street, five minutes away. We settled in, for a while, to a delightfully easy relationship.

It proved to be too easy. I was enjoying life in Fleet Street, with frequent pub sessions, and evenings in night clubs with Simon – or Gunn, who enjoyed night life. Towards the end of my time in Dublin the company had been predominantly male, but in London with a film contract there was Noelle Middleton, whose father owned the rights to the salmon fishing at Ballysadare in County Sligo; I had met her there when a few of us went over from Killadeas to try our luck in the pool, where the salmon waited for floodwater to allow them to swim upstream to spawn. And there were other girls, encountered with Simon. It did not occur to me that Rosemary might grow tired of my casual assumption that she would be around whenever I wanted her to be. When I woke up to the realisation – or rather, stayed awake to it – that the familiar footsteps on the rickety stairs leading to the flat were no longer being heard, it was too late. The sighs were as painful as they had been over Ruth.

I would work it out of my system, I decided, in the novel, which would present an 'I' in the same mould. Peter du Sautoy of Faber – who had just published my Ph.D. thesis as *The Freedom of the Press in Ireland*, thanks to funding provided through the Irish Historical Society – looked at it when it was finished and decided it was not quite good enough. Iain Hamilton, whose judgment I trusted, read it and told me I was too close to its theme for the reader's comfort. I should put it aside and come back to it later. I put it aside, with less angst than I have felt for some rejected articles.

Iain had heard about the novel because, by this time, I was working for him on the *Spectator*. Job-hunting after my return to London, I had tried the *Times*; Casey, unfortunately, had retired, and the deputy editor, Donald Tyerman, was unimpressed. I seemed unable to stay in any job for long, he commented. At the *Observer* David Astor was friendlier; in fact he left me with the curious impression that I had been interviewing him, to find whether he would be a suitable employer. But he had no job to offer. The obvious editor to approach would have been A. P. Wadsworth of the *Manchester Guardian*, as I had written for it in Dublin on occasion; but there was no chance of joining the London Office, Gerard Fay warned, without an apprenticeship in Manchester, which I did not fancy. But Jenny Naismith, who had been on the *Spectator*'s staff, was leaving to have a baby. In those days employers were not expected, let alone compelled, to provide paid maternity leave, or even to hold the job open; and Gerard suggested me as a replacement. A lunchtime exploratory session at a local pub with Iain and his friend and colleague Tony Hartley went satisfactorily, and I came in as an assistant editor.

16

The Spectator

The office at 99 Gower Street had once been somebody's town house; but behind it, where the garden had been, a two-storey pier had been built out in order to accommodate visitors. 'Within these now impeccable walls', according to Wilson Harris in his *Life So Far*,

> an adventuress of dubious, but mainly American, origin (for all that she claimed to be the extra-matrimonial offspring of the mad King Ludwig of Bavaria and the Spanish dancer Lola Montez), styled a little incongruously Angel Anna, conducted, with the aid of the husband of the moment and young girls attracted by various specious advertisements, operations commonly associated with angels of sombre hue.

It was a brothel until Angel Anna was prosecuted – by Sir Edward Carson, the Solicitor General – and put away for seven years.

The cubicles in the pier were tiny, even for a brothel's requirements; Peter Fleming, who had worked in one of them in the 1930s, surmised that they might have been designed 'either as oubliettes for very minor poets or as ferret-hutches for very large ferrets' – fanciful, he admitted, but not unfair. I was to have one of them, the others being occupied by Tony Hartley, John Scott the literary editor, Henry Fairlie the political correspondent, an office boy and the secretary, Joan Bayliss. The atmosphere was friendly, though a touch unsettled, owing to a minor power struggle in the main part of the building.

It had arisen after the sacking of Wilson Harris, in 1953. He had been editor for twenty years, and had doubled the *Spectator*'s circulation to just over 40,000; but its proprietors, Sir Evelyn Wrench and Sir Angus Watson, had decided it could do even better under a younger man. They had left Harris's deputy, Walter Taplin, in charge while they looked for one; settling for T. E. Utley, who joined the staff with the assurance that the succession would soon be his. Soon afterwards, however, they had received an offer from Ian Gilmour to buy the *Spectator*, which they had decided to accept.

Taplin had succeeded in making it less stuffy, more readable. Scott had brought in to his stable of reviewers some young novelists and poets who became collectively known as 'the Movement', among them Kingsley Amis, John Wain and Robert Conquest. The Labour MP J. P. W. Mallalieu (I had been taken with the rest of the Dragon rugger team to watch him, an Old Dragon, play for Oxford against Cambridge) contributed a perceptive weekly article on sport in general. Peter Fleming wrote the Notebook, signing himself 'Strix' (pseudonyms were still fashionable; he once explained why he chose to hide behind the ornithological name of a screech owl, but I have forgotten); and there were two other weekly columns, Compton Mackenzie's 'Sidelight' and John Betjeman's 'City and Suburban'. It was quite an impressive team; circulation had continued to rise; and Taplin could have expected to be confirmed in office by the new proprietor. But he was out of luck.

Gilmour had been a barrister with few briefs, and had not cared for the inactivity. He had no intention of sitting back in the conventional proprietorial role; the *Spectator* was to be the outlet for his energy. A clash was unavoidable, and Taplin, who held strong views on editors' rights and responsibilities, soon left. Gilmour found himself in a difficult position. With no journalistic experience he could not edit the journal, nor did he wish to. He needed an editor with whom he would be sufficiently in tune for a successful collaboration.

Utley's pronounced Tory views would have made such collabora-tion difficult. Gilmour had no party political affiliations, and he appeared more in sympathy with Labour, or at least with that element of the party which his friend Roy Jenkins represented, than with the Government. In any case, the fact that Utley was blind effectively ruled him out, as Gilmour needed an editor who would see, and oversee, the production side. And he had one to hand:

Taplin's deputy, Iain Hamilton. Hamilton, it was decided, would be editor; Gilmour, on the model of Lord Hartwell of the *Daily Telegraph*, editor-in-chief. For a weekly, however, this sounded too inflated. Gilmour became nominal editor; Hamilton, associate editor.

Right at the start, I had a stroke of luck. A 'Front' review which John Scott had been promised failed to materialise. He had given me a Sir Charles Petrie's biography of Lord Liverpool, to try me out with a small review. I offered to expand it to Front length, there and then. This was not difficult: Liverpool had played a significant role, during his long premiership, in the events which I had dealt with in my thesis. True, he had been in the background; but as the man responsible for appointing the Irish administration for almost fifteen years he bore a load of responsibility for the unscrupulous treatment meted out to the Irish newspaper owners and editors by Wellington, Peel and other Chief Secretaries in Dublin. I would have found it difficult to confine him to a paragraph or two: to produce a workmanlike 'Front' took no trouble and very little time, to Scott's obvious relief – and probably Gilmour's. Hamilton's friends were of remarkable diversity, and some were more at home in a pub than in an office; showing an ability to act as long-stop in emergency must have helped to secure my position.

For Hamilton, too, having another ally in the power struggle with Utley, which continued, was welcome. Utley had not relinquished his ambition to edit the *Spectator*; he had some reason to feel hard done by, but he could hardly blame Gilmour, and he believed that his contacts in the higher ranks of the government could be used as a lever to establish himself on a footing independent of Hamilton. To Hamilton's indignation, he commissioned articles on his own which, however unwelcome, Gilmour felt could not be rejected.

Eventually, though, Utley overreached himself. When in 1955 Churchill retired and Eden decided to go to the country, Utley announced proudly that he had lined up the Foreign Secretary, the Chancellor of the Exchequer, and the Minister of Supply to provide Tory manifestoes. Hamilton had already made his own arrangements, avoiding the bigshots and relying on politicians who could be relied upon to write their own readable version of their party's case, rather than have it written for them – David Ormsby Gore (the future ambassador to the United States) for the Conservatives,

Jo Grimond (not yet leader of the Party) for the Liberals; Kenneth Robinson (later to be Health Minister under Wilson) for Labour. The need also to find space for Macmillan, Butler and Maudling meant that the *Spectator* for a couple of weeks appeared committedly and boringly Tory.

Under Wilson Harris it had been conservative only with a small 'c', independent of the party, as the Trust which had been set up to preserve its identity required. A new proprietor had to satisfy the Trustees that he was not going to try to make the *Spectator* the servant of any party; and Gilmour had pledged himself to preserve that tradition. Although the editorial preceding the election was balanced, he felt embarrassed. Hamilton felt let down, and the rest of us were on his side. Utley was made to understand that he had gone too far. Realising that there was going to be no chance of achieving his ambition, he decided to leave.

This was lucky for me, as it further consolidated my position in the office; and that summer yet another piece of good fortune came my way. In Dublin Ruth had often spoken of the glamorous Lesley, a friend of the family. On a visit to America, she had met John Huston; he had told her at their first meeting they would marry, which they did, and they had lived in Los Angeles during the war. After it, when the marriage split up, she had moved to Cagnes, on the Côte d'Azur. I had not met her until Rory Childers, back in London pursuing his medical career, brought her round to Old Burlington Street. It turned out that by this time she was again living in America, and her house in France was empty – surely a great pity, she told us. If any of us wanted a holiday, she would let Freda know; Freda would arrange for Monsieur Chenivesse's taxi to collect us from Montelimar and bring us to Alba, ten miles away; and Freda could be on the bridge waiting with the keys.

Alba, Lesley explained, was a village which had almost died, after the war, when the demand for silk slumped and the grapes produced barely drinkable wine. A group of artists, driven from Cagnes by the arriving tourists, had found they could buy dilapidated houses in Alba for little more than the cost of the deeds. Lesley had followed them there, found a house which she modernised with a terrace and a bathroom, both unknown in the village. Freda and Pat, young artists, had joined them from London. I fantasised Freda, sitting on the bridge, as beautiful; so she turned out to be. It was an idyllic holiday, banishing the sighs for Rosemary. Alba was to become, and has remained, the place where I have gone contentedly year after year, as often as finances and work have allowed.

For the next few months the combination of Ian Gilmour and Iain Hamilton – to avoid confusion, I shall stick to their surnames – worked well. Hamilton was effectively editor – deciding, for example, what should go into the *Spectator* each week. Gilmour began to learn the trade, coming out on Wednesday evenings to the printers at Aldershot to see the paper to bed; and he turned out to have a forceful polemical style. In particular he wrote devastating exposures of the conduct of the police and the prosecution in the case which led to the conviction of Lord Montagu of Beaulieu; and he turned the *Spectator* into one of the most vigorous backers of the campaign for the abolition of capital punishment, which it helped to launch, lashing the Home Secretary for his craven decision not to reprieve Ruth Ellis, the last woman to be hanged in Britain.

The article was the more effective because Gilmour contrived to make the whole ugly process, from the donning of the judge's black cap to the actual execution, ludicrous as well as macabre by bringing in such telling details as that when the Home Secretary, feeling the need for reassurance from his chief adviser in the Home Office, asked for him to be summoned, the summons reached him over the loudspeakers at Ascot. The Lord Chancellor, Gilmour recalled, had claimed that in Britain an innocent man could be hanged only if jury, judges, the Court of Criminal Appeal and the Home Secretary went mad. Could this be the explanation for the hanging of the wretched Evans for the Rillington Place murders, for which it had become obvious that Christie was responsible?

That the *Spectator* was gaining a new class of admirers began to become clear from the correspondence we attracted, and from a typically eccentric letter I had from Erskine Childers – temporarily out of office, as the Inter-Party government had returned to power:

> Dear Brian
> I have had an astonishing letter from Raymond Chandler, who I presume is the author of the lowest type of detective fiction, in which he wishes to write for the Spectator a detailed account of my father's execution . . .

> Has he ever indulged in decent respectable literature, as
> the Spectator does not seem to me to be his line at all?

To have attracted Raymond Chandler as a contributor would indeed
have been a coup; but it was not to be.

The *Spectator*'s greatest asset, though, at this time was its new
political correspondent, Henry Fairlie. As a colleague, Henry was
maddening. He had a remarkable attraction for girls, coupled with
difficulty in arranging his schedule, so that they were forever ringing
up to find where he was, and why he wasn't where he said he would
be to meet them. His copy tended to arrive long after it was
promised; he boasted that he had never missed a deadline, but our
Wednesday evenings were plagued by his near-misses. He was
infuriatingly elusive, his telephone at home either remaining un-
answered or, more commonly, off the hook. Yet he had that charm,
second only in my experience to Desmond Williams's, which made it
impossible to be angry with him when he eventually showed up at the
office – often needing to borrow a pound or two to finance his evening
out (it was still possible for two to fare quite reasonably on two quid)
and came out for a drink with us at the Marlborough Arms.

Henry had enviable qualities as a political correspondent: a
historical sense; hunch; and the ability to write interestingly about
political matters which were not in themselves of much interest. And
occasionally, he would produce a devastating broadside, as in his
onslaught on the handling of the Burgess and Maclean affair. The
government was producing a White Paper on their defection four
years earlier. Shrewdly, Henry used the excuse that as it would be
published just too late for the *Spectator* to comment on it that week,
he could not deal with its details, but he could deal with the
implications; in particular, that the Establishment was more powerful in Britain than it had ever been.

He had used the term before, casually; now, he defined it:

> By the 'Establishment' I do not mean only the centres of
> official power – though they are certainly part of it – but
> rather the whole matrix of official and social relations
> within which power is exercised. The exercise of power in
> Britain (more specifically, in England) cannot be under-
> stood unless it is recognised that it is exercised socially.

Anyone who has at any point been close to the exercise of power will know what I mean when I say that the 'Establishment' can be seen at work in the activities of not only the Prime Minister, the Archbishop of Canterbury and the Earl Marshal, but of such lesser mortals as the chairman of the Arts Council, the Director-General of the BBC, and even the editor of the *Times Literary Supplement*, not to mention divinities like Lady Violet Bonham Carter.

The 'Establishment' had been employed in this sense earlier, among others by A. J. P. Taylor; but it was this Political Commentary which brought the concept into common usage. The choice of some of his examples was curious – perhaps deliberately so, to arouse curiosity; although the Archbishop had indeed been near the centre of power in the 1930s, by this time his influence had waned. But one jibe, in particular, stung those who clearly had been close to the centre. 'No one whose job it was to be interested in the Burgess–Maclean affair from the very beginning will forget the subtle but powerful pressures which were brought to bear by those who belonged to the same stratum as the two missing men;' how effective those pressures had been 'may be traced in the columns of the more respectable newspapers of the time, especially of *The Times* and the *Observer*'.

Not surprisingly, the Establishment erupted in protest in the *Spectator*'s correspondence columns: the editor of the *Observer*, David Astor; the Warden of All Souls, John Sparrow; and, among others, Lady Violet Bonham Carter herself. The critics of the Establishment entered the fray: Robert Boothby, Colm Brogan and Malcolm Muggeridge. People in libraries and clubs who had regarded the *Spectator* as soporific were woken up to the fact that it was now beginning to mount a challenge to the *New Statesman* as the journal to be picked up first. Doubtless more people began buying it, too; but this was offset by the losses as its predominantly elderly readership died or cancelled their subscriptions out of dislike of the new courses which it was taking.

From the point of view of the older generation of *Spectator* readers, worse was to follow when, in the autumn of 1956, the Eden government launched the Suez campaign. On major issues the

Spectator could have been expected to support the government. This, we assumed, was what most of our readers would expect. But as it happened 'we' in this instance consisted of Gilmour and myself. Fairlie had just left, understandably, for a far better-paid job in Fleet Street (neglecting to warn us of his departure). Although Charles Curran, later to be Conservative MP for Uxbridge, was writing the political commentaries, he was not on the staff. Iain Hamilton had been offered a job in Hutchinson the publishers, which he had decided to take; he had never been happy about being denied the editorship, when to all intents he was the editor. And Tony Hartley, who was looking after the Foreign Affairs side, was out of reach on a Mediterranean culture cruise. Gilmour and I had to decide what should be done.

We did not want to make too violent a breach through the shock to the *Spectator*'s readers – in my recollection, Gilmour urged caution; he thinks I did – but we were in entire agreement that the nationalisation of the Suez canal did not deserve to be met with a declaration of war, and that the story about British forces going in 'to separate the combatants', Israel and Egypt, was manifestly dishonest. There was no alternative, we decided, but to call the invasion a grievous mistake.

Any excuses we could think of to include, we included. 'The original unworthy suspicion can now be banished,' we innocently claimed: 'the belief, widespread in other countries – and even here – that the ultimatum to Egypt was a product of Anglo–French–Israeli collusion.' But even the humiliating outcome when the campaign collapsed owing to the threat of bankruptcy, and the Canal remained firmly closed, did nothing to stem the shoals of letters from indignant subscribers, many of them intimating they would subscribe no longer.

17

What the Papers Say

My personal memories of the Suez crisis are less of the problems it confronted us with in Gower Street than of an evening in Manchester. On 5 November, a new television programme was scheduled to go out on the Independent Television network, *What the Papers Say*, and I was presenting it.

A year before, commercial television (as it was then usually described) had started up in London. Aidan Crawley, in charge of Independent Television News, had decided that he wanted newscasters – as distinct from news readers on the BBC model; they were to write as well as read their scripts. His producer, James Bredin, invited a number of journalists, few of whom had television experience, to come to a studio and deliver a short news bulletin, followed by an interview with one of the other journalists, to see if any of us were suitable. The quality was – for me, as one of the hopefuls – painfully high. Henry Fairlie seemed made for the job: attractive, fluent, authoritative. Christopher Chataway, who had become the world record holder at 5000 metres the year before, was also impressive, as was Ludovic Kennedy, who had an air of more academic distinction than the rest of us, and whom we looked on with some awe for capturing Moira Shearer as his bride. The others ranged from the experienced *Sunday Times* man, Cyril Ray, to a briefless barrister, Robin Day, who, I thought, was out of his depth.

I stumbled through my news bulletin, trying desperately to remember what I had composed – we were told to look direct at the camera throughout; and although the interview went better, it was obvious that I would not even make the short list. It included Ray,

Fairlie, Chataway and Kennedy. As could have confidently been predicted, Chataway and Kennedy were selected. Fairlie, however, did not turn up for the finals. The other job went instead, to my astonishment, to Day.

Although I was asked once to provide a couple of minutes on one of the news bulletins about some trade union controversy, thoughts of television as a career receded until the following spring, when Granada TV began broadcasting from Manchester. Sidney Bernstein and his chief producer Denis Forman determined they would try to confound the pessimists who had been arguing that the need to attract mass audiences, in order to secure advertising revenue, would mean a lowering of standards; and one of the ideas they thought up in rebuttal was a programme on the lines of the *New Yorker*'s Wayward Press column by A. J. Liebling, casting a critical eye, week by week, over the national press. There was one major problem – the insistence of the Independent Television Authority on Balance. This would certainly mean that the presenter would have to be regarded as 'safe', and would in all probability have to be tediously cautious. Why not, then, three presenters, Right, Left and Centre, alternating – leaving Balance to be established between them? To sugar this hitherto unswallowable pill, they proposed that the editors of the *Spectator* (Right), the *Economist* (Centre) and the *New Statesman* (Left) as the triumvirate. Impressed, the ITA agreed.

Kingsley Martin was delighted to accept, on the *New Statesman*'s behalf. So was Donald Tyerman, who had moved from *The Times* to edit the *Economist*; but his Board refused him permission (possibly because, as a later TV programme showed, he was not very good at holding his liquor. At a televised dinner party, the director had to find ways to keep the cameras off him; his presence was detectable only by occasional puffs of smoke from his post-prandial cigar). For the *Spectator*, Gilmour suggested Hamilton – only to hear, a few days later, that he was leaving the *Spectator* for Hutchinson. So I went to Manchester for the trial run.

On the train, I realised it was likely to be a repetition of the ITN test, only worse. I had been told to bring a twelve-minute script, and to stick precisely to it on performance. Practising two sentences was about my limit, before 'drying'. But in the Granada studio, when I reached it, there was a gadget on top of the camera like a miniature television set on its side; and there was the script coming down it, as if on a roller paper towel. I had never heard of a teleprompter; but it struck me as easily the most welcome new invention I had personally ever encountered. In Dublin, on Radio Eireann, I had learned to make a script which is being read sound as if it were being spoken. A deep peace descended upon me. The rehearsal went without a hitch.

By this time Denis Forman had observed that the *Spectator* could no longer safely be classified as politically on the Right. He had to move us over to Centre, to replace the *Economist* (which had declined to nominate a substitute for Tyerman); and Granada brought in John Connell, the *Evening News* leader-writer, on the strength of his connection with *Time and Tide*, (which was not on the Right, but nobody was likely to object; Connell certainly was). The intention had been that Kingsley Martin should write and present the first *What the Papers Say*, but on rehearsal he had the opposite experience to me; he couldn't read the teleprompter – except in such a way as leave the impression that he *was* reading it – peering at it, his eyes moving with the words to and fro across the screen. So on the opening day, I found myself again in the Manchester studio, preparing for the programme's first appearance.

Denis had been a little worried, earlier, that there might not be enough newsworthy material. That week, Israeli forces had invaded the Sinai peninsula, British and French aircraft had bombed Egyptian airfields, and Soviet tanks had moved into Budapest. The problem now was how to keep it from being simply a description of the week's events as seen through the eyes of war correspondents and the lenses of war cameramen, as distinct from the programme's design, to compare and contrast the handling of the news by different newspapers. Still, the script proved acceptable; the rehearsals went smoothly; and I was told to entertain myself for an hour or so until transmission time.

Granada had no hospitality room; I set out to look for the nearest pub. Eerily, the sky was full of flashes. On the tracts of waste land, still with the remains of buildings shattered in the blitz, were bonfires; whizz-bangs and fire-crackers were sounding off as if in a macabre salute to the campaigners in Hungary and Egypt. The teleprompter had relieved me of any nervousness about drying, but it was obvious that many things could go wrong – the captions could get out of order, or fall off their rickety, school-classroom easels. As the programme was to go out live, mistakes could not be remedied.

At the pub I ordered a whisky-and-soda, pressed down on the lever of the siphon and had the mortification of seeing the spurt remove all trace of the whisky from the bottom of the glass, shooting it up into the rafters. Nobody was looking; nobody noticed. I ordered another whisky, and switched to water.

The programme went without a hitch. It was the start, for me, of several congenial years of 'Papers', every three or four weeks – the original plan of Left, Right and Centre was adhered to for a time, but occasionally American journalists working in London would be brought in to add variety.

'Papers' had quite an impact on Fleet Street, as we could tell from the indignant reactions of editors who were criticised. It also led to the introduction of a lunch, early each new year, in which awards were distributed to journalists. In 1957 they went to Arthur Christiansen, editor; Cassandra (William Connor), columnist; Osbert Lancaster, cartoonist. Although the standard was never quite so high again, there have been few distinguished Fleet Street figures who have not at some point won one of the awards, chosen by a committee of people connected with the programme as presenters, producers and directors. The choice, in my experience, was rarely easy; and with producers such as Bill Grundy, Barrie Heads, Jeremy Isaacs, David Plowright and Michael Parkinson, the selection committees' gatherings have not been notable for polite decorum. But the level of the award winners has remained consistently high.

18

Deputy

The handling of the Suez crisis confirmed that the *Spectator* was now back on the course which it had followed, or at least was considered by its editors to be following, since its foundation: radical, slightly left of centre politically (though with the rise of Labour, it had moved to the right), independent. As soon as the dust had settled, and it had become clear that the defection of some thousands of subscribers, casual buyers and advertisers was not going to be a serious threat to the paper's future, Gilmour and I felt a sense of liberation. The fact that our views on the crisis, as on most issues which arose, were similar meant that I was able to move into Hamilton's role – Gilmour remained, in effect, editor-in-chief, but largely left it to me to introduce new features, and new writers to provide them.

An obvious source, as yet hardly tapped in Britain, was Dublin. I had been impressed by Brendan Behan's column in the *Irish Press*, which had shown what a seductive style he had on any subject he cared to write about. Although *The Quare Fellow* had been produced, he was not the familiar figure in London he was soon to become, lurching drunkenly in and out of pubs and newspaper stories; it was not until *Borstal Boy* was published in 1958 that his talent as a writer was recognised here. He was engaged on it when he received my letter suggesting he should write for us (the first paragraph refers to his spell in hospital when his diabetes was diagnosed):

A Bhriain, a chara
    Rory Childers and Synge's nephew brought me back from
the dead, and I am going to the Gaeltacht for a few weeks.

I got your invitation to write something for the *Spectator*, and thought it best to take a bit out of my book. Would you consider 'Bridewell Revisited' as a title?

It was used for another bit, that was published in France, but I don't think anyone in England would notice.

Despite everything, I owe that money to my handlers in London that I've to go to Mass in a cab. I am waiting for my royalties to catch up on my subs.

.Therefore, it would be a great stroke for me, if you sent fifteen guineas on as soon as you can to

Brendan Behan
c/o Post Office, Carraroe
Co. Galway
Slean beannacht
Brendan

PS Like George Moore, the discovery of the semi-colon has excited me.

Unfortunately the piece which he offered was a draft of the episode towards the end of *Borstal Boy* where the inmates were to join in a Nativity play in various roles, and they found that an attractive nineteen-year-old, the wife of one of the warders, had been invited to the meeting held to prepare for it. As she came in

'She's a smasher, all right', said Joe.
'She is that', said I.
Charlie looked at her and nodded and said 'She's in the Nativity Play. She's the Virgin Mary.'
'I know,' said Joe. 'I wish I could be the baby.'

There was more in this style, including the line which was to get the loudest laugh when I went to a performance of Joan Littlewood's adaptation for her stage version at Stratford East – though in deference to the Lord Chamberlain, without the banned word: 'He's a fughing sex mechanic.' Unwisely, I thought I might be able to win him over by pointing out that he would be read by the benighted Sassenach, who might be shocked; could he not write something like the stuff he had been contributing to the Irish Press, 'which was bloody good'. By the time the letter reached Brendan in the Gaeltacht he was back on the Guinness as if – friends reported in awe – he had decided that the appropriate cure for his diabetes was to make up for the lost drinking time in hospital as quickly as he could. A few days later I received a drunken scrawl: 'A fucking lot you'd know about good writing in the Irish Press or anywhere else' – followed by an illegible sentence, and ending with 'Take a drop dead powder, Brendan Behan.' Brendan thereupon sent the piece to the *New Statesman*, which gleefully used a mildly cleaned-up version. Kingsley Martin, when I met him on one of his visits to Manchester to do *What the Papers Say* (he soldiered on for a time at the programme but still found the teleprompter unmanageable; he once actually kicked the operator, in a fit of frustration) was congratulating himself on his Irish find. His euphoria did not last. In some controversy over the Hone family, Behan contributed a letter referring to 'Nathaniel Hone, Joseph Hone and Pogema Hone'. It was duly published, nobody in the *New Statesman* office knowing that *pogema hone* is a corruption of the Irish for Kiss my Arse.

Conor Cruise O'Brien also proved elusive. He was willing to review the books he wanted to review, but was not to be lured into the contract which we were prepared to offer. 'What *are* the financial advantages of which you speak?' he asked. 'The trouble is I do an odd book for the N S, and like to keep a foot in both graves, as it were.' The project of a monthly letter from Paris, working in and out with our correspondent there, the *Manchester Guardian*'s Darsie Gillie – Darsie concentrating on the political, Conor on the cultural, scene – attracted him; but before it came to anything he was moved back to Dublin.

Apart from attracting new writers, we needed something along the lines of the *New Statesman*'s perennial 'This England'; a feature which could be relied upon to renew itself, week after week, without our having to commission it and, better still, costing nothing. We found it, and ran it in tandem with *What the Papers Say*, in the form of contradictions and discrepancies in the dailies. Not merely were they remarkably frequent; they often took a curious form in which it was the unimportant details, which lent the story no point unless they were correct (and not much, even then) which diverged; as on the occasion when the reporters waited for Prince Charles – when he went to school for the first time in 1957:

Prince Charles Intelligence

The school was . . . five storeys high.
– *Daily Mail.*
 . . . six storeys high.
– *Daily Telegraph.*
 . . . seven storeys high.
– *Daily Sketch.*
He arrived . . . in a black Ford Zephyr.
– *Daily Sketch.*
 . . . in a green saloon.
– *Daily Herald.*
At . . . 8.55 a.m. – *Daily Herald.*
 . . . 9 a.m. – *The Times.*
 . . . 9.15. – *Daily Telegraph.*
 . . . 9.28. – *Daily Mail.*
 . . . on the dot of 9.30. – *Daily Express.*
He was wearing . . . a fawn overcoat with a velvet collar. – *Daily Mail.*
 . . . a grey topcoat with a rust velvet collar. – *Daily Sketch.*
 . . . his cinnamon-coloured cap. – *Daily Express.*
 . . . which he was carrying in his hand. – *Daily Mail.*
 . . . which he had left at home. – *Daily Mirror.*
He painted a ship . . . coloured black and red. – *News Chronicle.*
 . . . green. – *Daily Sketch.*
 . . . grey. – *Daily Mirror.*
which was . . . approaching Tower Bridge.
– *Daily Mirror.*
 . . . passing under Tower Bridge.
– *Daily Mirror.*
 . . . coloured black.
– *Daily Sketch.*
 . . . brown. – *Daily Mirror.*

He was in a class with . . . 8 other boys.
– *Daily Express.*
 . . . a dozen other boys.
– *Daily Mail.*
 . . . 16 other boys.
– *Daily Mirror.*
 . . . 17 other boys.
– *Daily Sketch.*
He signed his name . . . at the bottom.
– *Daily Sketch.*
 . . . at the top.
– *News Chronicle.*
The Prince is to be called . . . plain Charles.
– *Daily Mail.*
 . . . Prince Charles by the headmaster and Charles by the other boys. – *Daily Express.*
 . . . Prince Charles by both staff and boys. – *Daily Telegraph.*
The teaching staff . . . is all female.
– *The Times.*
 . . . has a number of masters. – *Daily Telegraph.*
The day came to an end . . . at 1 o'clock.
– *Daily Herald*
 . . . at 3.30.
– *News Chronicle.*
 . . . soon after 3.30.
– *Daily Mirror.*
 . . . at 3.42.
– *Daily Telegraph.*
 . . . at 3.45.
– *Daily Express.*

It had struck me that some of the readers we were attracting, and would like to attract, were of what might have been described as the Elizabeth David persuasion. In the rationing years, which had not ended until 1954, her early books on French and Italian cooking had been mouth-watering reminders of the existence of the taste of, for example, vegetables everywhere to be seen during such Continental holidays as the currency restrictions permitted, but rarely or never seen in Britain except in Soho, and a few other such centres. In the New Year of 1957 we introduced a column, 'Consuming Interest', the first of its kind – anticipating the publication of *Which?*, not long after. 'Leslie Adrian' pointed out in his/her first contribution – 'Leslie' was selected as leaving the sex of the writer uncertain; desirable in a column which had various contributors, though it was mainly the work initially of Amy Landreth, and then of Jean Robertson – how desirable it would be to be able to obtain crusty French bread and properly-smoked – not dyed – kippers; and offered to be a producers' and consumers' go-between, wherever the produce was available but rarely to be found in the shops. Leslie Adrian also recommended Peter Geale's restaurant which had begun as a fish-and-chips take-away (and in which it was still possible 'to get fish, chips, tea, bread and butter for 1s 5d'), but where the quality was so high that it had become a place of pilgrimage for connoisseurs. The column concluded with a denunciation of a firm of makers of Christmas crackers, each of whose contents consisted only of a motto and a paper hat which could have fitted only a young child. The hats were not even gummed together; they consisted of the two halves.

A second innovation in 1957 was further to confirm the impression that the *Spectator* was liberating itself from its earlier reputation of being respectable and respected but rather dull. Charles Curran had decided he could not continue to write the Political Commentary after Suez; the line the *Spectator* had taken would do his political prospects no good. George Gale was suggested; he was still regarded as a *Manchester Guardian* product, leftish but, in his case, well capable of seeing through Marxist cant, as he had just done in the *Spectator* in an article 'Soft on China'. He would have got the job, but demanded more money than the *Spectator* was prepared to offer. And as no other obvious candidate was to be found, I suggested that we should dispense with a political correspondent – where required, Gilmour and I could take on the role – and instead have an observer at Westminster, contributing a weekly sketch along the lines with which the *Guardian*'s Harry Boardman entertained readers day by day.

I knew who should do it: Bernard Levin. He had been working for *Truth*, a journal which had once enjoyed quite a formidable reputation as an uninhibited commentator on current affairs, but had declined into near obscurity under the control of a cautious management. Its editor, George Scott, had begun to revitalise it by collecting around him some young and as yet unknown journalists, among them Levin, Alan Brien, and Philip Oakes; but the circulation was so restricted that they had not been able to make much of an impact. In any case, we at the *Spectator* did not feel as compelled to read it as we felt compelled to read Kingsley Martin's *New Statesman* – for fear that he might have some new idea which would attract readers and push up its circulation, then nearly double ours. What had impressed me about Levin – curiously, in view of the job he was to be offered – was his weekly television commentary for the *Manchester Guardian*.

When commercial television started up in London in 1955, the *Guardian*'s TV correspondent did not have a set capable of picking it up in Manchester, and Gerard Fay had suggested that the early transmissions should be monitored and commented upon by Levin. His commentary, sometimes acerbic, sometimes jolly, impressed Wadsworth; Levin was asked to continue them on a weekly basis. It was these articles which had impressed me – just the man, I thought, to go to Westminster, the party conferences and other events as a detached but absorbed observer, roughly the equivalent of a theatre critic. We nearly had the same problem as with George Gale: Levin turned the offer down, on the ground that he was actually being paid more by *Truth* than the £1,200 we were offering.

When Gilmour bought the *Spectator* he had made it clear that it was not going to be run for profit – much to the anguish of John Strachey, a shareholder. Wisely, though, he was anxious that it should pay its way, making enough to prevent any drain on its capital resources. He would have liked to give larger salaries but any raise for an individual would have made it difficult not to give raises to the rest of the staff. The *Spectator*, I told Bernard, had a rigid salary structure, and the only way he could be given the £1,350 *Truth* paid him would be for everybody on the staff to be upgraded. 'Further to our conversation of yesterday's date (you see I have the *Spectator*'s style already),' he wrote, 'here is a word of amplification.' The word was, yes. He could no longer stand *Truth*'s political line – the owners had insisted on Scott backing the government over Suez – 'and your point about the wages structure (you see, more *Spectator* style) is a telling one, though of course a rise all round would have met the case, besides ensuring that I would be popular with the rest of the staff when I arrived.'

At least, Levin urged, we could let him write under his own name.

He did not care for pseudonyms, and 'if the *Spectator*'s parsimony means that a man of my outstanding ability is forced to pick up the odd crust elsewhere, it would be handy to have a visiting card to brush the dust off the crusts with.' I showed Gilmour the letter; he remained unmoved. The staff wages structure must remain sacred; there could be no general upgrading. On the pseudonym issue we were agreed. Odd though I would think it now, our idea was to let others hide behind it, if Levin's contributions proved unsatisfactory. The precaution proved unnecessary. 'Taper' was a hit from the start, and soon we had the satisfaction of hearing from the M Ps who came to *Spectator* parties that the Westminster Commentary was avidly read by their colleagues. There was particular joy when a few weeks later it began. 'If Sir Shortly Floorcross is trying to get himself slung out of the Labour Party, he is going the right way about it.' What conceivable advantages, Taper asked, had being an M P for a man like Hartley Shawcross, earning fabulous sums at the Bar. 'Why should he spend his time wandering about the sixth ugliest building in the British Isles, listening to the futile maunderings of his inferiors, eating vile food, breathing foul air, sitting cheek by jowl with cads?' This was language of a kind not previously used about the Houses of Parliament except by those who would have liked to blow it up; Taper, for all his contempt for many of those who sat on the benches below the press gallery, was clearly enamoured of the institution, irritated because it could have been more effective than in practice he found it.

The next recruit was Robert Kee, who took on the literary editorship when Tony Hartley left to do that job on the *Manchester Guardian*; but Robert – whom I had not seen since we were the black slaves in the Magdalen play – soon found office work tiresome, and recommended Karl Miller as his successor. Karl, a Scot with the traditional dour manner enlivened from time to time with spasms of infectious fun, proved to be another asset. He had the important gift for someone in his position, needing reviewers of ability but lacking the means to pay them at the rates which the newspapers' literary editors could offer (the *Spectator*'s standard rate was £10 per thousand) of offering books which would tempt the reviewers to take on before anybody else had thought of the same ruse; and he managed also to inspire the trust even of such pernickety reviewers as Evelyn Waugh and Conor Cruise O'Brien (writing then as 'Donat

O'Donnell'), who did not take kindly to any changes in what they wrote.

The next arrival was Cyril Ray. Ray, as he preferred to be called – he loathed the Cyril – was a graduate of the *Manchester Guardian* school, under W. P. Crozier's editorship; he had been one of the *Guardian*'s war correspondents, covering the North African and Anzio landings and parachuting into Arnhem. Then he had joined the *Sunday Times*; for two years, he was their correspondent in Moscow, the only correspondent of an English newspaper, other than the representative of the *Daily Worker*. It was in this capacity that I first read and admired his articles while I was still working in Dublin. When I was interviewed in 1950 by the *Sunday Times* editors (there were two, for some reason, at that time) who were looking for a Dublin stringer, I told them I would be using Ray as my model. Finding that he was out of work – he had resigned from the *Sunday Times* in protest against its support of hanging – I suggested he join us at a salary even lower than Bernard Levin's – the wages structure, again. Indignant that so experienced and accomplished a journalist should have to work for a pittance, Bernard marched in on Gilmour (who became accustomed to such intrusions, and indeed showed every sign of enjoying them) to protest. The *Spectator* could not afford more, he was told. 'You own it,' Bernard told him. 'Why not sell a couple of grouse moors?'

Initially Ray was brought in to take over foreign affairs after Tony's departure, but as well as editorials he was soon writing colour pieces about London life, ranging from a visit to Collins Music Hall, still lit by fishtail gas jets, to the Miss World Beauty Contest; and then, establishing a niche for himself at the back of the book with the wine column that was to make his reputation – saddle him with it, he has sometimes lamented – as journalism's leading wine buff.

Ray was a sociable socialist. He had a set of rooms in Albany, and became a member of Bucks, Brooks and the Athenaum; yet he was, and remained, a member of the Labour Party. If taxed with political hypocrisy he would cite the example of Raymond Postgate – classical scholar, historian, biographer as well as being one of the leading socialist propagandists between the wars, with an impressive string of books, and articles on Labour's cause, yet after the war he had founded and run the *Good Food Guide* and written in praise of wine. Nobody was surprised that a socialist should enjoy a night at the theatre; why should he not spend the money on dining and wining, if that happened to be what he liked?

Ray's value to the *Spectator* lay in a professionalism which none of the rest of us could claim. Whatever he wrote, whether it was a leader, or a report on a visit to Moscow, or a book review, it was always impeccably presented in his precise handwriting to fit whatever slot it was to fill. He also had style, unobtrusive yet characteristic, in the sense that it would not be long before anybody familiar with it would recognise it even in unsigned pieces. The same was true of Bernard, but Bernard's style was more idiosyncratic. The rest of us would also have liked to put a mark, discreet but unmistakable, on what we wrote; but we never quite managed it.

Ray was followed by Alan Brien, brought in to look after the arts pages. He had been with Bernard on *Truth*; the only occasion I had met him was when Gilmour had felt that George Scott should be invited to one of the *Spectator*'s parties, and Alan had come with him. I had taken an instant dislike to him, as I had to Seamus Kelly. Alan had the knack of raising hackles; it was to prompt Evelyn Waugh to note in his diary 'Randolph hired a Jew to insult me in White's.' On this occasion he persuaded Scott to linger, after the other guests had left, to try to get an invitation to the dinner which, they knew, Gilmour would be giving at a Charlotte Street restaurant. Gilmour was determined not to invite them, and eventually we left them in the office; they had an enjoyable though frustrating time, Alan told me later, riffling through the editorial correspondence in the hope, unfulfilled, of finding something incriminating they could make entertaining use of in *Truth*. It would not have crossed my mind to bring him on to the staff if I had not read a perceptive, unsigned film review in the *Observer*, whose resident critic was on holiday, and finding to my surprise that Alan had written it. When Bernard suggested him as arts editor, testifying – correctly – to his suitability as an agreeably gregarious member of the staff, in he came.

He also took on theatre, which was even more of a lottery; by his own admission he had not been an addict and he actually claimed he never went to the theatre. Theatre criticism at the time, though, was dominated by men who were identified *as* theatre critics – even Ken Tynan, for all his attempt to diversify by becoming a connoisseur of bull-fighting. It seemed possible that someone with a fresh eye might prove better-equipped to deal with the Royal

Court, kitchen-sink school of dramatists than most of the old stagers; and so it proved.

One of Alan's commitments was to produce 'Roundabout' a miscellany or pot-pourri of a thousand words of so, introducing the arts pages each week. He found it a chore, and this soon begun to show. Then, Roundabout suddenly brightened up. We all congratulated him on its recovery. Before long it transpired that he had farmed it out; as it was unsigned, he was paying a friend to do it for him. Earlier, this would have been difficult, out of the *Spectator*'s meagre salary; but gradually most of us were beginning to do rather well on the side, with TV and radio offers which began to come in when the *Spectator* began to be read and enjoyed by the producer class. Bernard even wrote the nightly calypsos sung on the BBC's new *Today* programme. For a fortnight, while he was on holiday, I stood in for him. Eventually Alan introduced us to the writer he was employing, at £3 a paragraph; Katharine Whitehorn. We were immediately impressed; it was not long before she joined us on the staff.

Katharine was just what we needed to break down what was not so much male chauvinism as male habits of mind. She was no feminist, in the sense that term was soon to acquire, but she was feminine, without being inclined to trade on her attractions. Having worked on *Picture Post* in its period of melancholy decline, she was relieved to find a job in which she could display her talent as a writer. Soon, her Roundabout – signed, by this time – was attracting admiring comment.

With a steadily rising circulation, and no falling-off in advertisers' support, everything seemed Set Fair. There was, however, a storm brewing, whose echoes are still occasionally to be heard.

19

'Death in Venice'

In the *Spectator* for 1 March 1957 Jenny Nicholson, daughter of Robert Graves and wife of Patrick Cross, Reuters correspondent in Rome, sent us in a report on an important conference which had just been held in Venice to decide whether the Socialist party under Pietro Nenni should follow him, and break with the Communists. The lobby of the Hotel Luna had been filled with the rival factions of the party; and there was also,

> the occasional appearance of Messrs Bevan, Morgan Phillips and Richard Crossman, who puzzled the Italians by their capacity to fill themselves like tanks with whisky and coffee while they (because of their livers and also because they are abstemious by nature) were keeping going on mineral water and an occasional coffee. Although the Italians were never sure if the British delegation was sober, they always attributed to them an immense political acumen.

I assumed that the trio would come in for some ribbing from their colleagues; it never occurred to me that they would sue, but sue they did. How should we react? Naturally the first step was to check with Jenny, Patrick Cross, and other journalists who had been at the conference. The report, they agreed, was correct; one evening the Italians were left in no doubt at all that Morgan Phillips was very drunk, as he had to be supported out. We even obtained a statement from the barman, about the drinks he had served to the trio. But

Gilmour claimed that his 'Master', Lord Hailsham, had laid down 'never try to justify', on such occasions. And it was not difficult to foresee counsel for the prosecution having fun at the expense of an Italian barman. We would apologise.

Our solicitor, Peter Carter-Ruck, offered them a draft apology. It was rejected. So was a second draft. They were then asked if they would amend the draft to their satisfaction. This, too, they declined to do. For our part, we could not throw Jenny Nicholson's account overboard; not merely because we knew it to have been accurate, but also because she could have won swingeing damages from the *Spectator* for impugning her journalistic honesty – as Honor Tracy had not long before from the *Sunday Times*, in similar circumstances.

Even so, our apology was grovelling. The article, it noted, had 'unfortunately been taken to mean that these leading members of the Socialist Party consumed such an amount of alcoholic refreshment at the National Congress of the Italian Socialist Party as to make the Italians seriously suspect their sobriety.' The article, from a reputable source, had been published in good faith, 'and we wish to take the opportunity of making it clear that any such imputation was never intended and, of course, would be quite untrue.' If it had been read in this way the passages were unreservedly withdrawn, and we wished to take the opportunity of tendering to the three men 'our sincere apologies, and of expressing our regret for any inconvenience or annoyance they may have suffered'.

The apology was rejected, and the case came up in November 1957. Lord Chief Justice Goddard elected to try it himself: this was ominous, partly because of his known aversion to the press; partly because he had reason to detest the *Spectator*. He was an avowed supporter of hanging; we had been one of the instigators of the campaign against it. And we had been rash enough to criticise him a couple of times in 1956 for his autocratic handling of cases of contempt of court.

In one of them, we discussed two of his decisions. He had found W. H. Smith and Son guilty of criminal contempt for having imported and sold copies of the American magazine *Newsweek*, which had committed the contempt; although Smith's were clearly innocent of any criminal intention, they were fined, and warned that they would be more heavily punished if anything similar happened again. And he had found the Sunday *People* guilty of contempt for calling for the prosecution of a man who, unknown to the paper, had just been charged. 'Contempt of court is what Lord Goddard says it is,' the *Spectator* had commented. Consequently criticism of his decisions 'must be on the grounds not that they were wrong but that – assuming that they were right – they show that it is high time that the law was changed.'

Even more rashly, as things were to turn out, we hinted broadly that Goddard was twisting precedents to suit his prejudices. For the defence in the *People* case Gerald Gardiner, soon to be Lord Chancellor in the Wilson government, had cited two, one from 1889 and the other from 1906, to show that knowledge was an essential ingredient of contempt. As the prosecution had admitted that the *People* could not have been expected to know that the prosecution had just been set in motion, he argued that the *People* should be acquitted. Goddard replied by citing two cases where lack of knowledge or intention had *not* been regarded as a defence, one from 1742 and the other from 1806. Apart from the fact that the later precedents, if precedents were being accepted, should have carried more weight, Goddard was deliberately brushing aside the fact that both his two cases had come up before the division of powers between executive and judiciary had begun to establish itself; Lord Chief Justices had then actually been in the government, openly and notoriously acting as an arm of the executive in cases of libel or contempt. 'The law of contempt is now itself held in contempt,' we concluded. 'It is up to parliament to restore the prestige of the law by reforming it.'

It had not occurred to us that 'Death in Venice' would eventually bring us to court, let alone that Goddard would be on the bench. If it had, we might have remembered what had happened to Wilson Harris, as he recalled in his memoirs. He had complained in the Notebook that it was demeaning for a Lord Chief Justice – Hewart, in this case – to contribute articles to the Sunday papers. Hewart made no secret of his wrath, 'and from that time the conviction prevailed in the *Spectator* that if ever we had a case before Hewart we should fare ill.' When such a case came up, Hewart duly 'took the opportunity to express in the most caustic language he could command (and he was not incompetent in that sphere) his amazement that a journal of the traditions of the *Spectator* should have been guilty of so outrageous a piece of defamation – and so forth.' Goddard was notorious for giving free rein to his prejudices in the very public privacy of the Savage Club; and although we did not hear of any reference specifically to us, we were well aware of his expressed readiness to help the prosecution in cases where he was on its side.

There he sat, on the bench, when the case of Aneurin Bevan, Richard Crossman and Morgan Phillips v The *Spectator* Ltd came up in the High Court. Goddard was modelled, it seemed to me, on Stevenson's *Weir of Hermiston*, relishing the power he wielded; and from the start, he showed where his sympathies lay. His task was made easier by the incompetent handling of our case, on the first day. W. Fearnley-Whittingstall was an eminent Q.C. and an able one, but he had been involved until the previous day in another case. He had made an inadequate study of his brief, and actually had to be prompted, from time to time, by Gilmour.

The plaintiffs were also prompted – by Goddard. Only Crossman was at ease in the witness box, though he was clearly a little startled to find himself being jollied along from the bench. Bevan, giving evidence, admitted he had drunk 'a little wine, certainly'; then, a little nervously added 'one glass of whisky', justifying this improbable assertion with a remark about whisky-drinking being unusual in Italy. To ease the strained pause that followed, Goddard intervened helpfully: 'whisky is rather expensive. The extremely nervous Morgan Phillips, under cross-examination, took up this suggestion gratefully: 'I had one with a French colleague. He drank whisky – and paid for it.'

When it was Gilmour's turn to enter the witness box the case for the plaintiffs was put by Gilbert Beyfus, Q.C., who did not scruple to break the convention by which negotiations with a view to reaching a compromise – in this case, an agreed apology – are held 'without prejudice' – in other words, they will not be brought up in court. If such negotiations were to be brought up, obviously they would not be held at all, in case one or other side, and sometimes both, were shown to have been willing to make concessions of a kind which would conflict with the case they were eventually making. Beyfus, a much craftier operator than Fearnley-Whittingstall, managed to make it appear that it was Gilmour who was the perjurer, when all he had been doing was trying to come to terms with the plaintiffs' demands.

Gilmour also had to contend with another cross-examiner – Goddard, who acted as if he had been briefed for the plaintiffs, 'behaving with such outrageous bias that it caused audible gasps in the court', as Bernard Levin has recalled; 'his summing up to the jury was not easy to distinguish from the final speech for the plaintiffs' counsel.' Goddard even went out of his way to dismiss the apology which the *Spectator* had published, on the ground that it had been too long delayed – though the delay had been simply because of the negotiations to find if the apology could be agreed. He also pointed out to the jury that a libel became more serious if it was published in a serious paper. The jury, which had been given no hint of what had happened in Venice, awarded damages of £2,500 each to the plaintiffs – hefty sums, for those days.

Not long afterwards I went to Chelsea, where Granada had their London studios, to take part in one of the experimental programmes for which the company was earning its good reputation – though this was perhaps the least successful: individuals answering questions as if spontaneously, but with the answers prepared in advance. Crossman was there, still full of the trial, professing to be shocked by Goddard's promptings, and freely admitting that Bevan and Morgan had been swilling down the whiskies. He had not himself committed perjury, he insisted, as he had been drinking Cinzano; but the other two had not told the whole truth when they had claimed to have drunk only a single whisky, and Morgan Phillips had been very drunk. It did not appear to worry Crossman that he had been aiding and abetting their perjury.

Crossman did not hesitate to tell the same story, whenever the subject came up; but it was not until 1978, after the deaths of Morgan Phillips and Bevan, that – freed from the threat of another libel action – one of his hearers, Auberon Waugh, related the story in *Private Eye*, as he had heard it from Crossman's own lips. Inevitably members of Morgan Phillips's family protested that the charge of drunkenness had been levelled only when he was no longer alive to rebut it. And why should Crossman's word be trusted, so long after the event? The two questions were to be answered in 1981 when the first volume of Crossman's *Diaries* was published. Referring to the trial, he had written that 'Directly Morgan got into the box, it was clear that he was a subnormal witness – shifty, fearful, sweating with panic (legitimately, for he had been dead drunk for most of the conference) . . .' Even if this entry had been the only evidence of Morgan Phillips's condition, it could hardly be dismissed as an invention. In view of the confirmation which we at the *Spectator* had at the time, the case for Bevan's and Phillips's perjury becomes unanswerable.

Why did they conspire – in the colloquial, if not the strict legal sense – to deceive the High Court jury? In his diary Crossman referred to 'the kind of gamble which no one should responsibly have undertaken, even though we did win it in the end.' It was not so much of a gamble – not, at least, financially. Meeting Howard Samuel later at a party, Alan Brien elicited the information that he had backed them, promising them he would meet their costs if they lost.

Samuel had made his fortune out of developing property in London at the end of the Second World War. In common with a number of other men who had found that the austerity of those years had not impeded their accumulation of wealth, he regarded himself as a socialist. Bevan was a friend of his; and he had become the backer of *Tribune*, which occasionally preached the nobly idealist creed that Bevan had presented in *In Place of Fear* in 1952. Bevan, he knew, disliked Kingsley Martin: according to Edward Hyams's history of the *New Statesman*, he thought Martin insufficiently militant and uncompromising, 'a curious judgment for a man who had himself compromised so thoroughly in the end'. In 1957 Samuel made a take-over bid for the *New Statesman*. It was assumed that this was to please Bevan; 'that Bevan knew of his manoeuvres is certain,' Hyams claimed, adding 'as it is that he disapproved of them.'

Bevan apparently did not disapprove of Samuel's backing in the court case; and Samuel, according to Alan, had no qualms about admitting what he had done. Never one to avoid embarrassing questions, Alan asked him how he felt about the three taking money off a rival journal by perjury. Unused to being interrogated in such a manner, Samuel was taken aback. Embarrassed, he overturned a tray of peanuts with a twitchy gesture, and started picking them up off the carpet; an unusual posture, Alan could not resist telling him, for a tycoon.

There is nothing to suggest that Crossman lied. It is extremely improbable that Bevan contented himself with only a single whisky, but quite likely that he remained sober. Anybody who spent an evening in his company at a Party Conference, as I once did, would testify to his ability to retain his political acumen while absorbing quantities of liquor. He may have told the truth about the 'one glass', but not the whole truth. As for Morgan, I have often wondered what would have happened if another Q.C., well-briefed, had been in charge of the cross examination, ready to probe with more finesse. But by the time the case reached the High Court, it was already all but lost; and with Goddard on the bench, there were few advocates at that time who would have risked tangling with him.

Somewhere, Mark Twain claimed that if somebody tried to steal his wallet he would resist; but if the threat was to take him to law to get it, he would hand it over. Any thought of relying on British justice since – or of advising others to rely on it – has been banished by the mind's eye picture of Fearnley-Whittingstall fumbling his way incompetently through the first day's proceedings, and of Goddard unblushingly acting for the plaintiffs from the bench.

I have a clear memory of seeing Jenny Nicholson, after the trial ended, standing by herself outside the court. When I called round to see her in Rome a few months later, she told me that, quietly and seriously, she had then been putting a curse on them. By their lies they had damaged her reputations and jeopardised the *Spectator*'s future to enrich themselves; she did not like to think of them getting away with it for long.

Gilmour also paused for a moment on the way out, to assure the assembled reporters and photographers that there was no question of the *Spectator* ceasing publication. But he was clearly shaken, as indeed all of us were. For the next few months the paper's tone was muted. In the new year of 1958 John Betjeman decided to discontinue his column, which was a blow. 'This is the last paragraph I shall be writing in "City and Suburban"', he wrote. '*I have not been sacked*, but the effort, week after week, of compiling this column is proving too much for me.' It was not strictly true; soon, he was compiling a very similar column for the *Daily Telegraph* for a great deal more money. But later he delighted us by coming in, as he did all too seldom, on a visit, and telling us how much he had preferred writing for the *Spectator*, apart from the remuneration. 'City and Suburban' had brought him a steady flow of comment, adulatory and critical. He never met anybody, he complained, who read the *Telegraph*.

He remained an occasional contributor, appearing in the only bright new note we introduced at this time: a series, 'John Bull's Schooldays'. The others in it included Cassandra, the most respected columnist of the time, hardly sane on most issues; the only occasion I can recall when he went overboard was when he had joined the pack screaming abuse at P. G. Wodehouse for broadcasting from Germany while he was interned there during the war; a foolish decision on Wodehouse's part, but his script could not have given the allies any cause for concern. Others were Kingsley Amis, Patrick Campbell, Angus Wilson and Philip Toynbee – Toynbee's displaying the ambivalence of so many former public schoolboys, and incidentally rousing Gerald Hamilton, the original of Christopher Isherwood's Mr Norris, to give *his* recollections of Rugby thirty years before Toynbee, in a house where he was an exact contempary of Rupert Brooke. Hamilton used to visit us at the *Spectator* occasionally. It was impossible, I found, to listen to him for long without the mind slipping back to visualise him in the Thirties, squirming in nervous uncertainty before the customs examination, or in ecstasy at the Berlin boot-fetishist establishment.

John Braine, too, recalled his schooldays for us. We asked him to do so so that we could ease him painlessly out of the job of television critic, which he had taken on in March. His *Room at the Top* had come out a few months earlier; he was very full of himself; his copy was boring; so, on his visits to deliver it, was he.

20

Sabbatical

The success of *What the Papers Say* ought to have given me the opportunity to take advantage of the prospects opening up for commentators in commercial television who were not identified with the BBC. Up to a point it did: I took on from Robin Day another of Granada's current affairs programmes, *Under Fire*, in which a studio audience in Manchester threw questions at a couple of MPs, or people eminent in industry or the professions, who were in a London studio. I was in the chair, in Manchester, and felt quite satisfied with my stint until I watched my successor, Bill Grundy, perform. Bill was by training an engineer who happened to have come into broadcasting through one of the BBC's radio quiz games; he turned out to be a television natural, able to combine the necessary attention to the needs of floor manager and director with the desired air of a man who is *not* paying any attention to them, but is concentrating on listening, and where necessary responding, to the arguments from the floor, and the MPs' replies.

A few performers have that ability, though none that I have watched have used it so smoothly as Bill. In my own case, conditioning to the teleprompter proved to be the equivalent of using water-wings while learning to swim; the attempted transition to spontaneity proved unnerving. In 1958 a bye-election came up in Rochdale, and Granada determined to cover it – something the BBC had not dared to do in the past, under the impression it was against Government regulations. This turned out to be incorrect. Interest was mainly centred on whether the Liberal candidate, Ludovic Kennedy, might cause an upset, as he did; Labour was to win the seat, but he pushed the Tory to the bottom of the poll. The three candidates agreed to debate; I was put in the chair; and the producer, Tim Hewat, informed me shortly before we went on the air 'live' that my function was not simply to keep the peace, but to act as a time-keeper. By the end of the debate, each of the three must have been allowed the same time as the others.

Tim had come to Granada from the *Daily Express*, and he had retained something of the authoritarian manner that was common enough in Fleet Street, rare in television, where most directors find that flattery is a more profitable method with performers. I was left with the impression, minutes before the programme was due to begin, that failure to ensure equal time for the trio would probably mean that he and I and Sidney Bernstein would be had up before the Bar of the House of Commons for contempt. Nothing I tried, however, could persuade the Labour candidate to talk as the other two were talking. Tim had rigged up a kind of clock, which showed me just how far Labour was behind. Then, miraculously, something set him off for the last couple of minutes, to even up. All I had to do was stop the others butting in, so that he could play out time.

More agony of mind promptly followed. Granada had managed to get permission to have the cameras in at the count. I was to set the scene, briefly, before the results were declared. Some delay occurred, and I was told to keep on blathering – with no script, no teleprompt, and no talking to the candidates. I happened to have met Moira Shearer not long before when she was playing in *Ondine* at the Bristol Old Vic, in her attempt to switch from ballet to the theatre; she forgave my *Spectator* criticism of the performance and an interview with her, as a candidate's wife, filled in some time. After that I would have been struck dumb; but Jim Phoenix, who was on the administrative side of Granada, came to the rescue, guessing my state of panic. He had once been returning officer at an election; he was able, for the benefit of viewers, to describe what was happening, how the counting was done, and who did it, answering many other questions which viewers would be asking, as few of them could ever have watched an election count before.

I did not need Tim's scathing comment on the interview with Moira Shearer – I had managed to look throughout not as if listening keenly to her replies, he said, but as if trying desperately to think of another question to keep the interview going – to realise that my career as interviewer and ad lib commentator was over. Henceforth the teleprompter or autocue would be the standby. Not that it was an entirely trustworthy ally. On one occasion, owing to last minute changes in the script the 'roller towel' had to be run back and forth a couple of times; and on the second of them the paper began to tear at a join. Had it come apart at what was to be my peroration – the programme was about the threat of atomic warfare – I would not have had the remotest notion what to say. In such circumstances it had been known for performers to mouth words, silently, to give the impression that it was the sound which had gone. But this proved unnecessary; the join held – just.

On another occasion the linkage between the operator and the teleprompter went awry so that it slowed down, the words coming up too belatedly. As I slowed down to match, it slowed down still further. This happened to come at the end of the programme; which I managed to finish, but not before Bernard Hollowood, editor of *Punch* and also its TV critic, had spotted what was happening, as he charitably but gleefully indicated in his next column. Still, the teleprompter/autocue has remained my favourite invention, in spite of creating a dependence so total that Bill Grundy, when he came to be my producer, used to claim that if the teleprompter stopped at 'Good' I would be unable to remember to say 'Night'.

That autumn of 1958 Denis Forman suggested that I had become so identified with Granada that I ought to join the company. As it happened, I had just decided to leave the *Spectator*, but for a reason which made me turn down his offer: I wanted more time to write books. Working for Granada, I suspected, would have been even more time-consuming.

The urge had come upon me through yet another curious twist of Fate. During my years in Dublin I had continued to enjoy the company of doctors, and to hear their views on medical controversies which arose. One of them had been 'psychosomatic medicine' – still, in those days, enclosed in inverted commas, and often with 'so-called' or some other qualification. That psychosomatic disorders occurred seemed to me so obvious that I could not understand the resistance of the medical Establishment to the idea that emotional stress can cause physical symptoms; yet it aroused strong feelings.

Sir George Pickering, one of Britain's most eminent physicians, rejected it as unworthy of serious consideration by medical science.

In an article in the *Spectator* I had challenged this view. The article was read in New York by the art critic of *Time* magazine, Clement Greenberg, whom I had never met. He showed it to his friend Sidney Phillips, publisher of Criterion Books; and Phillips wrote to ask me if I would expand the article into a book. To be offered an advance by an American publisher – soon backed by another from Hamilton in Hutchinson, for the British rights – was a heady experience; but it would mean I would have to do the homework. With *What the Papers Say* and other occasional programmes which I could continue to do as a freelance, to pay the bills, there would be more free time to do it. Enjoyable though the *Spectator* was, the time had come to leave.

Besides, I wanted to take time off for another reason. I was about to get married.

In 1957 a press officer in the American embassy in London, Brad Connors, had rung to ask me who was the *Spectator*'s defence correspondent. We hadn't one, I told him. 'Then you are,' he said, inviting me to join one of the facility trips which the State Department was laying on for journalists from the European countries in the hope of projecting a friendlier image (the 'almighty dollar' in the post war era had bred jealousy of the United States which the Marshall Plan had only just begun to erode). In three weeks nine of us, from different countries, were whisked around to more places than most Americans see in a lifetime, from Washington D.C. to Washington State, from Louisville to Lubbock. Apart from a brief visit to the Pentagon, we were not required to bother ourselves with defence, the aim being to show us how pacific the Eisenhower administration really was. We were well looked after, apart from the shock of finding that the five days we were to spend in Lubbock would be 'dry'; and at the end of it I had an excuse to stay on in New York and renew my acquaintance with Ruth Woodeson, who I had met briefly in Italy: I was to get people to promise to contribute to the *Spectator*'s projected American number.

As well as our Washington Correspondent, Richard Rovere of the *New Yorker*, the trawl netted Joe Alsop, J. K. Galbraith, Walter Lippman, Dwight MacDonald, Norman Podhoretz and Gore Vidal;

but the project came to nothing as the *Spectator*'s managing director, H. S. Janes, felt they were not well-enough known to attract the necessary support from advertisers in Britain. Still, I saw a lot of Ruth Woodeson – 'Boo' to her family. A Bostonian, she had spent much of her childhood in the Far East, where her father had been Consul General in Mukden and Singapore. I had met her in Italy five years earlier with her husband; she since had divorced him. In her capacity as press officer at Sarah Lawrence College she enlisted me to lecture on Bernard Shaw to a roomful of Bermuda-shorted students, who asked such hair-raising questions as 'What is the difference between Shaw's concept of the Superman and Nietzsche's?' We enjoyed the hospitality of Conor Cruise O'Brien, by this time in his country's service at the United Nations. And before I returned we had agreed to meet the following spring for a holiday in a village she knew south of Naples.

Up to this point I had not been able to get Rosemary Harris entirely out of my system – not surprisingly, as she had been an outstanding success in New York in Moss Hart's *The Climate of Eden* and, though it had flopped, had come back to the Old Vic to play Desdemona to Richard Burton's Othello, and Cressida (in an abysmal production by Tyrone Guthrie in which words were sacrificed to swirling movement; it was as if Guthrie had succumbed to the feeling which makes television directors fill awkward gaps by having cars arrive or leave). Not that Rosemary was affected by success. On the contrary, she was to remain as unaffected as it is possible to be, in such circumstances. We continued to laugh together; but we could not quite come to old terms with each other.

I had been having affairs. 'It used to be called "philandering", a pleasant word for a pleasant pastime,' Jill Tweedie has recently recalled. 'There is no place for such amateurism now. That olde worlde occupation has been bought out, asset-stripped, automated and renamed "womanising".' Whichever it was, for me it was enjoyable and without problems – except one. In Ireland, to have remained a bachelor until the age of forty was to excite envy. In London, I had found, it aroused suspicion. Bringing a string of different girls to parties actually suggested either that the man was a 'queer' – 'gay' had not then been corrupted into use – and using them as a disguise, or that the girls were finding out his inadequacies in quick succession.

Bernard Levin and our resident cartoonist, Rory McEwen, had ensured I would remember my fortieth birthday by filling my tiny office with junk from a nearby shop – a hat-stand, ludicrous vases and other useless accessories – so full that it was almost impossible to get into it. I did not begin consciously to look for a wife, from that time; but I was ready for the prospect of marriage. Boo was attractive and amusing; we shared the same tastes; and the fact she had a two-year-old daughter, Diana, by her former husband appealed to me – as did Diana – as providing a ready-made family. Fortunately Boo liked the idea of living in London. Our holiday in Italy in the summer of 1958 decided us that we could go ahead without too many qualms.

Our plan was that marriage would be followed by a honeymoon coupled with a three month sabbatical which I claimed the *Spectator* owed me, to be spent in Italy. I would have another go at the novel, and at writing a play. But when I told Ian Gilmour of my decision to resign, his reaction was to ask me to stay on – as editor. It had not occurred to me that he might be ready to step aside, and let me take over; but apparently he felt it was only fair to let me have the nominal title – to make way, as he might have put it, for the older man. The offer was too good to turn down. I was not prepared to sacrifice the sabbatical; but in November, it was agreed that when I came back from it Gilmour would step aside.

21

Election Year

Boo, Diana and I spent the sabbatical partly in Rome, partly in a villa we had found the year before in Maratea, south of Naples. The novel was dusted off, and re-jigged; the play was written; both of them were to attract encouragement – to write something better. Eventually I would, I decided, but in the meantime the *Spectator* must have priority. And an idea I had had for a time suddenly burgeoned, thanks to a chance meeting with Charles Curran.

Curran had ceased to be our political commentator because, as prospective Conservative candidate for Uxbridge, he would have been embarrassed at the connection; but we had remained on good terms. I was to be reminded how little I knew him when Victoria Glendinning's life of Rebbeca West came out in 1987; 'Rebecca made one of the best friends of her life on the *Evening Standard*,' she noted, 'the lawyer Charles Curran, then features editor of the paper, a clever, witty and ugly man ten years younger than herself.' Sardonic rather than witty, in my recollection, and *joli laid* rather than ugly; his expression was engaging. I knew neither that he had been a lawyer – he was very much the straight journalist – nor that he was a Catholic with the moral scruples about sexual intercourse that enraged Rebecca West. So far as I was concerned whatever he wrote was sound and well-reasoned; and though I was astonished when he offered us a ten thousand-word piece about the way in which Stalin had contrived to be the chief beneficiary of the decision to drop atom bombs on Japan, I said yes, please, sight unseen.

When Truman told Stalin of the United States' intention to use the atom bomb, Stalin welcomed the information; and in 'Stalin Merely

Smiled' Curran set out to show why. As it would take up more space than all the 'middles' put together usually did, it had to be planned for; and as things turned out, when it appeared on 18 September the *Spectator* was confronted with the need to make a delicate decision. Macmillan had just decided to go to the country; we would be expected to pronounce a verdict on his stewardship since he had succeeded Eden, and to indicate how we hoped our readers would vote.

A couple of weeks before I had surveyed Macmillan's premiership in a leader, contrasting the respect that could be felt for his early career – as the preacher, in the 1930s, of what was later to be described as 'caring' conservatism; as wartime minister in North Africa; as the Master Builder in the peacetime Churchill government – with the suspicion aroused by his role over Suez, when he had breathed fire at the outset, then said the invasion would have to be called off, or bankruptcy must follow. Although his government's popularity three years after he had succeeded Eden was at its height, his parliamentary performances were lamentable – 'he had become mannered in the worst sense of the word, a parody of himself.' And his attempts to portray himself as a man of influence internationally ought to have been a joke: a trip to Moscow had ended in humiliation, and Britain had become more unpopular with the French and the German governments than she had been since the war.

This having been said, the *Spectator* could not enthusiastically endorse Macmillan's claim to be given another five years in office. But could we break with the Tories altogether? There was no way of telling what proportion of the 40,000-odd readers of the *Spectator* still regarded it as fundamentally conservative, even if not Tory. Could we safely return to the tradition established by its founder Rintoul and his nineteenth-century successors, becoming again truly left of centre?

Gilmour and I had had no disagreement, thus far, over editorial policy; but, realising that the election was going to present me problems, he set out his views in a memorandum. It came quite close to outlining the line I was proposing to take. Two main questions arose: should we come out for any of the parties? And if so, which party? 'A newspaper has no duty to advise its readers how to vote,' the *Observer*, chastened by its loss of readers and revenue over Suez, announced at the beginning of the campaign. I disagreed: 'the *Spectator* is read by many people with formed political opinions which are not going to be altered by anything which they read in an editorial; but this does not make it unnecessary or presumptuous to give an opinion of our own.'

In his memorandum, though, Gilmour counselled more caution than I liked. The *Spectator*'s influence, such as it was, was derived from being considered Conservative; if we advised our readers not to vote Conservative it would need to be on Conservative grounds, and in fact there were good Conservative grounds for wishing for a Conservative defeat. But in view of the mess the Labour Party had got itself into over the notorious Clause Four of its constitution, committing it to the nationalisation of the means or production, we could not support it; and although the *Spectator* was in agreement with much of the Liberals' policy, it would be absurd to jump on what was obviously a rickety band-wagon – the Party would be lucky if it won six seats. The line, he felt, should be that the balance was still slightly weighted in the government's favour.

I would have preferred not to temporise; and three days later, Gilmour agreed, irritated by Macmillan's decision to make his foreign and colonial policy his main plank – the government's record was so bad, he thought, 'that it is an insult to the electorate to fight an election on it.' It would be wise to leave the final decision to the last moment; but as things stood, if the polls continued to suggest a Conservative victory we should say that although we had usually supported them, 'we cannot support them this time.'

As we were now in harmony, Gilmour decided he would make the visit he had already arranged to Franco's Spain, leaving me to play by ear anything which might come up in the course of the election campaign; and as things turned out there were no surprises. Remembering the fiasco of the 1955 election issues, I was determined to keep the party heavyweights out of the pages; the week before the election we simply had thoughtful pieces from John Simon, Financial Secretary to the Treasury; Roy Jenkins, perhaps Gilmour's closest friend in politics at the time; and Mark Bonham Carter, who had just won Torrington for the Liberals (that he was to lose it again at the election was a severe blow to them). We waited until the week after, when the *Spectator* would be appearing on polling day, to commit ourselves editorially.

In Macmillan's 1955 election article in the *Spectator*, we recalled, he had claimed that the primary task of the free world must be to forestall aggression. Yet he had been one of the most vigorous backers of the Suez campaign, until it fell apart; he had been presiding over the continuing futile attempt to keep Cyprus in the Commonwealth; and he must bear much of the responsibility for the ugly repression of nationalism in Kenya and Nyasaland. We could not support a government which had so catastrophic a record in its handling of foreign and colonial affairs.

We could not endorse Labour, either, in view of the control still exercised by the trade unions. The best advice we could give voters was to register a protest by voting Liberal, where a Liberal was standing. Failing this, the choice should be made between the candidates on their merits. And where the choice unfortunately had to be made between, say, a supporter of Suez and a trade union hack, 'on balance, and with some reluctance, we can only recommend a vote against the government candidate'.

To get around the difficulty of publication day and polling day coinciding – which meant that although copies would be in the bookstalls in London that afternoon, postal subscribers would not receive their copies until later – we came up with a gimmick which might have proved embarrassing, but turned out better than we could have expected: we would ask a number of well-known people, not party politicians, why and how they were going to vote. The trawl netted Kingsley Amis – 'I shall never forgive the Tories for the grubby bravado of their Suez venture', he explained, though he regarded Labour as 'sinister and fatuous as well as revolting'; Lord Beveridge, predictably Liberal; E. M. Forster, who recalled he had voted at general elections for half a century and 'no one for whom I have voted has ever got in'; Christopher Hollis, Conservative but anti-Suez, who hedged; Wolf Mankowitz, who proposed to vote Labour 'without enthusiasm or even very much interest'; Angus Wilson – 'the Communists since the war had made "peace" a dirty word', he complained, 'Tory propaganda during this election has done something of the sort with "prosperity"'; and Evelyn Waugh, who hoped the Tories would be returned, but would not vote for them: 'if I voted for the Conservative Party and they were elected I should feel that I was morally inculpated in their follies – such as their choice of Regius professors' (Macmillan had appointed Trevor-Roper to the Oxford Chair).

How would Gilmour react? When it arrived, his letter, from Barcelona, was enthusiastic, both about the leader and about the use of the pundits. He was reassured by the fact the *Observer* had eventually changed its mind, and come out against the Government; had we pushed David Astor off the fence? He felt sure we had taken the right line: 'my original idea that we had to support the Conservatives was based upon a false premise, and even from the few newspapers that we saw here I should have been very uneasy if we had been on the other side'.

In his letter Gilmour mentioned that he was prepared for a falling away in circulation, as there had been over Suez. In the event there were few cancellations; and we were heartened by messages from people, some of them unexpected, who welcomed the return to the Rintoul tradition. One letter gave us particular pleasure. For many years, in Wilson Harris's time, Harold Nicolson had contributed a page of 'Marginal Comment' which had been one of the paper's most popular features: 'I never did as good a piece of work for the *Spectator*,' Harris had written, 'as when I persuaded Harold Nicolson, at the beginning of 1939, to write a weekly page for the paper.' It was not just that for fourteen years Harris was able to rely on the weekly contribution being readable: 'No other editor can ever have had a more ideal contributor,' he added; not merely did the copy always arrive on time, it was 'so rarely as almost to create a sensation that "Marginal Comment" was a single line over or under its allotted space'.

What a paragon, I had thought, and had tried without success to lure him back. Now, he wrote after the election,

> I read your last number with great interest and apprecia-
> tion. I am indeed glad that you have come out so openly as
> a liberal radical and I hope that, while you may lose the
> support of a few schoolmasters and clergymen, you will
> gain the support of a large number of the younger
> generation.
>
> I do much admire the manner in which you have
> rejuvenated the dear old Spectator and I wish you every
> form of good fortune.

The circulation appeared not to have been harmed, but there was another source of worry. From his managing director's chair, H. S. Janes exuded gloom; advertisers, he feared, would leave us in droves. One test would be their reaction during the weeks leading up to Christmas, ordinarily the most profitable.

The *Spectator*'s Christmas number, which appeared in late November, had become an indicator of its popularity and prosperity, as the number of writers it could accommodate was related to the quantity of advertising it could attract. Although as proprietor Gilmour did not regard the paper as a money-spinner, he wanted it kept, as we appreciated, financially stable, turning in a small profit each year; and the libel action had made it seem even more important to regulate the number of pages, week by week, with reference to the revenue. If advertisers had been offended by the paper's line on the election, it would show.

In the event, there was no need to worry; we had sixty-eight pages to fill, and on the feathers of the turkey-cock which Quentin Blake painted for the cover were some of the contributors: Kingsley Amis, John Betjeman, Patrick Campbell, Roy Jenkins, Hesketh Pearson, Evelyn Waugh and Angus Wilson. At the annual office party we could celebrate, and did, undeterred by the message in Patrick Campbell's 'Maintenance Work on the Hangover':

> What we've got, without going into too much detail, is an iron band round the head, felted piano-hammers playing Ravel's Bolero on the back of the eyeballs, little jackets of matted Angora wool around the teeth, nerves leaping on miniature pogo-sticks, magnesium flares in the oesophagus and a general feeling of stiffness, as though we'd been rolled at some point the previous evening off a low roof into a heap of old bicycles

Janes remained convinced that it was only a matter of time before the weight of boardroom Conservatism made itself felt in advertising departments. Advertisers, he warned Gilmour in a memorandum in January, thought the paper irresponsible, and had 'indicated that they might no longer feel justified in advertising in or recommending a journal which seemed to be becoming increasingly subjective'. Gilmour's reply was tactful, but firm; some advertisers defined 'responsible' as Conservative and 'irresponsible' as Labour, and it ought to be made clear to them why the *Spectator* felt differently. As things turned out only a handful of advertisements, most of them reports of company meetings, were lost.

That the political shift did not have the dire consequences Janes feared was mainly due to a rise in what might be described as station-bookstall purchases. The *Spectator* in Wilson Harris's time had been largely read in the home – or at least displayed there: country houses, and many more modest residences, usually had a selection of periodicals – *Punch*, the *Illustrated London News*, the *Tatler* – for browsing through when it was raining. This habit was slowly declining; periodicals were gradually giving way to coffee-table books. But at the same time commuting was on the increase. More and more business and professional men were on the look-out for something they could enjoy on the train, and which their wives would like at the weekend (or, in some cases, vice versa).

For these readers, the *Spectator* was challenging Kingsley Martin's *New Statesman* where earlier it had enjoyed its main advantage: at the back. In the arts section Alan had asked Irving Wardle, then on the *Times Educational Supplement*, if he knew anybody who would take on Music: Wardle had suggested a young colleague on the *TES*, David Cairns; David wrote a couple of specimen articles and was taken on. His pieces immediately began to attract attention, including a note from Seamus Kelly in Dublin, a hard man to please: 'so refreshing to get a music man who not only can write, but is not afraid to kick'. Another newcomer was Clive Barnes, who up to that time had chafed under the restricted column inches he was allowed by the *Daily Express*, to cover Ballet; invaluable practice for his move to the wider Theatre to become, as the *New York Times* critic, one of the 'butchers of Broadway', though more humane in that capacity than some of his predecessors.

We were to find, later, that our arts pages were causing alarm to John Freeman, deputy editor of the *New Statesman* and by this time heir apparent. We accepted the stock belief which had grown up over the years that half the *Statesman*'s readers bought it for its socialism, and threw away the back (except occasionally for the Competition, if it was something simple like inventing clerihews), while the other half turned to the back and ignored the front, except for a quick look at Sagittarius's topical verse and the 'This England' selection. The appeal of the straightforward brand of Socialism offered in the front under Kingsley Martin was being threatened by divisions among the faithful about disarmament and Clause Four. If the back lost ground to the *Spectator*, the prospect of the *Statesman*'s circulation continuing to reach six figures, as it then promised to do, would be jeopardised.

In the book pages, particularly, Karl Miller was busy eroding the *Statesman*'s former undisputed supremacy with, among other achievements, a telling selection of front reviews – Leavis on D. H. Lawrence, Waugh on Frank Harris, Philip Larkin on Auden, Conor Cruise O'Brien on Edmund Wilson. And the *Statesman* had nothing to compete with Consuming Interest, Roundabout and Postscript – or with the cartoonists we had begun to use: Trog, who provided a weekly comment on the news (with George Melly as his ideas man), and lighter drawings from unknowns, or little-knowns: Timothy Birdsall, who was to die tragically young; Blake, Heath, Ed. Fisher and the self-effacing Maurice Bartlett.

The *Spectator*'s 'front' was also undergoing a change, with a succession of longer 'think-pieces' on Charles Curran's 'Stalin merely smiled' model.

It had been quickly followed up by an article from an unexpected source: Erskine Childers III – grandson of the executed republican, son of the Fianna Fail politician – sent in another long, and obviously well-researched, article on the background to Suez.

I had not known 'young Erskine', as the family called him, in Dublin; he had left to complete his education in the United States before I came to know them. But I knew he could be relied upon to fit the theory to the facts, and not the other way round, and his thesis – that the Suez campaign had been cooked up in advance between the British and the French governments – was entirely convincing. Collusion had, of course, been suspected, but it had been vehemently denied; one Tory MP, Monty Woodhouse, had gone so far as to commit himself to resign his seat if collusion were to be proved. Childers could not prove it, but his account of the events leading up to the invasion, with information leaked from French sources, in fact told English readers for the first time how and when the assault had been planned, and how and why it had gone wrong.

By that time, however, too many people had invested in 'My country, right or wrong' for the article to have any impact, in the sense of persuading those who had backed the crazy adventure to change their minds about it. Eden, they had come to assume, had been right to do what he did. If there was some collusion, in the circumstances that was forgiveable; and if the campaign had ended in humiliation, that was the fault of John Foster Dulles and the State Department, persuading poor old Ike to refuse American support.

Other long pieces followed; among them Ian Gilmour on Franco's Spain, which won a tribute from Salvador de Madariaga, the most eminent of the Spanish Socalists in exile; 'With Mac through Africa', a cool appraisal by Robert Manning, *Time/Life* bureau chief in London (soon to become editor of *Atlantic Monthly*), of the way in which Macmillan came to feel and appreciate the strength of the wind of change; and 'Traffic planning – or town planning?', by Malcolm MacEwen, then Chief Information Officer at the RIBA, with a prophetic warning about the absurdity of town planning, for London, when there was no authority capable of making, let alone enforcing, a plan for traffic. These articles flowed in, without commissioning. I initiated only one; but as things turned out it was later to be curiously influential, and important for me: Geoffrey Murray's 'Fringe Medicine'.

Murray was the Religious Correspondent of the *News Chronicle*, a more demanding job than it now sounds, as the paper had an extensive circulation in non-conformist circles. I had read, and been impressed by, his *Frontiers of Healing* when it was published in 1958; it dealt with unorthodox methods of treatment sympathetically but shrewdly, and when the *News Chronicle* ceased publication in 1960 it occurred to me that he would be free to survey them for us, which he was glad to do. They had no accepted common designation at the time, except perhaps 'quackery'. Taking a hint from the Theatre – the Fringe at the Edinburgh Festival was by this time well-established, and Londoners had just been enjoying *Beyond the Fringe* – I settled for 'Fringe Medicine', which was soon to become common currency. Even the *British Medical Journal*, though patronising, was editorially intrigued.

For variety we had a sporadic series 'Come here till I tell you' from Patrick Campbell; the occasional 'John Bull's Schooldays' – from Malcolm Muggeridge, Quentin Crewe, William Golding, Ken Allsop and Peter Forster, the novelist who had become our TV critic; a short story from Kingsley Amis; a short play from Harold Pinter; and the serialisation of Evelyn Waugh's forthcoming *Tourist in Africa*, a diary of his travels there in 1959. But the most impressive article – or series of articles, as it was to become – during the year was Bernard Levin's 'The Prisoners of St Helena'. It not merely drew attention to a particularly repellent legacy from Britain's imperialist past, but also actually succeeded in its aim, in spite of some ugly opposition, of getting something done.

Under the amended Colonial Prisoners Removal Act of 1869, prisoners sentenced in a British colony or protectorate could be moved to another; and in 1956 the St Helena Government Gazette announced that three men would be arriving from Bahrain to serve their sentences there, as they later did. By accident Donald Chesworth, a Labour member of the London County Council, came to hear about the case, looked into it, and alerted lawyers and Bernard to what had happened.

What had happened was barely credible. Five Bahrainis had been campaigning for, among other things, a legal code to be established in Bahrain. They were arrested; 'tried' on trumped-up charges by a 'court' composed of three relatives of the Ruler of Bahrain; and – as Bernard put it in his summing up of the affair – not merely were they found guilty and sentenced to terms of imprisonment of from ten to fourteen years, but 'the verdict was announced five days before the court met, and two before it was even convened'. Even more disgracefully, the announcement of the impending arrival of three of them in St Helena '*was made before the trial began, and before the court was even brought into being*; the whole farcical and shameful travesty had been hugger-mugger arranged with the British government in advance.'

The case might not be on the level of enormity of the Dreyfus affair, Bernard commented, but 'there are places in the long story at which it seems at any rate more squalid'. One of those places was Westminster; only one member of the Tory party took up the cause of prisoners, and he soon reneged. That the case did not make more impact, and was soon forgotten, may have been because it *was* a long story, and a complex one, in journalistic terms. The full realisation of the discreditable nature of the deal that had been done did not finally dawn even on the prisoners' supporters until after a judicial committee of the Privy Council had turned down their initial appeal, largely because the Foreign Secretary, Selwyn Lloyd, was able to convince the committee that the 'trial' had been genuine, and the removal to St Helena justified.

Only then did somebody realise that the time at which the warrant for the prisoners' removal from Bahrain had been presented to the captain of the warship which was to take them to St Helena, had been earlier than the time at which their removal had been sanctioned by the necessary Order in Council in Britain. It was this error – in other circumstances it might have been called a technicality – which left the judge who heard the second application for Habeas Corpus no option but to declare the warrant was a nullity. He added, for good measure, that by invoking the Removal Act the Ruler of Bahrain had automatically waived his jurisdiction over the prisoners. This made the removal itself illegal, (which their embarkation would not have been, if they were still under the Ruler's jurisdiction). They were consequently free both from the threat of being returned to Bahrain and from their prison sentence.

Because the story came out in bits; because of the legal complexities; because the men were not British citizens; because they were Bahrainis; because St Helena was far away, some readers lost interest. A few expressed their irritation: why go on about it? But others subscribed to the fund set up to fight the case; and they had the satisfaction of reading about the men's gratitude for their eventual release, and its expression in a lunch they gave, not only to their solicitors and counsel but to their prosecutors and their jailer, which included melons they had grown in the St Helena prison kitchen garden.

'We have always believed in British justice', they announced when their freedom was toasted in champagne, 'and our belief is vindicated.' They might have toasted luck, as well; with Selwyn Lloyd's odious buttering-up of the Ruler of Bahrain ('the official walrus pledges himself in every case', as Bernard Shaw had put in the Preface to *John Bull's Other Island*, 'for the kindliness of the official carpenter') they would have had to serve out their sentences, but for a trivial mistake on the part of the Ruler's staff, and a chance realisation that the mistake was crucial. 'It is, for all its shaming quality, a heartening story', Bernard concluded.

Heartening it remains; but it should also serve as a reminder of the ruthlessness of official carpenters, and the readiness of official walruses to support them.

22

Rupture

During 1960 Gilmour had occasionally been serving the *Spectator* as a travelling Foreign Correspondent, and that autumn he decided to watch Nixon and Kennedy on the campaign trail. He had some difficulty in being temperate about Nixon, and he hardly attempted to disguise the admiration he had come to feel for Kennedy. Kennedy's victory, he commented 'was so generally predicted that it is easy to forget what an extraordinary achievement it was'.

Kennedy had won, Gilmour felt certain, not just because he had been so much the more impressive of the two in their TV debates, or that he had 'brought a panache and a sense of style that have been missing for a long time; and in this as in so much else the contrast was total', but also because of the feeling Kennedy generated which had been expressed by the man he had defeated for the Democratic nomination, Adlai Stevenson. When Cicero finished speaking, Stevenson reminded his audience to whom he was introducing Kennedy, the people said 'how well he spoke'; when Demosthenes finished speaking they said 'Let us march'. Kennedy was not yet a great orator, Gilmour admitted, but the comparison was apt; 'Europe will need monkey glands to keep up.' He had said at a rally, 'Let's go'; Britain, Gilmour clearly felt, needed to follow the same path. The fact that the *Spectator* was so in tune with this feeling, we assumed, must be a source of gratification to him.

The following spring, however, while I was with the family on holiday in Maratea a letter arrived from Gilmour which both baffled and angered me; baffled because of its contents, angered because he had given no indication of them before I left. The *Spectator*, he contended, had become too light-weight. One of his specific examples was justified: the flow of long pieces had tended to dry up. Although with the exception of Fringe Medicine they had not been commissioned, they had come in frequently enough not to need commissioning; this source had been failing. For the rest, though, what Gilmour seemed to be saying was that he no longer wanted the *Spectator* to continue on the course he himself had helped to set. He would have preferred to have more serious attention paid to the design and the texture of what earlier he had regarded as the emperor's clothes.

When I returned it was to find that Bernard, acting editor in my absence, had been puzzled by Gilmour's fault-finding. We could understand he might be worried over Karl Miller's decision to move over to the *New Statesman*, though in a sense it was flattering; according to Edward Hyams in his history of the *New Statesman*, John Freeman had been planning it for a long time, aware of Karl's outstanding talent. Freeman's lure had been the offer of a wider control of the back of the paper than I had been prepared to offer Karl, as I was less confident of his judgment outside the literary field.

Alan Brien, too, had just been prised loose from us by the new *Sunday Telegraph*, to take on the Theatre; an offer which, we had to agree, he could not refuse. Disappointing though this was, however, it brought Bamber Gascoigne in to us as Theatre critic, on the recommendation of his uncle – hardly a reliable source, but the uncle happened to be Quentin Crewe, whom we felt we could rely on, and the nepotism was immediately justified. Karl's successor Ron Bryden was also able to establish his reputation securely, as his 'front' reviewers soon indicated: among them Auden on Beethoven, Golding on Tolstoy, Waugh on Cecil Beaton, and Amis on Waugh.

Other newcomers were soon making their mark. Julian Critchley, just elected Conservative MP for Aldershot, began contributing political commentaries of the kind which his constituents have had to learn to live with, leading off with 'Principles of Conservatism' – 'the truth is, of course, that Conservatives do not have political principles. They have prejudices guided by facts'. John Cole, who had arrived from Ulster to work on the *Manchester Guardian*, began to cover trade union affairs for us; and we had entertaining pieces from Simon Raven and John Mortimer.

It seemed to us as if Gilmour was finding it hard to justify his captiousness; for a while an uneasy truce was signalled, perhaps assisted by the addition, at the back, of some newcomers dealing with more serious subjects – though not ponderously: Maurice Goldsmith on science, Gavin Lyall on motoring, and Monica Furlong on religious affairs. On medicine we had Jonathan Miller, fresh from *Beyond the Fringe*; he was working as a houseman down Gower Street at University College Hospital. Somehow we managed to persuade Raymond Postgate and Elizabeth David, who had pleaded too much work and too little time, to write on Food in alternate weeks. People were starting to read the paper from the back, we soon found; Ray had taken his wine paragraph and fused it into a Postscript with his wry comments on the week.

Payments for these contributors was in peanuts: still at £10 or £12 a thousand words. Yet their copy continued to tumble in, and space could be found for them because circulation and advertising revenue continued to rise. During the 1950s there had been many gloomy predictions about the future of the serious weeklies, chiefly based on the success of the *Sunday Times* under Denis Hamilton, with its serialisations of the life of Field Marshal Montgomery and other military leaders. Why, it was asked, should people who for ten pence could get both the *Sunday Times* and the *Observer* delivered together, spend ninepence on the *Spectator*? And why should advertisers bother with a journal which reached so few people? Replying to this in *Advertisers Weekly* in 1960 I pointed out that far from regarding the posh Sundays (as they were then commonly called) as a threat, we believed they were actually bringing us new readers – themselves created by the expansion of higher education and greater economic prosperity.

Betjeman had provided us with the clue when he told us he got no feed-back (not a term, I suspect, he would ever have used) from the *Telegraph* column. People who bought the *Spectator* bought it for pleasure, and so long as they could be reasonably sure of finding sufficiently interesting and entertaining material they would continue to buy it without making comparisons with newspapers bought out of habit and duty. But a great deal depended upon maintaining variety, and I was relieved to get a good response from a small group of writers who were asked that summer if they would like to join in a revival of the *Spectator*'s Notebook, this time to be written from outside the office, to start that winter. The five, all of whom agreed, were Kingsley Amis, Freddie Ayer, Graham Greene, Roy Jenkins and Evelyn Waugh.

Before the Notebook had been re-launched, however, Gilmour came in one day to the office and suggested the two of us should go round to the Marlborough Arms, something he had not done for some time. When he had bought our drinks he told me that he had put his name down for consideration as a Conservative candidate, and it had been accepted by the Conservative Central Office. Immediately, all became clear. I ought to have realised, months before. At a party I had met the then MP for Isleworth, Gilmour's home constituency, and he had said how pleased he was that Gilmour had become an active member of the party there. Teased with this, Gilmour had said he had decided it was a social, rather than a political obligation, and made light of it sufficiently convincingly for me to accept the excuse. Now, the reason for his dissatisfaction with the paper was obvious. Facing questions from a constituency election committee, he would certainly be held to account for what had been appearing, and some of it was highly critical of the Party.

By yet another of Fate's twists, I had just been asked by Denis Forman whether I would take on *All Our Yesterdays* from James Cameron, who had been presenting it for a year and wanted to return to journalism. I had regretfully declined, realising it would be impossible to combine the research and the writing which the programme required with editing the *Spectator*. As soon as I got back to the office I was on the telephone to Denis, praying that he had not found somebody else. He had not found somebody else. I tendered my resignation as editor forthwith, to take effect when a successor had been found and installed.

On reflection, we in the office thought we realised what had happened. Gilmour had not thought of a political career because he had not considered himself to be a politician, and had no strong party preference. His *Spectator* connection, though, had brought him into closer contact with many leading politicians. Doubtless some of them, impressed by his grasp of politics, had suggested he ought to try for a seat.

Simply in terms of his views he was closest to the Liberals; but at the time they offered little hope of mounting a recovery. If Labour had been firmly under Gaitskell's control he might have been tempted to join it, but he could have found his wealth, his social connections – he was married to a daughter of the Duke of Buccleuch – and even his looks – *Krokodil* might have used him as a model for an English aristocrat – against him. The hanging-and-flogging aspect of Toryism repelled him, and he deeply mistrusted Macmillan; but his views were not far removed from the 'Butskellite' centre, in particular those of Iain Macleod, Leader of the Conservative Party in the House of Commons and Chairman of the Party Organisation.

Macleod, we decided in the office, would certainly have been relied upon to recruit Gilmour, if he thought there was a chance. The chance had come – or so we surmised – because Gilmour had seen what Kennedy had managed to achieve in spite of the far more formidable obstacles of his Catholicism, his Boston origins and – in retrospect, more startling that it was at the time – his notorious womanising. All that Gilmour himself would need to live down, or at least play down, if he went before a constituency election committee, would be the *Spectator*.

His relief at my decision to depart must have been as great as mine that James Cameron was leaving *All Our Yesterdays*. Gilmour, too, was able to persuade Iain Hamilton to return, this time to editor – an ideal choice, I thought, as it would preserve continuity, Hamilton being well-known and well-liked by those who had joined us after he had left. I could leave, too, on a rising tide of prosperity for the paper. The circulation, which had been 39,000 in 1959, had risen to over 48,000. In one heady week the figures were circulated through the office weekly – it actually exceeded 50,000, including 'returns'. And the Christmas number, the barometer of the mood of advertisers, was so well supported that it could be expanded profitably to eighty pages.

I was given a farewell party on 14 February. Coming in, blearily, to say formal farewells the next day, on my way to Manchester to do *What the Papers Say*, I was handed a copy of that week's issue, which had just been brought in from the printers. Its cover read, simply

THE SPECTATOR
CODOLOGICAL
BASIC SLAG

–

LEAVE IT FOR
THREE MONTHS

The hand of Levin was immediately apparent. He had persuaded the printers to set one copy with a cover which would encapsulate what had come to be recognised as my distinguishing characteristics in the matter of dealing with the day-to-day problems which arose with contributors and correspondents whom we did not care to offend, yet were reluctant to find space for. 'Codology' covered a range of irritations, from the worthy-but-dull to the academically-distinguished-but-unreadable; 'Basic slag' applied to editorials, which we often longed to dispense with. The other injunction dated back to Charles Stewart Parnell, who claimed that nearly every letter answered itself within six months, if it were let alone.

I cannot visualise having a more congenial bunch of colleagues. We were lucky in having some serious stabilisers: Charles Seaton, an almost alarmingly efficient sub-editor; Isabel Quigly on films; Nicholas Davenport, whose financial column helped to ensure that we would not be regarded as too flighty to be taken seriously in the City. But we were unable to take ourselves too seriously. The notorious weekly conference which most newspapers and journals held was dispensed with; instead, on Thursdays, after the paper had been put to bed in Aldershot the night before, we had an informal lunch in the boardroom – to which contributors, along with visiting journalists and writers, could be invited – consisting of bread, butter, paté, salami, cheese, fruit and wine brought in from Charlotte Street, occasionally supplemented by home produce. They were light-hearted occasions, but out of them came ideas which would rarely have emerged in formal discussions.

Spectator parties, held every few months, became an institution which people did not care to miss. Gilmour had liberated them from the staid occasions they had been under the Watson/Wrench proprietorship. At the first one I attended after I joined, the wife of a now eminent journalist carried out a reconnaissance to find which of the women present had kicked off their shoes, to stand talking in their stockings; she abstracted, and hid, one of the pair from each of them. Ian Fleming was almost always the first to arrive, and the first to leave; it was as if he felt he had to put in an appearance. Even Waugh came once. I felt in duty bound to talk to him, where he sat holding his ear trumpet. His deafness, he maintained, was psychosomatic, a protection against boredom . . .

We tried to make the *Spectator* a co-operative enterprise. Looking back, I can claim only one of the contributory elements for my own. To show our appreciation for their help, I suggested that our regular contributors should be sent a Christmas present of a bottle of V S O P brandy, doubtless selected by Ray. The thank-you letters intimated more than conventional gratitude; clearly the burgeoning network extended beyond 99 Gower Street. And there seemed no reason, as Hamilton had never left it, why it should not continue to flourish.

My departure, Gerard Fay explained in the *Guardian*'s London Letter, did not mean that any personal or political differences had arisen, as was clear from the fact I had been asked to stay on as a director. This was hardly the whole truth, but in the circumstances forgivable. Fay, anxious to ensure that his old friend Hamilton would not be thought to be trimming, went on to insist 'nor is there to be any change in political stance'; Hamilton saw eye-to-eye with Gilmour, 'though he is perhaps a little more to the left of centre'.

Hamilton had earlier been distinctly further to the left; but during his time in Hutchinson, like so many of his contemporaries and friends – Tony Hartley, Robert Conquest, Kingsley Amis – he had been moving perceptibly to the right. But in a letter thanking Gilmour for the party and for the editorship he had given me the chance to enjoy, I offered one word of warning: 'I do not believe that you will find it possible to continue to control the *Spectator*'s policy without directing it along the lines that you, within the Party, want it to go.' This would make it hard for him 'to take a dispassionate view of what constitutes the *Spectator*'s attitude, as a journal which must preserve some consistency'.

As an example I cited its attitude to Macleod. One of Gilmour's complaints, earlier, had been that we had not sufficiently stood up for Macleod as Secretary of State for the Colonies in 1961, when Lord Salisbury had derided him as 'too clever by half'; it was possible to approve of the strategy and yet be critical of the tactics. But soon it became clear that politics were not the problem – except for Ray, who was ill-at-ease in a Tory journal. The powerful pull from Fleet Street continued, extricating first Bernard, then Ray and Katharine, so that by the end of the year all three had left. Hamilton was able to attract some useful contributors, notably Henry Fairlie, to do occasional pieces, and Tony Hartley returned; but the loss of the regulars was soon reflected in a circulation slide.

Unexpectedly, too, Hamilton turned out to be an ineffectual editor. He was basically a writer – 'of divine quality, full of quirk and character', as Sir Robert Lusty, his boss at Hutchinson, was to recall in his obituary; and a shrewd talent-spotter. 'Iain, with his immense and varied range of friends, cronies, associates and crackpots, made an immense contribution to the "new" Hutchinson group image' – it was he who had pulled in Brendan Behan, Edna O'Brien and Michael Farrell. But in the firm he had Lusty in charge, and an experienced team to work with; back in the *Spectator*, he revealed an unexpected degree of indecision and administrative inefficiency, which exasperated the management.

Writing the occasional piece for him, and coming in with it, I began to sense a year later the same frosty atmosphere that I had encountered myself two years before; but I was not prepared for the shock of hearing, while I was rehearsing for *What the Papers Say* one afternoon in Manchester, that there was a paragraph in the *Evening Standard*'s Londoner's Diary claiming that the *Spectator* was to have a new editor: Iain Macleod.

What made things worse was that Hamilton, too, read of his dismissal in that *Evening Standard*. Gilmour had asked Macleod to keep the news a secret until Hamilton had been informed, but Macleod had leaked it to a journalist. As a director of the *Spectator* I too should have been informed in advance of the move; and I thought there was one possible way to thwart it. The appointment clearly broke the terms of the Trust which had been set up to try 'to maintain the best traditions and political independence of the *Spectator*'. The Trust consisted of the Chairmen of the LCC and the Headmasters' Conference, along with the Presidents of the Royal Society, the Royal Historical Society, the Law Society and the Institute of Chartered Accountants; it was convened whenever there was a change of ownership, with a view to vetting the newcomer to ensure that he would accept and honour the obligations the Trust imposed on him.

A *Daily Telegraph* reporter, despatched to find out who the Trustees had been when Gilmour bought the paper, contacted two of them and asked for their opinion. Victor Mishcon, who in 1954 had been Chairman of the LCC, recalled that, as one of the Trustees, he had actually asked Gilmour for an assurance that he had no intention of taking up party politics, which Gilmour had given. If he had foreseen what was to happen he would not have agreed to allow Gilmour to buy the paper. Frederick Jessop, who had been President of the Law Society in 1954, agreed: 'had I known that he intended to take up politics I would not have approved of him.' Lord Adrian, who had been President of the Royal Society, was in New York at the time; the *Telegraph* correspondent there sought him out. 'When I heard Mr Macleod had been selected as editor I naturally assumed he would cease to play a very active part in the Conservative Party,' Lord Adrian said: 'But if he carries on as an important figure in the party I should think it would certainly be a contravention of the *Spectator* Trust.'

The Trusteeships were *ex officio*; none of the three men who were living still held office. The *Telegraph* named the men who would have to be called upon, if the committee were reconvened. Under the terms of the Trust, however, no provision had been made for a review of the original decision, should the beneficiary change his mind. The assumption, presumably, had been that he would not change his mind; or that if he did, and entered politics, he would arrange to sell the paper. Gilmour made it clear that there was no intention of convening a meeting of the Trustees; that he did not intend to sell the paper; and that Macleod would be brought in as editor.

There remained the *Spectator*'s own board meeting, at which I put the case against Macleod's appointment. But as the board consisted of Gilmour, Janes and the company accountant, F. G. Elliot, Hamilton and I were outvoted, and that was that. I resigned my directorship, and severed the connection which had meant so much.

Yet it has never quite been lost. In 1964 Nick Tomalin, one of the brightest and best of the young journalists who emerged in the 1950s, was in charge of the Atticus pages in the *Sunday Times*. In one of them he described his research into 'Networks'. 'A Network is a Club without premises, constitution or life membership,' he explained. 'Not simply a clique. Not quite an elite. Not exactly a Trades Union. But with some of the qualities of all these alliances.' It might have its origins anywhere – in politics, art or sport. Journalism, he thought, was the perfect nursery. He cited the *Manchester Guardian*, the *Observer*, and the *Queen* under Jocelyn Stevens as examples of papers which were its breeding grounds;

'but perhaps the *Spectator* in 1959 was the most romantic example', he thought, 'treasured by its Networkers with unrivalled nostalgia'.

Twenty-five years later, this still holds. When I wrote in 1989 to David Cairns to ask him how he came to take on our Music column, his reply came from the University of Davis, California, where he was holding Mozart courses. 'It was a, if not the, big break for me,' he commented. 'It was, no need to say, a marvellous paper to work for' – a view which, I feel sure, the rest of us shared.

Points of View, a selection from *Spectator* which Longmans published in 1962, helps to explain why the Network still flourishes. 'Perhaps the *Spectator* may be permitted one small boast,' I wrote in the introduction. 'Between a third and a half of the contributors here included were unknown as writers before they began to contribute to it; or at least not known in the field where they were to make their reputations – reputations, in most cases, which now extend considerably beyond the limits of the *Spectator*'s circulation.' Some had consequently moved on to lusher pastures, 'but weeklies are by now resigned to such defections and indeed rather proud of their alumni.' I suspect I am not the only one of us who still feels proprietorial gratification when one of those alumni obtains such rave notices as, for example, David Cairns has had, some thirty years after he joined us, for his Berlioz biography.

23

All Our Yesterdays

The formula of *All Our Yesterdays* was so simple that the mystery was why nobody had thought of it before. The BBC's *Scrapbooks* had recalled single years, arbitrarily chosen; the Granada series, devised by Sidney Bernstein's brother Cecil, dealt week-by-week with the week of twenty-five years before. At first it ran for only quarter of an hour, with James Cameron as writer and presenter; he made such a success of it that in 1961 the decision was taken to extend it to half-an-hour, and to screen it at a peak time – seven o'clock on Monday evenings.

Flattering though this was for James, he realised it was going to make things difficult. Granada had contracted with Movietone to use its newsreel material, exclusively. It added up to no more than twelve minutes for each programme – some of it, James knew only too well, abysmal. As there would be no more film, the longer programme would mean more writing, and writing of a kind – links – that bored him. It was time, he decided, to return to journalism.

Barrie Heads was producing the programme when I took over. A former journalist, he had been with Granada from the start and was already established as a mentor to the young directors and producers arriving from the universities; among them Jeremy Isaacs, fresh from his spell as President of the Oxford Union, who was now to take on *All Our Yesterdays*. It soon became clear to us that Movietone would have to be dispensed with; for the rest of the programme's life we switched to Pathé, which not only had more of the newsreel footage which cinema audiences had seen in the 1930s, but also its Gazette – snippets of fashion, show biz, odds and ends – and a fair

257

amount of unused film which, for some reason, had been rescued from the cutting-room floor, and which George Marshall of Pathé was able to sort out for us.

We were lucky: the fact that the half-hour series was launched in the autumn of 1961 meant that we were dealing with the Abdication of Edward VIII. Although for most of the build-up period in 1936 the newsreels, like the newspapers, had been silent, it was possible to make a feature of this restraint by setting it off against, for example, stills of what was appearing in the American newspapers at the time, and material taken from diaries and memoirs of people who had been involved. The fire which burned down the Crystal Palace, the day before Fleet Street's self-imposed dam broke, provided a fine climax for the programme which looked at the background; and to our relief the programme on the Abdication itself, which had to compete with an elaborate BBC Special, won the approval of the critics in two of the posh Sundays. Maurice Richardson in the *Observer* thought ours had been 'brisker, less pretentious', and Maurice Wiggin in the *Sunday Times* called it 'a clear winner over the BBC'.

This was important to us, as it helped to establish that the programme was not just a filler, to be dispensed with whenever some other idea caught the fancy of the programme committee. And we had another piece of good fortune when Granada decided to risk putting on a sitcom – or pubcom – immediately after us. It had been looked at, nervously, by the committee, but they had let it through for lack of anything else at the time; to their astonishment *Coronation Street* quickly climbed to the top of the ratings. Viewers switching on early found themselves watching *All Our Yesterdays*, and our ratings benefitted. In the mid-1960s we were usually in the 'Top Twenty', sometimes in the 'Top Ten', a couple of times second to 'The Street'.

The series reached its peak during the showing of the war years. For most of them, Bill Grundy was the producer and Raye Farr the researcher; they were both to become as happily involved in the programme planning and making as I was. The raw material we had to work with – the newsreel footage – was for the most part dire, for the obvious reason that the camera crews were rarely on the spot – except at the receiving end of bombing raids, as in the Blitz. In the Western Desert campaigns, which occupied so much of the early years of the war, they could show guns firing, but the targets were usually out of sight. This had led to some crafty faking.

In 1966 we showed an episode in which it appeared that the cameramen had actually filmed a successful burst by anti-aircraft gunners in the Western Desert, shooting down a German plane at night. It could be seen on fire, tumbling out of the sky, with an inimitable portentous commentary hailing it as a notable feat of marksmanship. A few days later a letter reached me from Bill, in Manchester:

> Yesterday afternoon a lorry driver, Mr H. Russell of Stoke-on-Trent, came to see me and revealed that the whole thing was phoney. It wasn't in the Western Desert . . . The plane that came down in flames was cut out of a cigarette carton. Two holes were cut for where the engines would be. Two zinc pots were inserted in these holes. It was filled with petrol – the whole thing suspended on a wire – then the petrol was ignited and our Mr Russell lowered the burning cardboard fake slowly down as the cameras rolled.

We had often suspected such cheating, Bill commented, but this was the first time we had proof; we should use the film again, in a later programme, as a warning.

With the exception of a rumpus over our programmes on the fall of Singapore, when our strictures were mistakenly taken by some *Daily Telegraph* readers to refer to the defenders, the correspondence which came in about the series was consistently friendly, including a congratulatory letter from Lord Avon – Anthony Eden: 'I thought you might like to have this spontaneous reaction from one who was closely concerned with many of the events you discuss.' But the letter which gave me personally the most satisfaction came from Sir Alan Cunningham, whose fame as a general stood high after he had driven the Italians out of Abyssinia, but who was sacked by Auchinleck for his failure to cope with Rommel, and who had been freely blamed for botching the Desert campaign. I had emphasised the point that Cunningham could have had little experience of tank warfare. 'I owe you my thanks,' he wrote,

> for your humane and objective handling of those parts of last night's presentation which dealt with a difficult part of

my own career. It may amuse you to know that although experienced in the handling of motorised infantry etc. I had *never* had a chance of handling real armoured forces until I was set up to meet Rommel. On paper, yes, but not otherwise.

All Our Yesterdays was always interesting to prepare. We could hope for surprises, such as the sight of some well-known politician spud-bashing in his army days. That never happened, but endlessly we received requests for the source of our material from men and women who had seen themselves, or relations, or friends. Because it was a straightforward studio show, too, it could be exploited to give young trainee-directors, who Granada was then attracting from universities, some not too taxing experience. Naturally Bill and I have claimed the credit for the fame of those who went on to higher things: twenty years later Mike Cox was in charge of Granada's impressive drama output; Mike Apted's *Gorillas in the Mist* was being nominated for Oscars: Mike Newell had directed several admired films. Out of all of the trainees I can remember only one who made such a botch of the programme that in the New Theatre pub, afterwards, I asserted that we would hear no more of him. Nor did we, at the time. But when in 1988 I teased him with the cock-up he had made, John Birt could afford benignly to acknowledge it; by this time he was just about to become Deputy Director-General of the BBC.

In addition to being so enjoyable to prepare, *All Our Yesterdays* provided me with nearly fourteen years of a subsidy to do whatever research I wanted to do, for whatever books I might want to write, without the need to worry too much about the size of the advance on royalties which Graham Watson of Curtis Brown would be extracting for me. This was just as well, as advances then were small except for established authors; for *West Briton*, £175.

A biographer can describe and comment upon a writer's output; for the writer himself this presents some intractable problems. All I can do is recall how and why the books came to be written, to account for their apparent disconnectedness. My intention was to exploit the opportunity *All Our Yesterdays* provided to seek out historical subjects; but as things turned out the first commission was to present a survey of the main varieties of unorthodox therapies, based on Geoffrey Murray's *Spectator* article.

Shortly after it had appeared Murray had been approached by Faber & Faber to expand it into a book. He had agreed, with the proviso that I should contribute the sections on those aspects of the subject which he had not gone into, in particular the branches of psychotherapy which orthodox psychiatry either neglected or denounced, and which I had become interested in while doing the research for *Emotional Stress and Your Health*. This was agreed; but almost immediately, Murray was offered a job by the World Council of Churches in Geneva. He decided to accept it, leaving the book project to me.

Interested though I became in the therapies, and convinced that they were not so ridiculous as some of them appeared, by the time *Fringe Medicine* was with the publishers I had just the kind of commission I had hoped for. Peter Ritner, then a senior editor with the Macmillan Company in New York, had decided the time was ripe for a book on the abdication of Edward VIII, twenty-five years before; and he had asked John Gross whether he knew of anybody in England who would write it. Unable to think of anybody off-hand, Gross asked his friend Jeremy Isaacs if *he* could think of somebody. Jeremy, who had seen how interested I was in the affair during the weeks we had been covering it on *All Our Yesterdays*, suggested I might take it on.

Before the research was completed, though, the earlier work for *Fringe Medicine* had sprung two other books which could be written off-the-cuff, as it were – luck, again, playing a leading role in prompting the first of them. It came as the result of a call from a man who claimed to be a freelance reporter working for a broadcasting company in Canada, who wanted an interview. He duly brought his tape-recorder along, and did the interview; but in the conversation which followed it gradually became clear that his real purpose was to sell me life insurance. The interview was simply his way of gaining access to potential clients. Before this dawned on me, however, he had found another way to keep his patter going; he remarked on my interest in fringe medicine, which he had grasped from some cuttings and books on the desk. Did this include osteopathy? I told him, yes. Had I met Stephen Ward? I had never even heard of Stephen Ward.

Ward, the life insurance salesman assured me, was *the* fashionable osteopath in London, and I would be doing myself a disservice if we did not meet. He offered to ring up, there and then, to fix an appointment, which he did. A few days later, the three of us met for lunch. Ward was affable and, up to a point, engaging, though he was a chronic name-dropper (among his 'friends' were Winston Churchill and Elizabeth Taylor), and more inclined to lecture us on the merits of Maoist Communism than to discuss osteopathy. Still, he agreed to read the typescript of my chapter on the subject, and took it away with him.

A few days later the papers carried the story of the shots which the West Indian Johnny Edgecombe fired at the lock of Ward's mews flat, trying to get in because Christine Keeler, who had had a row with him, was there. When Ward rang to say he had read my chapter and would like to have a word about it, he clearly found the whole mews episode vastly entertaining. After we had met at his consulting rooms – where he showed me some of the drawings he had made of celebrated patients, and their names in his appointments book – he took me to the mews, and showed where its by this time most notorious attraction, a two-way mirror enabling voyeurs to watch lovers in the bedroom, had been, its place still indicated by a hole in the wall.

On this occasion Ward launched into a light-hearted but genuine apologia for osteopathy. He had been trained in the United States, where osteopaths who had qualified were just coming to be granted the right to regard themselves as on a par with the medical profession, much to the indignation of the American Medical Association; but in his experience, hunch and psychology were of much greater importance than mere manipulative skills. As soon as new patients came to him, he claimed, he would know instinctively – even before examining them – whether he would be able to treat them successfully. In some cases he actually knew in advance; usually if they had been sent by somebody who was a firm believer in Ward's ability. It was as if they had been infected with optimism, and this had made them physically and psychologically tractable, in both senses of the term.

With sceptical patients Ward sometimes resorted to a form of brainwashing. Some of them came to him, he suspected, because they had heard eulogies, but rather hoped to be able to say that they had tried Ward, and found his treatment for backache useless. Members of Parliament, Ward had found, were particularly prone to stand on their dignity, already compromised by having an appointment with a quack – American qualifications were not taken seriously in Britain. They had to be made to realise who was the master. Ward told them to undress; when they were stripped to all but their underpants his receptionist would tell him he was wanted on the telephone, and he would leave them for a few minutes, as long as he deemed necessary to break their pomposity. The method worked wonders, he had found. The Houses of Parliament furnished him with some of his most enthusiastic supporters.

I did not expect to meet Ward again, but some weeks later he rang to ask me to lunch. All the bounce had gone out of him; he had come to realise that the Establishment was out to get him. This I knew, up to a point, because I had earlier found myself in the unexpected position – having heard him relate the full details of the Profumo affair, as it was about to be called, from his point of view – of being able during the period of speculation and rumour before Profumo's resignation to dine out on the story, enjoying the reputation of having access to inside knowledge. It had not then occurred to Ward that he would be held responsible for the blow to Tory morale when, as he knew was inevitable, the facts came out; but soon, I was getting indications of the Establishment's determination to destroy him. Even so, I was unprepared for the account which he gave over lunch of the way in which the witnesses who were to appear against him were being suborned – told that unless they gave the evidence the prosecution required they would be charged with prostitution, and perhaps more serious offences.

From what Ward told me about his relationship with Christine, Mandy and the others, the notion of his living on their immoral earnings was ludicrous. But the fact that this was going to be the charge was sinister; he wanted me to write an apologia which, he believed, the *New Statesman* would publish, setting out the facts. I told him that I had no inclination to act as his ghost, but that if he wrote it, I would do for him what he had done for *Fringe Medicine*; offer him comments and criticisms. He neither accepted nor rejected the proposition; and I did not hear from him again. After his death, a journalist who knew him well told me that there was never any possibility that Ward would have written the apologia himself. He was no writer; the only example of Ward's writing the journalist had ever seen was his suicide note.

The facts have since been set out in *An Affair of State*, by Philip Knightly and Caroline Kennedy, and they are even more disgraceful than was suspected at the time. Even the new Lord Chief Justice Parker, who had been welcomed as a more judicial mind than Goddard, was evidently an accessory to the Establishment's conspiracy – not too strong a term, though the conspirators did not need to meet to plan Ward's downfall; they appear to have acted independently, as if knowing each other's minds.

The Profumo affair, along with some other scandals – the revelations about the Argylls when they were divorced; the exposure of sleazy press methods by the Vassall tribunal – led to a spate of articles about the state of morality in Britain, including a *Punch* series to which I contributed; and this led to an offer from André Deutsch to write *Private Conscience–Public Morality*, a survey of the way attitudes to crime and vice had been changing, so that much which convention, as well as the law, had put in those categories had become socially more acceptable.

Drugs, Doctors and Disease, which followed, arose out of *Fringe Medicine*, which prompted the management of a small pharmaceutical firm, DDSA, to send me material about some disreputable practices engaged in by its larger competitors. Pfizer, for example, was charging the National Health Service £60 a thousand tablets for its antibiotic tetracycline. DDSA was offering tetracycline to the NHS at £6. 10s. a thousand, and could make a profit, if allowed to; but Pfizer had claimed that its patent must be protected, and the Ministry had agreed. Yet in 1961 the Federal Trade Commission had shown that Pfizer had 'made false, misleading and incorrect statements for the purpose of inducing the US patent office to grant a patent on tetracycline, and caused said patent to be issued as a result of said misrepresentations' – one of many examples of the pharmaceutical industry's ruthless methods which the book dealt with.

In the meantime *Abdication*, which owed its conception to *All Our Yesterdays*, was in gestation: and the continuing popularity of the programme – even among people who would not normally have watched commercial television, or television of any kind, at that hour – proved to be a distinct asset in the research. Many of the individuals who had played leading, but behind the scenes, roles were still alive;

but most of them initially, and understandably, were suspicious of anybody who approached them for inside information. Yet the only one who refused point-blank was the Duke of Windsor himself. He left it to his lawyers to vet the typescript. Most of the points they wanted changed were reasonable; I could not, though, comply with their request that no reference should be made to the feeling among those who knew Edward that he had some fascist sympathies, as this was so well supported.

One of the courtiers of the time I would have liked to interview was Peregrine Brownlow, who had been Edward's Lord in Waiting. When Wallis Simpson fled to France, after the newspapers had at last broken the story to the British public, it had been Brownlow who accompanied her in the hectic journey through France, chased by reporters. To add to his discomfort, the flask of whisky he had brought with him broke in his pocket; when they got out to have lunch at the Pyramide in Vienne, he and the car's upholstery stank of it. Brownlow had stayed on in the South of France as her adviser, until after the Abdication.

Brownlow, however, was in the Bahamas. I sent him a letter, with some questions I hoped he could answer. 'I am perfectly glad to help you and to answer your questions,' he replied, 'not only from a historical point of view, but mostly because "All Our Yesterdays" is my favourite TV programme, and has been for a long time.' Not only did he answer the questions, but added bits of information marking them 'speculative' or 'not to be quoted', which were precisely what I needed.

Peter Ritner, when he read the typescript, liked the approach and suggested a successor along roughly similar lines; a biography of the welfare state, its origins, development and achievements. Again the aim would be to explain the phenomenon to American readers who, in his experience, found it baffling. How had it come about?

It would be necessary, I realised, to have an introductory chapter on the Poor Laws as they stood until Lloyd George began to sweep them away. This took me back to their inauguration in the 1830s; and then beyond, into territory which was more familiar, to me, from both the theses at Oxford and TCD. Eventually the 'introduction' ran to about 30,000 words, and they were painfully superficial. There was nothing for it, I decided, but to abandon the welfare state idea for the time being, and concentrate on a reassessment of the Industrial Revolution and its effects.

What Peter Ritner would have made of this switch from his welfare state project I do not know; by the time the typescript reached Macmillan in New York he had himself switched to Harcourt Brace. To my relief, Macmillan raised no objections, and published it under the curious title of *Men of Conscience*. Robin Denniston, then of Hodder and Stoughton, had taken on *Abdication*; now, he too accepted *Poverty and the Industrial Revolution*. My next book, he suggested, should be a biography: what about Sir Roger Casement?

24

Sir Roger Casement

On the clubhouse walls at the Island, in the days when I played there, were photographs of the members who had won the Irish Women's Golf Championship; the first being Mabel Casement, who won it three years in succession before the First World War. She had been a friend of my mother's and, as I was to find out when I first came across an account of his life, a cousin of Sir Roger. His name was never mentioned in our Malahide circles, though he had had friends there, and used to visit the village occasionally. I knew nothing about him until I found that for Irish nationalists he was one of the patriot martyrs of 1916; not quite on a par with the men of Easter Week, as he had not been directly involved in the Rising, but a martyr nonetheless.

Casement had come of Unionist stock, and had entered the British consular service as a loyal servant of the Crown. In that capacity he had been sent to the Congo, where he had uncovered the atrocities through which the Belgian rubber-planters were amassing profits for King Leopold II, with slave labour. Later, as a British consul in South America, he had made a similar and even more devastating exposure of the methods used by the planters to collect rubber in the Amazon basin; and on his return to Britain he had been given a knighthood.

But he had also become disillusioned with English imperialism, like Wolfe Tone before him and Erskine Childers a few years later; and he had decided to serve the Irish cause by enlisting support in Germany during the First World War. Captured after landing in Ireland in 1916 he had been tried for treason, sentenced to death and hanged – a fitting end for a patriot, securing him a place in the Pantheon with Pearse, Connolly and the other 1916 leaders. However, it had become known that the attempt to secure a reprieve on the ground of his earlier notable career, which had won influential backing, had been silenced by the production of certain diaries, allegedly his, revealing him to be a practising homosexual. The diaries had been shown around by, among others, F. E. Smith, the state prosecutor at his trial. They had then disappeared; the British government declined to acknowledge their existence. Why? Clearly they had been forged, to discredit Casement. Yeats had expressed what was the common opinion

> Afraid they might be beaten
> Before the bench of Time
> They turned a trick by forgery
> And blackened his good name.

I accepted this verdict unquestioningly; and when in 1955 the controversy was stirred up again, I took the opportunity to argue in a *Spectator* leader that it was time the issue was settled.

The controversy had been stirred up again by the publication of a biography of Admiral Sir Reginald Hall. With Sir Basil Thomson, Hall had been Casement's inquisitor after his capture; he would presumably have been responsible for arranging for the forgeries. His fellow-admiral and biographer, Sir W. M. James, dismissed the allegation as baseless; and in a follow-up article in the *Spectator* he argued that although Hall and Thomson would have gone to any lengths to stop the activities of a traitor, 'they were far too astute to devise a plot which, if exposed, would cause their downfall.'

This was answered by Desmond Williams, pointing out the many grounds for suspicion, and Robert Kee, who added another: Thomson, after his retirement from the Criminal Investigation Department, had himself been convicted of an indecent offence in Hyde Park, and it had been disclosed he had tried to bribe the policeman who arrested him. The correspondence rambled on until it was formally closed; only to break out again after the publication of René McColl's biography of Casement the following spring. I criticised it for, among other things, accepting that the diaries were genuine. Why, I wanted to know, if they were genuine, were they not produced by the Home Office for inspection?

A couple of months later, copies of the diaries were produced for inspection; not by the Home Office, but by Peter Singleton-Gates, who brought them round to the *Spectator*. They were, or purported to be, typed copies of two of the three diaries, for 1903 and 1910. Singleton-Gates had been given them in 1922, he told us, when he was working as a journalist in London, in return for some service – he was cagey about what the service had been. His intention had been to use them for a book; but the Home Office, getting to hear of it, threatened him with prosecution for refusing to divulge his source. His publishers were informed they, too, would be prosecuted under the Official Secrets Act.

As a sop, Singleton-Gates had been told he could have a look at the actual diaries if he pledged himself not to publish any of the material. Realising that no publisher would risk bringing out his book, he had accepted; and the originals had been shown to him. It was this claim of his that made me, for the first time, doubt the case for their being forged. It would not have been too difficult to forge the typed copies; but Singleton-Gates insisted that one of the theories – that the diaries were genuine, but the homosexual bits had been slotted in – was untenable. Not merely was Casement's handwriting distinctive, 'he filled all the space. The horrific entries in innumerable instances occur in the middle of a day's recording'.

Still, the only way the issue could be settled would be for the Home Office to produce the diaries for public inspection. Our request was refused, the excuse being that the government did not want to stir up antagonism in Ireland – a particularly absurd piece of reasoning, as it was precisely the refusal to exhibit the diaries that for over forty years had been periodically fuelling Irish resentment. In 1959, however, Singleton-Gates came to a deal with Maurice Girodias in Paris; the two diaries of which Singleton-Gates had copies were published as *The Black Diaries* by the Grove Press, with a preface explaining how (though not why) they had come into his hands, an introduction, and a commentary on Casement's career. R. A. Butler, Home Secretary at the time, decided that there was no further point in trying to keep the diaries out of the public eye; interested researchers were invited to apply for permission to inspect them at the Public Record Office.

The diary for 1903 was fairly innocuous, containing little more than hints of Casement's homosexuality; but the diaries for 1910 and, still more, for 1911 described his sexual encounters with native boys in loving detail. The descriptions, too, were in a form which, as Singleton-Gates had insisted, banished any possibility that they had been inserted. This left only the possibility, which some people still cling to in Ireland, that the diaries as a whole had been forged; but as I felt compelled to emphasise, this too was untenable. It would have been a mammoth task, and even the most accomplished forger would have blenched at the idea of imitating Casement's idiosyncratic handwriting for page after page. Besides, who would have paid for the forgery? If Hall, Thomson and the others had been unscrupulous enough to decide to employ a forger, they certainly would not have made him write at such unnecessary length when, say, a few letters would serve their immediate purpose.

Robin Denniston's idea of a biography of Casement had naturally appealed to me; it would be challenging. Most of the research had to be undertaken at the Public Record Office in London. It proved to be a protracted and daunting task; Casement turned out to have been a compulsive writer of letters and memoranda, as well as his diaries. The book took me three years to complete; and it began to sort out for me some unresolved problems of my own.

Casement, I found, was 'cracked' in two ways. One split was the consequence of his homosexuality. As it had to be hidden both from his employers and from his social circle in Ulster, where he liked to spend most of his time when he was on leave, his affairs had to be with youths who were not of his own class; this made it difficult, often impossible, to express the love which he longed to link with his sexual appetite.

The other division was in his loyalties. So long as his work took him to places such as the Congo and South America, the growing involvement in the Home Rule campaign did not trouble him: but when he was on leave he was confronted by the three-way pull of Unionism in the British sense; Ulster Unionism – in effect, Protestant nationalism; and Home Rule. The confusion of the years leading up to the First World War, with Carson and the English Unionists in effect backing rebellion in Ulster – 'Ulster will fight, and Ulster will be right' – confused Casement, too, until he decided, disastrously, that it justified his going to Germany to win support for the Home Rule cause he had embraced, thereby making himself in British – and many Irish – eyes a traitor.

But for fortune's grace, I might have found myself in a similar situation. I had been spared from having to make the disturbing, and eventually destructive decisions which divided loyalty can demand – as it would have demanded, if there had been a British invasion of Ireland in 1940.

Tracking Casement through his career, though, I was continually being jolted into introspection; and paradoxically the main effect was to upset preconceptions about the ordinary everyday business of living. Casement was a conventional man, insofar as circumstances allowed, who would have liked to lead a normal conventional self-satisfied life. It was nagging frustration which lifted him out of the rut, prompting the secular discontent which never relaxed its hold over him. Lacking that spur, I had been complacent.

25

'Ireland Awakes'

There had been plenty of excuses while I was engaged on the research for Casement to visit Ireland; some of his correspondence was to be found in the National Library. I was struck by the changes that were beginning to take place. Throughout the 1950s there had been little sign of movement away from the old political divisions, created by the civil war, or the futile anti-Partition campaign; and the economy had remained stagnant. I happened to have been in Dublin just before the *Irish Times* 1959 centenary celebrations; wandering through the office I came upon a notice which could be held to typify the country's, as well as the company's, condition at the time:

Irish Times Centenary 8th June, 1959

To mark the above occasion the directors have decided to give to each member of the staff a bonus of five pounds or one week's wages, whichever is the lower.

Yet 1959 also marked the turning of the tide. De Valera left the Premiership for the Presidency; and Sean Lemass took over. He had begun the process of dismantling Protectionist legislation the year before, and by the time I did a tour of Ireland in 1962 – for Mark Boxer, editor of the *Sunday Times*'s new colour magazine – the difference was striking enough to justify the headline Mark put on it, 'Ireland Awakes'. It was not just the signs of capital pouring into the country from abroad that was impressive; there were also

272

the indications of a fundamental change of attitudes. In 1952 I had heard the then Minister for Justice explain in the Dail why there was no need to ban *Ulysses* – it was too vile for any bookseller to stock. Now, ten years later, it was in shop windows, and when the architect Michael Scott opened up the Martello Tower in which the story begins, the new Minister for Justice attended the opening ceremony.

When *West Briton* was published in 1962 I had another indication of the way things were changing in Ireland, in the form of a letter from Dan Breen. In 1919 Breen had led a group of Volunteers in Tipperary in the ambush which triggered off the War of Independence; 'one of the great berserkers of the war', Tim Pat Coogan had described him in *Ireland since the Rising*, who had eventually become 'in many ways the most colourful figure in the Dail'. I had thought Breen an incorrigible Republican hardliner, but in his farewell speech to the Dail in 1961 he had included tributes to some of the men he had fought against in the Civil War, and had actually urged reconciliation with the Ulster Orangemen, in place of the anti-Partition campaign. Now, 'You will I know be surprised' he wrote,

> to get a letter from me. Your grandmother would not like it – in fact she may now turn in her grave at you reading it. I only want to congratulate you on your book 'West Briton'. You surely got to grips with the real position. It's sad for Ireland to lose men like you – you are needed back here to build up an Ireland not rich, but with a culture.

The handwriting was at times barely legible; he had been ill for some time, he explained, and found it hard to write, 'so excuse my effort'. As I wrote back to tell him, I could think of no letter which had given me more pleasure.

The book's reception in Ireland gave me the urge to promote a better understanding in England of Ireland's problems – one of them being that the English found it impossible to take the idea of an Irish economic revival seriously. *Private Eye* reflected the general impression in a take-off of my *Sunday Times* piece, describing how pleased a German entrepreneur was to find the natives coming to the gates of his new factory 'with their traditional Celtic greeting "Boggerough"'. In 1963 Granada agreed to a programme *The Troubles*, to try to show British viewers how and why a legacy of problems had dogged the Republic, as it had become, from the start. Jeremy Isaacs produced it; I wrote the script and did the 'voice over'; and we were relieved to hear from people both sides of the Irish Border that they thought it fair. Gerard Fay, a Catholic Southerner in his family background, wrote to tell us how emotionally stirred he had been; the Ulster Protestant John Cole – 'from the wrong half', as he put it – congratulated Jeremy on 'a superb job, both in television terms and historical ones. When even I thought the balance was right, it must have been good.'

Either *The Troubles*, or a memorandum I had been asked to provide for the committee which had been set up earlier to decide on what kind of form Irish television should take – should it be on the British, or American, or some other model? – or both, prompted the business man who had been appointed Director-General of Radio Telefis Eireann, Kevin McCourt, to invite me to dinner in London to suggest I should become the company's programme controller.

I had just had, and turned down, what could have been a thoroughly enjoyable job away from London on the ground that I did not know enough about the background: an offer of the editorship of the *Sydney Morning Herald*. It sounds more grand than it was; the editor had charge only of the leader pages. The publishers had been impressed by the success of the experiment they had made earlier by bringing in John Douglas Pringle from the *Observer* in London to edit the paper, from 1953 to 1957; and they wanted to repeat it. In the case of RTE, however, I knew the background only too well. In practice the job would have been hell, sifting and dealing with the demands of all the pressure groups – and with the attentions of the Irish newspapers which, then as now, tended to be well-disposed to Irish men and women who make a success of jobs in Britain, but are ready to savage them if they think this qualifies them to take on greater responsibilities back in Ireland. Even in 1974, when both marriage and *All Our Yesterdays* were over, I would have not have been tempted by the RTE job for which, according to Seamus Kelly, I was again being suggested.

By 1967 Seamus had been drama critic of the *Irish Times* for twenty-one years; and diarist, four or five times a week, for eighteen (barring the months he had spent in the making of *Moby Dick*). I laid on a party for him at the Irish Club in Eaton Square with his friends from theatre, film and Fleet Street. He had been in a shaky position under Alec Newman; but the new editor, Douglas Gageby, gave him (and, as it turned out, the *Irish Times*) a new lease. He was to carry on both jobs for a further twelve years; surely unmatched in journalism in our times.

Paddy Campbell declined the invitation; he was curiously uneasy, I found, at the prospect of an evening of this kind. But in his *My Life and Easy Times*, which came out that year, he described what the *Spectator* 'Come here till I tell you' series had meant to him.

I had seen him only once in the intervening years. Finding myself with another old friend of his near his home in the country we had called in, to realise that the visit was unwelcome; it became obvious that his second marriage was in difficulties – not surprisingly, as the book was to show. He was rarely at home, spending much of his time enjoying himself at the expense of his three employers, *Lilliput*, the *Sunday Dispatch*, and the Rank Organisation. As he recalled, they were 'getting almost nothing in return', except his company. He had become a master of the art of churning out whatever was required, whether it was one of his stock columns or a snippet of additional dialogue. Quite suddenly, it was as if all three had rumbled him. Rank withdrew his retainer; *Lilliput* gave him six months notice; and although the *Dispatch* column continued, a succession of changes of editor had begun to show him how unsafe his position was there, too. And his second marriage was indeed collapsing.

My invitation to him to write a dozen pieces for us had not merely put fresh heart into him; he 'found himself concerned for the first time in years with the long-lost graces of style'. And infuriating though it must have been for him at the time, he was grateful in retrospect because I returned some of them to be re-written whenever I thought he had crept back into his 'old refuge of automatic writing'. The *Dispatch* job was soon lost, but to his astonishment his agent Irene Josephy told him that the *Sunday Times* – still, then, a Kemsley paper – were interested. If he had not been able to find anything to interest *Dispatch* readers, his first thought was, what hope would he have with the infinitely more sophisticated readers of the *Sunday Times*? 'And then I remembered the *Spectator* pieces. I knew they'd held up well in comparison with the work of the other contributors, and many of them had been distinguished writers. Perhaps the *Sunday Times* had been encouraged to hire me because of them?'

Few aficionados of Campbell rated his *Sunday Times* columns as among his best; he was at times to grow desperate again, wondering where the next one was going to come from. But when he succeeded to his father's title, and part of his wealth, as the third Lord Glenavy, he was able to settle down with his third wife Vivienne in the south of France, mellowing in the process, and turning out weekly Provençal sitcoms, usually gently readable and sometimes up to the old mark. By that time, too, he was reaching an even wider audience in *Call my Bluff*.

Soon there was to be a different form of temptation for me to return to live and work in Ireland. 'When, a hundred years from now, they are casting round for suitable centenaries to celebrate, I like to think that 1970 will be remembered as the year when poets first began to be repaid for their services as the unacknowledged legislators of the world', I wrote at the time. 'In the Republic of Ireland, this financial year, anybody who produces or has in the past produced "a book or other writing, a play, a musical composition, a painting or sculpture which is original and creative and which is regarded as having cultural or artistic merit" will no longer be required to pay income tax on the proceeds.' The Minister for Finance in the Lemass government, Charles Haughey, had belied his reputation as 'the Hard Man' by introducing the measure 'to create a sympathetic environment here in which the arts can flourish'.

It was a noble gesture; but, as Haughey himself admitted, it was unlikely to bring artists and writers in droves to Ireland. Few of them earned enough to pay much income tax anyway. Those writers from Britain who took advantage of it were mostly in categories where 'cultural and artistic merit' needed some stretching to accommodate them; and by this time, though I was engaged on Casement, it was hardly likely to bring financial security. In any case I had no confidence in my ability to settle down to write in Ireland. I had known too many writers whose works were never finished –

Desmond Williams was one; and some whose projects were never even begun.

One friend from the past, too, now became inaccessible. Erskine Childers had enjoyed what could have been regarded as a successful political career, culminating in the deputy premiership under Jack Lynch. He had also been one of the most effective advocates of reaching agreement with the Northern Unionists in speeches in his constituency – Monaghan, one of the three counties ripped out of Ulster by Partition. Now, on de Valera's retirement, he was proposed as the next President, and was elected.

One English newspaper described him as 'a nice old gentleman'; but at the age of sixty-eight, I wrote in a comment on his elevation, 'in mind as in appearance, Erskine Childers remains almost absurdly young; rather more serious, and certainly more sedate, than when I first met him twenty-five years ago, but with the enthusiasms of youth always ready to break out.' Nobody, I thought, was better equipped to continue to lubricate relations between North and South – and Britain – if protocol allowed.

Protocol did not allow. Erskine was effectively muzzled. Nor was he able to make his official residence into the kind of cosmopolitan meeting place which his Highfield Road home had been. Touched by what I had written, which he thought 'quite perfect', he urged me to visit him at Aras an Uachtarain. But the prospect of the formality involved was daunting; we were not to meet again.

By this time, the urge to do more for Ireland in Britain had been brought back forcibly by the renewed 'Troubles' in the North; and an opportunity had just arisen. Con Howard, press attaché at the Irish Embassy in London, invited a small group of Hibernophiles, including Robert Kee and Iain Hamilton, to lunch to discuss forming a British Irish Association, with the aim of improving relations between the Republic, Northern Ireland and Britain on an apolitical level. We welcomed the idea; Robert allowed himself to be persuaded to take on the Hon. Secretaryship; and at a meeting in June 1972 we formally approved a constitution which stated, among other things, the BIA's objects: 'to further educational, cultural, artistic, social and other relations'. Politics was not mentioned.

That autumn, however, the young barrister Nick Stadlen, who had been appointed Secretary, presented a programme in which the 'social and other relations' took on a different complexion. 'An annual conference on a topical aspect of British–Irish relations, modelled on the successful Anglo–German Königswinter conference, will be arranged,' it asserted. 'This will bring together politicians, civil servants, academics, journalists and other men and women in public life.'

This was far from Con Howard's intentions, and Robert was further alarmed when he had a letter from David Astor, owner-editor of the *Observer* at the time, not merely insisting that the BIA must become more political, but 'suggesting Lennox Boyd and Callaghan as twin political heads'. Clearly the BIA was being hijacked; 'I rather rue the day,' Robert commented, 'when we allowed ourselves to be drawn in.' We did manage to insist that practising politicians should be excluded from the Association's executive, but at the price of accepting the idea of a politically-oriented annual conference; and although eventually there were a couple of cultural evenings, politically-oriented the BIA was to remain.

The first conference was held in Magdalene, Cambridge, in 1973. Realising that no Ulster politician would attend if either of the extremist elements, the IRA and the UVF, were present, they were not invited. Even so, Paisley and some other leading Unionists declined. But a few others came, as did John Hume and Austin Curry of the SDLP; and from Dublin, the Republic's Foreign Minister, Garret Fitzgerald, and Conor Cruise O'Brien. At meals, and in the bar, politicians and civil servants met who had never spoken to each other before. In the small hours Unionists were to be heard joining in 'Kevin Barry', and nationalists in 'The Sash My Father Wore'. The British civil servants who were there took note; from that time on the BIA's annual conferences were to be used as occasions for informal contact at the highest level. There is no doubt in my mind that they provided the sociable occasions through which progress to the Hillsborough accord was lubricated.

Incongruities often continued to irritate some of those who attended the conferences, notably John Hume. The original notion of a cultural organisation led to the Anglo–Irish aristocracy and the Guinness connection being prominent; Lord Longford and his heir Thomas Pakenham; Lord Moyne; the Marchioness of Dufferin and Ava. Somebody – I suspect Tim Pat Coogan – dubbed us 'Toffs against Terrorism'. Nevertheless the compromise which had been effected whereby the running of the BIA by our Secretary, Marigold

Johnson, and the eccentric executive were kept apolitical, while the events staged were heavily into politics, worked out more satisfactorily than any of us who were in at the first stage would have believed possible. If the quality, as well as the quantity, of the applicants for places at the conferences was a reliable criterion, they certainly fulfilled a need.

26

Beyond the Fringe

Until 1973 *All Our Yesterdays* had for twelve years provided me with security and plenty of time to write. But the series itself was now insecure. When our week-by-week progress had brought us up to 1945, it had come to be identified with the war. Could it survive into the peace?

James Butler, Rab's son, had succeeded Bill Grundy as producer, and periodically the series' future came under discussion, but it had been so successful in terms of ratings that there seemed to be no serious threat to its continuance. We became worried, though, at the rapidly deteriorating quality of the newsreel material, reverting 'to the pap of the 1930s', as Mike Murphy, who took on from James, observed in one of the memos which went back and forth: 'Eisteddfods, Dog Shows, Battles of Flowers, and the latest addition to the London Zoo'. There was, however, one change: regular interviews with men and women who had been in the news twenty-five years before.

I had forgotten, until I looked up the list of those we had on the programme in the first eight months of 1972, the extent to which the interviews had become the main feature of the series; they included Michael Balcon, Roger Bannister, R. A. Butler, Denis Compton, Lord Exeter, Carl Foreman, Sir Bernard Fergusson, Michael Foot, Lord Franks, Lord George-Brown, Douglas Jay, 'Gannex' Kagan, Lord Listowel, Lord Longford, James Mason, Ian Mikardo, Emanuel Shinwell, Denis Mack Smith, Laurens van der Post, Harold Wilson, and George Woodcock, then General Secretary of the TUC. But they had consented to be interviewed, I pointed out in a memo, mainly because of the programme's past reputation; and now, the tide had turned against us.

One reason why our ratings had been so consistently high was that those of the BBC programme on at the same time, *Tonight*, were low. *Tonight* was an uncommonly intelligent magazine programme, well-produced and presented; but *All Our Yesterdays* from 1964 to 1970 had the advantage that it rivetted two groups of people: those who had lived through the war, in the forces or in civil defence; and their sons, for many of whom the war was fascinating. Reluctant though the BBC must have been to take off *Tonight*, it was eventually decided to replace it with *Z Cars*; *All Our Yesterdays* ratings inevitably slumped, as a result. We were taken out of the Monday 7 p.m. slot, and transplanted to Sunday afternoons. Next, whereas we had been on all over the country at the same time, some regions started shifting us to different times of day. Although various suggestions were discussed with the idea of re-animating the series, in 1973 the decision was made to axe it. James Cameron, Bill Grundy and I together presented the final programme, looking back over the highlights of its predecessors, from the spectacular film of the crash of the zeppelin Hindenburg to the delightful spoof of Nazi soldiers goosestepping to 'The Lambeth Walk'.

All Our Yesterdays was an early victim of the BBC's decision to compete with Independent Television at all levels, down to *Dallas*. Granada would have found it hard to get the other regions to accept any replacement, if somebody had thought of one; but in any case the innovatory skill which had made the company's reputation in its early days was no longer in evidence. As Granada grew larger, too, it had become less flexible, more bureaucratically muscle-bound – illustrated in one of the last instructions we were given. When a new researcher was required, the producer and I always conducted the interviews. In future, we were informed, the appointment would be made 'by Management'. Although for a while I continued to do the occasional *What the Papers Say*, my earlier close connection with Granada was now severed.

The demise of the series could not have come at a worse time for me. I have said nothing about marriage and family. Our son, Neil, was born in 1962, and for a while all had gone smoothly; but gradually the tie began to loosen. Boo took a job on *Nova*, a magazine which for some reason enjoyed a higher reputation among its readers than among the advertisers necessary to keep it going; she began to extend her own circle of friends in Fleet Street. Diana had left school, going to live with some friends in a flat. Neil, always remarkably self-contained, had decided he wanted to go to Westminster, as he eventually did; in the meantime he was at Westminster Under School. I had rented a small flat as an office to write in, and periodically to stay in during the week; not always alone. Almost imperceptibly Boo and I eased apart, until it became clear she would prefer to separate. This would mean alimony, with no secure income out of which to provide it. And in three years time I would be sixty . . .

Rescue, temporary but crucial, came through Judy Froshaug, a colleague of Boo's on *Nova*. Her lover was involved in a part-work, one of the many which burgeoned at the time, coming out in weekly segments. Its editors needed somebody who could provide articles on paranormal phenomena: telepathy, dowsing, ghosts and so on. I was the expert on the subject, Judy assured them. They gave me the job.

At one remove, I owed it to Arthur Koestler. We had been introduced by his friends John and Patsy Grigg when he was still at the height of the fame which *Darkness at Noon* had brought him. He was about to return to his old love, science, he told us; though he declined to tell us what the next book would be about – he was almost superstitious, I later found, about disclosing his intentions. I had been warned that he could be 'difficult', either if he got drunk or if, while he was still sober, he was contradicted by anybody on subjects he felt strongly about. That evening he was genial, with only the occasional flicker of impatience, as when the subject of water-divining came up. I had the feeling, though, that he was dismissive about it only because he regarded it as letting the side down; that he was prepared to accept the existence of unexplained phenomena, and would welcome research into some of them, but found it impossible to take seriously the traditional forked hazel twigs and other such gadgets.

He and his wife Cynthia, who had been his secretary, were friendly, in spite of my attempts to defend the art of water-divining. I plucked up the courage – for at the time Arthur seemed to me awe-inspiring – to get Faber to send him a pre-publication copy of *Fringe Medicine*; he reviewed it in the *Observer*, on balance favourably, though again mocking me for having included, and taken seriously, so obviously spurious a therapy as acupuncture. They came to dinner; Boo and I went to dinner with them in their Montpelier Square home; and we settled down to what turned out to be a sporadic, protracted tussle between Arthur and me, with me endlessly questioning, and Arthur endlessly seeking to justify, his opinions and attitudes – a role he enjoyed so long as the questioner was basically on his side, trying to elucidate, not to demolish, his developing ideas.

Arthur was another sufferer from a split mind. As a child he had begun to have a passion for science, and the scientific method. But he was also psychic, so much so that he was in demand when friends wanted to have table-turning seances – still a popular pastime in the early years of the century. Conventional science, then as now, denied that the kind of experiences he had actually witnessed could happen; and when he grew up and became science correspondence of a leading German newspaper chain, though he did once ask its readers to send him experiences of the kind usually regarded as psychic, for the most part he stayed within convention's bounds.

Conversion to Communism meant that his curiosity about ESP, aroused by the results of the research which J. B. Rhine was doing in the 1930s in the United States, had to be altogether suppressed. And when he broke away from the Party, although *Darkness at Noon* was conceived and written primarily as an anti-materialist manifesto, it was hailed as a political tract; as a result, he had become too involved in the Cold War to return to his old interest. In the 1960s, when he picked up the threads again, he felt it was wise not to tax tolerance too far. His reputation was enough to ensure that for a while, at least, his criticisms of the condition of science – of physics, biology and psychology, in particular – would be taken seriously even by scientists who disagreed with his unpopular opinions. If he asked them to accept ESP, they might use it as an excuse to look the other way.

While he was keeping the paranormal at a safe distance in *The Act of Creation* and *The Ghost in the Machine*, he was encouraging me to join the Society for Psychical Research. So by the time the part-work offer arrived, I was reasonably well briefed to cope with it; and it had the inestimable advantage of prodding me into more careful research, particularly on the historical side. This revealed a curious gap in the otherwise very extensive literature; no history of the subject had been published for a century. Encouraged by Judy and Arthur, I decided to write it myself.

The project was obviously going to take time, and meanwhile there was another gap which would be easier to fill. Preparing *Drugs, Doctors and Disease*, I had found several histories of medicinal drugs, but none of those which were consumed for pleasure or relief, nicotine, alcohol, opium, cannabis, coca. It happened that in the late 1960s and early 1970s the drug which was arousing most alarm was cannabis – 'pot'. A few campaigners were seeking to legalise it on the ground that it was less lethal than alcohol or tobacco; but the more general view was that pot was not merely dangerously addictive on its own, but also led on inexorably to heroin addiction. A committee had been set up to investigate, chaired by the redoubtable Lady Wootton, the leading authority in Britain in the area where sociology, criminology and psychiatry overlap. It reported in 1969: on the available evidence, it was able clearly to show that cannabis was not responsible for aggression, crime or ill-health; it was less dangerous, both to the user and to society, than alcohol; and it did not lead on to heroin addiction.

Although the implication – that cannabis could safely be legalised – did not appeal to the Home Secretary, James Callaghan, who unhestitatingly rejected the committee's findings, the controversy had continued; and this encouraged me to write *The Forbidden Game* (Baudelaire's description of drug-taking for the pleasure of hallucinating), surveying the use of drugs in history. I started with few preconceptions, but the lesson which emerged was that considerably less damage has been done by drugs than by governments' clumsy efforts to control them – Prohibition in the United States being only one example. Another, the attempt by the Chinese government to ban opium, then gave me the excuse to describe it in a spin-off from the research, *The Opium War*.

In the meantime, a course which events were taking in the early 1970s had begun to provide me with the subsidy no longer coming from Granada. In 1971 James Reston, the *New York Times'* Political Correspondent, went down with appendicitis while he was on a visit to China; and in one of his despatches he described how he had been successfully treated for post-operative pains by acupuncture. Of all the forms of fringe medicine, acupuncture had provoked the most derision in the medical profession; but when three of the most eminent physicians in the United States were invited by the Chinese government to investigate it for themselves, they felt bound to accept. To the chagrin of many of their colleagues, when they returned they reported that they had witnessed the use of acupuncture as a pain-killer, and there could be no doubt that it worked. Within months, people all over the western world were watching it working, on television programmes.

At the same time, one of orthodox medicine's most cherished dogmas was being demolished by research in the United States. Generations of medical students had been assured that the mind cannot learn to control the body's automatic functions – temperature, pulse rate, blood pressure. With the help of techniques of meditation imported from the Far East, this was being shown to be fallacious. Blood pressure, in particular, could be lowered, and kept low – all the more important in that research was also demonstrating that high blood pressure is a risk factor in connection with heart attacks. But it took time – in fact is still taking time – for the medical profession to digest these unpalatable findings. Largely as a result, more and more people began to turn to the 'Fringe' – now to become better known as 'alternative medicine'. As features editors, needing somebody to satisfy their readers' curiosity, found my name linked to the subject, I was to benefit.

As a bachelor again, and as a freelance working from home, I also could begin to liberate myself from convention. Looking back, I suspect that the initial impulse had come earlier as the result of a mildly ludicrous episode. When Colleen Stafford and I had met again in London she had been so entertainingly scathing about my behaviour as a junior reporter on the *Irish Times* that we had greatly enjoyed each other's company; and after the founding of the Wexford Festival she invited me to come over to stay at her home there. Her husband had driven me down from Dublin Airport just in time, she told us, for us to dress for the opera.

It had not occurred to me to bring a dinner-jacket. For Glyndebourne, yes, and Covent Garden; but Wexford? I would have to wear one of her husband's, Colleen said when I admitted leaving it behind. Luckily, she said, looking at me, it would fit.

I knew it would do nothing of the kind; his waistline obviously far exceeded mine. Humiliatingly, it didn't; the fit was perfect. All was now well, I thought. And then I came upon the tie. Of all the social solecisms that it was possible to think of, during my Anglo–Irish Descendancy days, the wearing of a made-up tie was for some reason the worst. It was what waiters wore – as we could see any evening at the Dolphin; one of them had a long neck, and the clip at the back was frequently visible. Stafford's was an even greater horror: the clip was at the front. All there was, was the bow; nothing to go round the neck. I put it on in a state of shocked embarrassment. It would surely fall off.

The opera turned out to be *I Puritani*, with the then unknown Mirella Freni. The old-fashioned cinema used as the opera house was wonderfully resonant; she sang ravishingly; by the end of the evening, especially after a session in the Talbot Hotel, I did not care what happened to the tie (in fact one clip parted from the shirt, leaving it hanging down sideways). What fools, I realised, we had been – all the more because true dedication to the principle would have entailed wearing double-end bows, while we secretly settled for single-ends.

It took time for the implication to seep through: that there might still be areas of mental and emotional, as well as social, arrested development. Whenever there was a reminder of how enslaved we were to fashions in clothes, it was to give another push to introspection. Soon after the demise of *All Our Yesterdays* Barrie Heads and I, who share a birthday, were having lunch to celebrate it, and he recalled how earlier, almost every morning of his life, he would put on a shirt to which a collar had to be attached with the help – help, indeed! – of a small stubby white bone collar-stud at the back of the neck. The collar would then be fastened to the shirt with another stud, longer, collapsible, and tortoiseshell-backed, so that he could put on a tie. I had gone through the same absurd performance.

I had mocked girls for slavishly following fashions without realising how ridiculous mine were. Take that comical form of male cleavage, the trilby hat! Many of us felt undressed without one. The more pretentious among us wore 'Anthony Edens', or bowlers, but everybody wore a hat – or, in the country, a cap. We kept up our socks with sock-suspenders or bought socks with elastic tops, and a gap for the calf to bulge out of. We wore armbands to keep the cuffs of the shirtsleeves just visible at the end of the jacket sleeves, at the end of which were buttons, never used. We wore waistcoats which, as Ronald Frankau used to sing, if a gentleman was quite correctly dressed, 'he would leave the bottom button undone and do up all the rest.' And so on.

The conventions of a lifetime are not easily overturned. I had, and still have, some prejudices which I am unlikely ever to shed. But gradually I began to rebel against them, starting with the easiest of the changes to make, at least for anybody who is living either alone or with somebody who will not be embarrassed. Moving into a flat, I escaped from pyjamas.

At school, pyjamas had been subject to much the same tyrannical rules as day-time wear. Convention ruled that flannel was the obligatory material for douls, and anything flashy would in all likelihood have ended up with the wearer dumped in a cold bath. When they came back from the laundry, the cord had invariably been pulled to one end. It would have been easy enough to thread it through again with the help of a large safety-pin, but safety-pins of any kind were not usually found in boy's dormitories; the threading took ages. And to wear pyjama tops outside pyjama bottoms was inconceivable.

The tyranny which pyjamas came to exercise on former public schoolboys can be judged from the fact that on his first day in New York in 1913 Rupert Brooke, who might have been expected to have much else to think about, fussed in a letter home about the loss of his, on the voyage. When Orwell's Winston Smith was summoned from his bed in *1984* by the two-way TV alarm signal, he was naked because 'a member of the Outer Party received only 3,000 clothing coupons annually, and a suit of pyjamas was 600.' In one of Patrick Campbell's last columns, although he was living in Provençal warmth, he described how he had gone as usual to 'a distingué gentleman's emporium' in London to replenish his stock, and was staggered to hear the assistant say they did not have any; 'You see, sir, pyjamas are really no longer being worn.' It had been difficult in my own case, too, to imagine life without pyjamas. Now, it became difficult to contemplate ever voluntarily wearing them again.

At the same time, I was the beneficiary of another form of liberation. I have inhibitions about dealing with it, of the same kind that Arthur Koestler used to recall in connection with his autobiography; he had determined to make it rigorously honest, but when it came to his private life he found himself shying away from detail. Marriage for me had worked out much as Boo and I had planned from the start; we would lead our own lives, so far as the children allowed. If either of us had affairs, they would be conducted discreetly. I did, and very enjoyable they were. But we found, as so many people taking the same course have found, that marriage can eventually break up for lack of any sanction except the children; and when they cease to hold it firmly together, it can disintegrate.

Gradually I had begun to learn the lesson that what had seemed to me to be the love I had felt for Ruth and for Rosemary was too tinged with self-love to deserve the name. About one of her characters in *Company*, Françoise Sagan has said that 'he had read enough to know that anxiety – perhaps even more deeply than jealousy – is love's great accelerator.' So it had been with me. Now, I was to learn it was possible, though still difficult, to love somebody without the anxiety that loss of possession breeds.

At the end of *All Our Yesterdays* Isabel James, who had succeeded Raye Farr as researcher for *All Our Yesterdays*, had herself moved on to become a producer on BBC Radio 4's *You and Yours*; and among the people she met in the course of her work was one who worked for the National Consumer Council. Isabel insisted I must meet her. It turned out to be Rosemary Delbridge, who in turn introduced me to her circle of friends, several of them just down from Cambridge University, most of them in their early or mid-twenties. While married Boo and I had tended to meet, to entertain, and to be entertained by, friends of about our own ages, except for those who we encountered in the course of work. To be on the loose among this generation, the product of the Sixties, was a stimulating bonus.

Rosemary was the great demolisher of outmoded habits of dress, of conversation, of thought. She had a particularly acute mind, paradoxically derived partly from her ability to live out her fantasies; she left me, as she left many of her friends, with the impression that she had a Ph.D. in history from Cambridge. Yet the impression remains that she could easily have had, if she had put her mind, second in my experience only to Desmond Williams's when it came to discussing historical subjects, to academic study, rather than to lobbying M Ps to get them to vote for Bills, or clauses of Bills, for the benefit of the consumer. She was an extremely effective lobbyist, but she found that twisting back-benchers round her little finger tedious; much more enjoyable was to ring up and demand to come round for the evening to talk about other things, and to mock me if she spotted something slipshod in one of my articles.

Rosemary was scatty, as one of her postcards, from Lindos, testifies:

Dear Brian
1) Had no passport.
2) Left money behind.
3) Started a major fire in exquisite villa bathroom (what a saga . . .)
4) Body pink and peeling.
How are you?
Love, Rosemary

To have fallen in love with her, as men often did, would have been a nerve-racking experience. As for marriage, she herself used to give the same reason for saying, 'No', as Groucho Marx did for not joining a club. But simply to be one of those who loved her was a delight. Her vitality was extraordinary; it was as if she had burned herself out when, in 1981, she died of a stroke. She was only thirty-two. Her friends still forgather each anniversary when an award is presented, in conjunction with the Hansard Society, to the lobbyist or journalist whose work, we feel, would have excited her admiration.

When at last I had finished the history of paranormal phenomena – up to the outbreak of the First World War in 1914, a convenient break, as it was getting too long – it was published by Hodder and Stoughton in the new year of 1978, the launch assisted by a pre-publication commentary which appeared in Bernard Levin's *Times* column. He had read it in proof, thanks to an arrangement which we had come to earlier to proof-read for each other; and mindful of protocol, he insisted that his intention was not to review it but simply to predict, and discuss, what the knee-jerk reaction of rationalists would be. He was fascinated 'by the terror that seems to seize many intelligent and large-minded people at the suggestion that the universe may contain, may even be run on, principles beyond either their control or their understanding.'

My aim had been to try to de-fuse this explosive material by treating the evidence along the lines laid down by the great mathematician Pierre Laplace. 'We are so far from recognising all the agents of nature and their modes of action that it would be unphilosophical to deny phenomena simply because they are inexplicable in the present state of our knowledge,' he had written in his *Essay on Probabilities*. The further the phenomena are from everyday experience, however, the more important it is to make sure that the attestation is sufficiently trustworthy to provide 'a probability superior to the reasons for not admitting them'. It should be possible, I had assumed, to distinguish between those phenomena for which the evidence is well-supported and those which, as Laplace put it, 'are so extraordinary that nothing can balance their improbability'.

In other words, I approached the subject as an agnostic. If asked, say, 'Do you believe in ghosts?' my reply was, and is, that it is a misleading question. Ghosts have been reported from every part of the world, in every era, often by men and women whose word would be accepted unquestioningly about any other experience they had. The question should be, 'Can you explain ghosts?' On this basis it is possible to survey the evidence dispassionately, and consider whether it suggests that ghosts have some kind of an existence 'out there', where they are seen or heard, like Hamlet's father; or whether they are hallucinations, like Macbeth's dagger. But to say 'I don't believe in ghosts' is simply childish.

On this basis, I thought, I could present and discuss the historical evidence about the paranormal on precisely the same lines as I had presented and discussed the historical evidence about drugs and their effect on societies. But, as Bernard had warned, rationalists declined to accept it. Believing as they did in the materialist model of nature laid down in the nineteenth century, they were certain that extra-sensory perception, the action of mind on matter, ghosts and the rest do not happen, because they *cannot* happen. Had I been prepared to relate each case history with an indication how those who had the experiences, or had witnessed them, could have been deceived, or have deluded themselves, *Natural and Supernatural* would have been acceptable. To relate them as if they might have happened was unforgivable.

I have to admit that I gave rationalists, and indeed many people who would repudiate that label, every excuse to deride the evidence. I had assumed that many of the phenomena in the paranormal category could safely be rejected on Laplace's ground that they were too extraordinary to take seriously. Common sense suggested that people do not levitate, or become immune to great heat, or emerge in the form of ectoplasmic materialisations. The historical evidence, though, for all three happened to be strong; so well-attested that I knew it could not be dismissed out of hand. Would it not, then, be safer to omit it, or fudge the issue in some way?

Here, though, I came up against the principle that Senior at Shrewsbury, McFarlane at Oxford and in particular Moody in Dublin had instilled; that anybody who omits good evidence because it is an embarrassment is almost as guilty as somebody who omits it because it would demolish the case he happens to be making. Inevitably, the inclusion of such phenomena provided rationalists with just the excuse they needed for derision; and although *Natural and Supernatural* was on balance surprisingly favourably reviewed, it tended to be regarded by both sides less as a history than as a manifesto. Introduced to a very eminent scientist at a reception, Bernard was not surprised to hear himself criticised for giving publicity to such rubbish; but even he was startled when the scientist, who had not read the book, began to turn purple in the face as he fulminated, beads of sweat breaking out on his brow.

The only hope of breaking the rationalist hold of 'promissory materialism', as Sir John Eccles has called it – materialism based on the assumption that everything will eventually be explained in terms of physics and chemistry, including our minds – is that quantum theory, which has overturned Victorian physics, will provide a rational basis for paranormal, as indeed in connection with 'non-locality', interaction of nuclear particles at a distance, it has begun to do. In his life time, Arthur Koestler decided that when he died he would leave his money to found a Chair of Parapsychology. Meanwhile, he would back any research projects which were scientifically conducted. In 1980 he and I and Instone Bloomfield, a London banker, formed the KIB Foundation in the hope of raising funds and support for such projects, with Ruth West as secretary and general organiser; and it was able to give some support to ventures lying outside orthodoxy's boundaries in parapsychology and alternative medicine. But it has been unable to attract the funds which would have established research on a scale substantial enough to attract the scientists Arthur hoped would become interested.

Occasionally people who are willing to accept the reality of the paranormal say to me, 'So what?' Is it really worth anybody's while, they are implying, to continue beating his head against rationalism's wall? For me, it is; because the role of the supernatural – that is, psychic phenomena of the kind attributed to divine or diabolic intervention – and more recently of the paranormal – anomalous phenomena – is of incalculable significance. A great range of history, in fact, cannot properly be written until the supernatural is naturalised – an end Alfred Russel Wallace strove for. And science will not really be scientific, until the anomalies can be fused in.

Postscript

At a meeting of the British Irish Association in 1984 I was introduced to Margaret van Hattem, Dutch by birth, West Australian by upbringing. At the time, she was Political Correspondent of the *Financial Times*. It was 'hard to imagine anyone who looked more unlike the stereotype of a high-powered journalist,' as Ruth Dudley Edwards wrote in an obituary; Margaret was 'youthful, tiny, curly-haired, jeans-clad and gentle-voiced, with a face of flower-like prettiness constantly lit up with laughter and mischief. But as a journalist she was multi-talented: acute, tough, tenacious, single-minded and fearless.'

The 1980s for me are too bound up with Margaret to write about them; but a curious link with my memory of her was given to me shortly before she died, in a letter written to my mother by an admirer. I had seen little of my parents after my father retired from the Wallingford Hydraulics Research Station in 1958 (right to the end, his obituary in *The Times* noted, 'his most evident personal characteristic was a drive to meet the opposition in battle,' the opposition chiefly being those who frustrated his plans; 'the most hated of all was the Ministry of Works'). He and my mother went to live in Sussex; Boo and I took the children down to see them every few months, but the old constraint remained between my mother and me. When she died in 1972 she left quantities of letters, photographs and cuttings related to me, but only a handful of correspondence concerning her own life. One fragment of a letter to her, she had mentioned earlier to me as coming from a man who had fallen violently in love with her. She had refused him; the letter described the 'bewilderment and desolation' he had felt before he 'grew up'. He was no longer desperate; but he still could not face the prospect of meeting her just as a friend:

> Since those days till now . . . you can fill up for yourself. Don't you know quite well that one can't feel like that twice? I wonder why you don't think it is serious? I suspect that it is just your kind heart that makes you try to believe that, for my sake. Do you think I am such a fool as not to realise what I'm losing by not being able to drop my romantic notions? What I'd gain if I could be just an unromantic friend?

He would continue to hope against hope; although 'nine down with nine holes to play', he thought that the faint chance she might change her mind was worth waiting for.

She had not changed her mind. Eventually, she told me, the man had married, and she could feel that she had handled the problem well. But she had not told me who he was, and the pages of the letter which she had kept did not give his name. I did not find who he was until after I had completed *Downstart*, and happened to look up something in a copy of a diary which she had produced, and had printed, during the war in India. It had two days to each page, each with a quotation and with space between them in which her friends and relations, to whom she gave copies, could remind themselves of birthdays to be remembered, or put in their own favourite quotations. Browsing through hers, I came upon one which I recognised as having been taken from the letter. Under it she had put the writer's initials: W.F.C.

So the frustrated lover had been Casey. Committed as she was to Claude, Vera must have shared Casey's feelings but refused to be swayed by them. She felt proud that eventually he had got over his disappointment, so that they had been able to enjoy each other's company when she returned on leaves. If they had not come to terms, she would not have brought me to meet him, and I would not have thought that journalism, otherwise unthinkable, might be worth trying, after all.

When a man 'loses his head' – the extract from Casey's letter in the diary ran –

> over a woman of intelligence who returns the compliment, and when both have similar interests and when also (this is rare) the most passionate part of their regard is built on the solid foundation of comradeship, then for these two, especially for the man, there is I think what Gissing calls the Crown of Life. Very few are lucky enough to gain it, but for those who do there is a lifetime of the finest happiness.

For a few all too short years, Margaret gave me that crown.

Index

INDEX